HYPOTHETICAL THINKING

Hypothetical thought involves the imagination of possibilities and the exploration of their consequences by a process of mental simulation. Using a recently developed theoretical framework called Hypothetical Thinking Theory, Jonathan St B. T. Evans provides an integrated theoretical account of a wide range of psychological studies on hypothesis testing, reasoning, judgement and decision making.

Hypothetical thinking theory is built on three key principles, implemented in a revised and updated version of Evans' well-known heuristic–analytic theory of reasoning. The central claim of this book is that this theory can provide an integrated account of some apparently very diverse phenomena including confirmation bias in hypothesis testing, acceptance of fallacies in deductive reasoning, belief biases in reasoning and judgement, biases of statistical judgement and a number of characteristic findings in the study of decision making. The author also provides broad ranging discussion of cognitive biases, human rationality and dual-process theories of higher cognition.

Hypothetical Thinking draws on and develops arguments first proposed in Evans' earlier work from this series, *Bias in Human Reasoning*. In the new theory, however, cognitive biases are attributed equally to analytic and heuristic processing and a much wider range of phenomena are reviewed and discussed. It will therefore be of great interest to researchers and post-graduates in psychology and the cognitive sciences, as well as to under-graduate students looking for a comprehensive review of current work on reasoning and decision making.

ESSAYS IN COGNITIVE PSYCHOLOGY

North American Editors:
Henry L. Roediger, III, *Washington University in St. Louis*
James R. Pomerantz, *Rice University*

European Editors:
Alan D. Baddeley, *University of York*
Vicki Bruce, *University of Edinburgh*
Jonathan Grainger, *Université de Provence*

Essays in Cognitive Psychology is designed to meet the need for rapid publication of brief volumes in cognitive psychology. Primary topics include perception, movement and action, attention, memory, mental representation, language and problem solving. Furthermore, the series seeks to define cognitive psychology in its broadest sense, encompassing all topics either informed by, or informing, the study of mental processes. As such, it covers a wide range of subjects including computational approaches to cognition, cognitive neuroscience, social cognition, and cognitive development, as well as areas more traditionally defined as cognitive psychology. Each volume in the series makes a conceptual contribution to the topic by reviewing and synthesizing the existing research literature, by advancing theory in the area, or by some combination of these missions. The principal aim is that authors provide an overview of their own highly successful research programme in an area. Volumes also include an assessment of current knowledge and identification of possible future trends in research. Each book is a self-contained unit supplying the advanced reader with a well-structured review of the work described and evaluated.

Titles in preparation

Gernsbacher: *Suppression and Enhancement in Language Comprehension*
Park: *Cognition and Aging*
Mulligan: *Implicit Memory*
Surprenant & Neath: *Principles of Memory*
Brown: *Tip-of-the-tongue Phenomenon*

Recently published

Gallo: *Associative Illusions of Memory*
Sarris: *Rational Psychophysics in Humans and Animals*
Cowan: *Working Memory Capacity*
McNamara: *Semantic Priming*
Brown: *The Déjà Vu Experience*
Coventry & Garrod: *Seeing, Saying, and Acting*
Robertson: *Space, Objects, Minds, and Brains*
Cornoldi & Vecchi: *Visuo-spatial Working Memory and Individual Differences*
Sternberg *et al.*: *The Creativity Conundrum*
Poletiek: *Hypothesis-testing Behaviour*
Garnham: *Mental Models and the Interpretations of Anaphora*

For continually updated information about published and forthcoming titles in the Essays in Cognitive Psychology series, please visit: **www.psypress.com/essays**

Hypothetical Thinking

Dual Processes in Reasoning and Judgement

Jonathan St B. T. Evans

Psychology Press
Taylor & Francis Group

HOVE AND NEW YORK

First published 2007 by Psychology Press
27 Church Road, Hove, East Sussex BN3 2FA

Simultaneously published in the USA and Canada
by Psychology Press
270 Madison Avenue, New York, NY 10016

Psychology Press is an imprint of the Taylor & Francis Group, an Informa business

© 2007 Psychology Press

Typeset in Times by RefineCatch Limited, Bungay, Suffolk
Printed and bound in Great Britain by TJ International Ltd, Padstow, Cornwall
Cover design by Lisa Dynan

This publication has been produced with paper manufactured to strict
environmental standards and with pulp derived from sustainable forests.

British Library Cataloguing in Publication Data
A catalogue record for this book is available from the British Library

Library of Congress Cataloging in Publication Data
Evans, Jonathan St. B. T., 1948–
Hypothetical thinking: dual processes in reasoning and judgement/
Jonathan St. B. T. Evans. – 1st ed.
p. cm. – (Essays in cognitive psychology)
Includes bibliographical references and index.
ISBN-13: 978–1–84169–660–7 (hard back)
ISBN-10: 1–84169–660–9 (hard back)
1. Reasoning (Psychology) 2. Judgment. 3. Thought and thinking. I. Title.
BF442.E93 2007
153.4 – dc22 2006037166

ISBN: 978–1–84169–660–7

Contents

Foreword and acknowledgements

This book is my third contribution to the *Essays in Cognitive Psychology* series, following *Bias in Human Reasoning* (1989) and *Rationality and Reasoning* (with David Over, 1996a). It has some features in common with these earlier books, including an attempt to integrate work from the psychology of reasoning with that on judgement and decision making, and a framing within dual-process theory. However, the current volume represents, I hope, considerably more than an update of these previous works. Of the three books, it is the most theoretically ambitious. I present here a recently developed theory of hypothetical thinking, including a revised and extended version of the heuristic–analytic theory of reasoning. The claim on which the book is based is that phenomena on a wide range of apparently diverse cognitive tasks in the psychological literatures on hypothesis testing, reasoning, statistical judgement and decision making can be understood with reference to a common and relatively simple set of principles. In support of this, I present an extended review and discussion of the relevant studies.

As befits the series, this book is an extended essay and not a textbook. For this reason, I have given more weight at times to discussion of studies that I feel are particularly relevant to the theoretical objectives of the book, including those run in my own laboratory. However, the book includes a fairly comprehensive review of the main findings in the fields covered and should hence prove useful also as a broad introduction to these topics.

I am indebted in this work to my two closest collaborators of recent years, David Over and Simon Handley. In particular, David and Simon helped me to develop the three principles of hypothetical thinking that form the foundation of hypothetical thinking theory. They have also collaborated with me on a number of experimental investigations of the key phenomena in the study of hypothetical thinking. In addition, I am grateful to several colleagues who read and criticized a draft manuscript of this book, including Keith Stanovich, Valerie Thompson, Shira Elqayam and an anonymous reviewer. The book was certainly improved in response to their thoughtful and constructive comments.

Writing books is a time-consuming enterprise and best undertaken with the minimum of distraction. For this reason, I am very grateful to the ESRC who supported this work with the award of an extended research fellowship (RES–000–27–0184), thus freeing me from all normal university duties.

Jonathan Evans
Plymouth, March 2007

CHAPTER ONE

Introduction and theoretical framework

It is evident that the human species is highly intelligent and well adapted. Some of our intelligence we clearly share with many other animals: we have well-developed visual and other perceptual systems, complex motor skills and the ability to learn in many ways to adapt to the environment around us. We also seem to be smart in ways that other creatures are not: we have a language system that is complex and sophisticated in its ability both to represent knowledge and to communicate with other humans; we study and attempt to understand a multitude of subjects including our own history and that of the universe; we have devised systems of mathematics and logic; we design and build a huge range of structures and artifacts; we have constructed and mostly live our lives within highly complex economic and social structures. All of these distinctively human things imply an extraordinary ability to reason, entertain hypotheses and make decisions based upon complex mental simulations of future possibilities. I will use the term "hypothetical thinking" as a catch-all phrase for thought of this kind.

It is equally apparent that evidence of human error and fallibility surrounds us. The world is plagued by wars, famines and diseases that in many cases appear preventable. Stock markets collapse under panic selling when each individual acts to bring about the outcome that none of them wants. Doctors sometimes make disastrous misjudgements that result in the disability or death of their patients. Experts often fail to agree with each other and may be shown in hindsight to have made judgements that were both mistaken and overconfident. At the present time, governments of the world are well informed about the likely progress of global warming and its consequences but seem to be making minimal progress in doing anything to prevent it. Criminal courts continue to convict the innocent and acquit the guilty, with alarming regularity. And so on, and so forth.

It seems vital that psychologists should be able to provide understanding of the mental processes of reasoning and judgements that underlie the actions and decisions that people take. A fundamental premise of the current book is that there are two distinct kinds of thought, which for the moment I will call intuitive and deliberative. Many of our everyday decisions are made rapidly and intuitively because they just feel right. Others are made much more slowly, involving conscious deliberative thinking. Sometimes we have no time for deliberative thought and just have to react quickly to some situation. In fact, the great bulk of our everyday cognitive processing is carried out rapidly and implicitly without conscious thought. Such processes enable us to accomplish a multitude of necessary tasks, as, for example, when we recognize a face, extract the meaning from a sentence, keep our car safely on the road when driving to work (and thinking consciously about something quite different) or attend to the voice of one person in a room containing the babble of many conversations.

Much of our judgement and decision making takes place at this level also. A lot of our behaviour is habitual, so we are not conscious of choosing our direction at a junction on a familiar drive to work. However, something very different happens when we drive to a new location in an unfamiliar town, following verbal directions or trying to read a map. Now we have to engage conscious and deliberative thinking and reasoning to work out the route, identify landmarks, turn at the correct places and so on. In general, novel problems require much more deliberative thought than do familiar ones. When we have to do this kind of thinking it takes time, it requires effort and it prevents us from thinking about other things. Conscious, deliberative think-ing is a singular resource that can only be applied to one task at a time. This is one reason that we allocate this kind of thought to tasks and decisions that have great importance for us and make snap intuitive decisions about less important things. However, there is no guarantee that thinking about our decisions will necessarily improve them (see Chapter 5).

Folk psychology – the common-sense beliefs that we all hold about our own behaviour and that of our fellow human beings – involves the idea that we are consciously in control of our own behaviour – we think, therefore we do. The opinion polling industry, for example, is built on the common-sense belief that people have conscious reasons for their actions which they can accurately report. Psychological research, however, seriously undermines this idea (Wilson, 2002). Not only is much of our behaviour unconsciously controlled, but many of our introspections provide us with unreliable infor-mation about the extent and the ways in which our conscious thinking controls our actions. Working out the relative influence of intuitive and deliberative thinking and the interaction between the two systems is a complex problem that must be addressed with the methods of experimental psychology. This enterprise lies at the heart of the current book.

Many of the phenomena to be discussed in this book are described as cognitive *biases*. It may appear that the demonstration of bias implies evidence for irrationality, and it is impossible to study these topics without taking some view on whether and in what way people are rational. Cognitive psychology as a whole studies the workings of the mind at a number of levels. Basic cognitive processes (still incredibly complex and sophisticated) form the building blocks for our behaviour and thought. These include such functions as pattern recognition, language comprehension, memory for events and the acquisition of conceptual knowledge about the world around us. None of these topics has generated debate about human rationality. Our visual systems have limited acuity and our memory systems limited capacity, we assume, because that is simply the way our brains are designed: the way they were shaped by evolution to be. The study of higher cognitive processes, on the other hand – thinking, reasoning, decision making and social cognition – has been somewhat obsessed by the notions of bias, error and irrationality. Author after author provide us with evidence of "bad" thinking: illogical reasoning, inconsequential decision making, prejudice and stereotyping in our view of people in the social world. The study of cognitive biases is something of a major industry.

What exactly is a cognitive bias? One definition is that it is systematic (not random) error of some kind. This then begs the question of what is an error. Psychologists have largely answered the second question by reference to normative systems. Thus reasoning is judged by formal logic; judgement under uncertainty by probability theory; choice behaviour by formal decision theory and so on. Some authors go further and claim that people who fail to conform to such normative standards are *irrational*. Most of the biases studied in cognitive psychology have been defined in this way, and yet this notion is today highly controversial. Some authors claim that people's behaviour only appears biased or irrational because the wrong normative theory is being applied. For example, if standard logic requires that propositions are clearly true or false, then people's reasoning in an uncertain world might better be assessed by norms based on probability theory (see Oaksford & Chater, 2001).

In fact, we do not necessarily need to invoke normative rationality in order to think about cognitive biases. We have much lower visual acuity than does a bird of prey, but vision researchers do not accuse us of being biased against distant objects. Similarly, memory researchers do not accuse us of irrationality if we cannot remember a phone number more than seven or eight digits in length. Researchers in this area rarely use the term "bias", but their findings certainly indicate the constraints and limitations of human information processing. So we could think about biases of thought and judgement also as indicators of the design limitations of the brain. This is an approach that emphasizes what is known as *bounded* rationality (Simon, 1982). According to this view, we are not inherently irrational but we are cognitively constrained in the way we can reason about the world. For example, it may not be possible to calculate the best choice of action in a given situation, so we settle for one that is good enough.

Another concept of cognitive bias is dispositional: for example, people have different styles of thinking that may be related to personality or to culture. A widely cited claim is that Western people have a more analytic style of thinking, while Eastern people are more holistic or intuitive (Nisbett, Peng, Choi, & Norenzayan, 2001). One style is not necessarily better than the other, but each may fare better or worse on different kinds of task. Combining the dispositional and bounded rationality approaches, we might conclude that people's ability to think in particular ways is biased or constrained not only biologically, in the design of our brains, but also culturally. Either or both kinds of explanation might be induced, for example, to account for biases in social cognition. For example, people seem compulsively to employ stereotypes when thinking about people from an "out-group" with whom they do not share social membership (Hinton, 2000). This could reflect some innate form of social intelligence shaped by evolution, learning of cultural norms passed from one generation to the next, or an interaction of the two.

As we shall see in this book, psychologists studying higher cognitive processes have discovered and documented a wide range of biases. In most cases, these biases have been defined as deviation from a normative standard, leading to a debate about whether or not they should be termed irrational. I have discussed the rationality issue in detail elsewhere (Evans & Over, 1996a), and it will not be the main focus of interest in this book. (I will, however, consider the issue in my final chapter.) The study of cognitive biases should be seen as important for two reasons, whether or not they are deemed to provide evidence of irrationality. First, they establish the phenomena that have to be explained. Second, they may have practical implications for reasoning and decision making in the everyday world. Hence, each bias gives rise both to a theoretical question: "Why do people think in this way?" and to a practical question: "How will this bias manifest itself in real-world behaviour and with what consequences?"

As an example, psychologists have accumulated much evidence that people's evaluation of logical arguments is biased by whether or not they believe the conclusions given (Chapter 4). This is regarded as a bias because logical validity depends only on whether a conclusion follows necessarily from some assumptions and not on whether assumptions or conclusion are actually true. I suppose one could try to move directly from this result to its practical implications without any real theoretical analysis of the cause of the bias. Such an analysis might, however, conclude that human reasoning is automatically contextualized by prior knowledge and belief and that only a strong effort of deliberative conscious reasoning will overcome this. In my view, understanding of the likely practical implications of the bias is greatly assisted by this kind of theorizing.

In this book, I shall be viewing the phenomena discussed within both a broad and a more specific theoretical framework to be introduced later in this chapter. The broad framework, generally known as "dual-process" theory, has been applied to a wide range of cognitive studies, including learning (Reber, 1993), reasoning (Evans & Over, 1996a; Stanovich, 1999), conceptual thinking (Sloman, 1996), decision making (Kahneman & Frederick, 2002) and social cognition (Chaiken & Trope, 1999). Dual-processing approaches assert the existence of two kinds of mental processes corresponding broadly to the idea of intuitive and deliberative thinking and to more general distinctions between implicit and explicit cognitive processes, such as those involved in learning and memory. Within this general framework, I will, however, present a more specific dual-process theory of hypothetical thinking that updates and extends my earlier heuristic–analytic theory of reasoning (Evans, 1989). In support of this theory, I will discuss phenomena that are drawn mostly (but not exclusively) from two separate but related literatures: the psychology of reasoning on the one hand; and the study of judgement and decision making on the other. Before presenting my general and specific theoretical framework, I shall outline the nature of these two fields of study, including the methods and theoretical approaches that have tended to dominate them.

THE PSYCHOLOGY OF REASONING

I ought, perhaps, to start with the distinction between implicit and explicit inference (see also Johnson-Laird, 1983). Any kind of inference involves going beyond the information given and may technically be regarded as deductive or inductive. Inductive inferences add new information, whereas deductive inferences draw out only what was implicit in assumptions or premises. Both deductive and inductive inferences may be either implicit or explicit in terms of cognitive processing. I shall illustrate this with some examples.

Pragmatic inferences are almost always involved in the comprehension of linguistic statements (see Sperber & Wilson, 1995, for discussion of many examples). Because they typically add information from prior knowledge relevant to the context, they are generally inductive as well as implicit. As a result, such inferences are plausible or probable but not logically sound and may turn out to be incorrect. In accordance with the communicative principle of relevance (Sperber & Wilson, 1995), every utterance conveys a guarantee of its own relevance, and this licenses many pragmatic inferences. Consider the following dialogue between an adult son and his mother:

"I think I am going to be late for work"
"My car keys are in the usual place"
"Thanks, Mum".

There will be a context behind this exchange that is mutually manifest to both parties. For example, the son usually travels to work but his mother sometimes lets him borrow her car, which takes 15 minutes off the journey. Hence, the first statement is interpreted as a request to borrow the car, and the reply acquiescence to this request. Neither speaker has actually stated that the car is to be borrowed, so the inferencing is clearly implicit. It is also hardly deductive and can be incorrect. Suppose the dialogue actually went like this:

"I think I am going to be late for work"
"My car keys are in the usual place"
"I am going for a drink after work. Can't you drop me off?"

The son's reply clearly signals that the mother's original inference that he wanted to borrow the car was wrong. This is cancelled by the reply with a further implicit inference: the son wishes to drink and will therefore not drive home afterwards. This kind of inferencing occurs all the time in everyday dialogue, but it is not what the psychology of reasoning is (apparently) concerned with, as we shall see shortly. Note that such implicit inferences can be deductive in nature, as in:

"I can't play golf this weekend; my sister is visiting"
"Surely, she can spare her brother for a few hours?"

By the conventions of relationships, it follows logically that if X (male) has a sister Y, then X is the brother of Y. This inference is included in the riposte above, but it is most unlikely that either party would have required any conscious reasoning to deduce it. Such inferences are also implicit or automatic but cannot normally be cancelled, unless the premise on which they are based is withdrawn.

What is described as the psychology of reasoning should really be known as the psychology of *explicit* reasoning as it has, at least on the face of it, nothing to do with these kinds of conversational inferences. Instead, psychologists in this field have concentrated on giving participants in their experiments verbal statements from which explicit conclusions need to be inferred. Explicit reasoning tasks can in principle be deductive or inductive, but the field has been generally dominated by the former, using what is known as the "deduction paradigm" (Evans, 2002a). This method involves giving people some premises, asking them to assume that they are true and then asking them to decide whether some conclusions necessarily follow. This method allows people's reasoning to be assessed against the normative framework of formal logic. For example, people might be presented with a syllogism that has two premises and a conclusion, such as:

Some of the blue books are geography books   1.1
None of the large books are geography books
Therefore, some of the blue books are not large.

The logical question to be asked is, does the conclusion of this argument necessarily follow from its premises? To put it another way, if the premises of the argument are true, must the conclusion be true as well, no matter what else we assume about the state of the world? The above argument is valid in this sense. The first premise establishes that there exists at least one blue geography book. Since none of the large books are geography books there exists at least one blue book that is not large. Hence, some (meaning at least one) of the blue books are not large. Suppose, we reorder the terms of the conclusion:

Some of the blue books are geography books   1.2
None of the large books are geography books
Therefore, some of the large books are not blue.

Now is Argument 1.2 still valid? The answer now is no. The conclusion would be false if all of the large books are blue. Although there is at least one blue geography book (that is not large), it is perfectly possible that all of the large books are blue. The actual state of affairs, for example, might be:

10 small blue geography books
20 small red geography books
30 large blue history books.

Given this collection of books, both premises of both arguments hold: some of the blue books are geography books, and none of the large books are geography books. The conclusion of 1.1 also holds: some of the blue books are not large. However, the conclusion of 1.2 is demonstrably fallacious because all of the large books are blue. What this illustrates is the semantic principle of validity: an argument is valid if there is no counterexample to it. This principle is favoured by psychologists in the mental model tradition (Johnson-Laird, 1983; Johnson-Laird & Byrne, 1991), who have built a popular theory of human deductive reasoning around it.

In contrast with conversational inferences, which are automatic and effort-less (though not necessarily logically valid), explicit deductive reasoning tasks of this kind are slow and difficult to solve for most people. In fact, psycho-logical experiments on deductive reasoning show that many mistakes occur with ordinary participants (Evans, Newstead, & Byrne, 1993). In particular, people make many fallacies: that is, they declare arguments as valid when their conclusions *could* be true given the premises, but do not need to be true. Hence, many people would indicate if asked, that both 1.1 and 1.2 above are valid arguments. Syllogistic reasoning is also known to be systematically biased by several factors as we will see later in this book.

How do ordinary people engage in deductive reasoning? For many years, the psychology of reasoning was dominated by two apparently contrasting theories. According to a tradition known as mental logic (Braine & O'Brien, 1998a; Rips, 1994) people have a logic built into their minds comprising a set of inference rules. In the mental logic account of reasoning it is assumed that the content of a particular reasoning problem is stripped out so that the underlying abstract logical form is recovered. Reasoning then proceeds like a proof in formal logic, by application of standard inferential rules or schemas. Consider the following argument:

The car is either a Ford or a Mercedes   1.3
If the car was built in the USA then it is not a Mercedes
The car was built in the USA
Therefore, the car is a Ford.

It is quite easy to see that this is a valid argument, but how exactly do we do this? According to the rule theory we first strip out the content, reducing it to an abstract form:

1. Either A or B
2. If C then not B
3. C
Therefore, A.

Reasoning now proceeds as a mental proof, citing inference rules and the assumptions they require:

4. Not B (Modus Ponens, 2, 3)
5. A (disjunction elimination, 1, 4).

According to the rule of Modus Ponens, if we know that "if p then q" and "p" we can infer "q". Substituting C for p, and not-B for q, we conclude not-B. The other step requires this inferred statement to be combined with the first premise: "Either A or B". The rule of disjunction elimination states that if one component of a disjunctive statement is false, then the other must be true. This leads us to the conclusion A, which can be restated as "the car is a Ford". The theory requires both that people have such logical rules built in to their minds and that they have a set of effective procedures for applying such rules to draw inferences (see Rips, 1994, for a full computational implementation).

According to the rival mental model account, people do not use inference rules. Rather, they construct what I will call (for reasons that will become apparent later) *semantic* mental models. Such models represent possible situations in the world. Consider the first premise of 1.3:

The car is either a Ford or a Mercedes.

This disjunctive form is ambiguous as it sometimes is used in an inclusive sense (both disjuncts are possible) and sometimes is exclusive. Context (which can influence the construction of mental models) indicates here that the disjunction is exclusive as cars have only one manufacturer. Hence, the statement is represented by two models:

Ford
          Mercedes

The second premise was:

If the car was built in the USA then it is not a Mercedes.

According to the model theory such conditionals are compatible with three possibilities (a highly contentious assertion, as we shall see in Chapter 3):

Built in the USA   not Mercedes
Not built in the USA   Mercedes
Not built in the USA   not Mercedes.

However, people represent only one model initially in a short-hand form:

Built in the USA   not Mercedes
. . .

where ". . ." is a "mental footnote" that there are other possibilities in which the antecedent is false. This makes Modus Ponens a trivial inference, as once it is asserted that the car is built in the USA it is consistent only with the explicit model in which it is not a Mercedes. This inference in turn eliminates the second model of the disjunctive premises, leaving only the model in which the car is a Ford, hence supporting the conclusion as a valid argument.

The debate between mental logic and mental model theorists has been difficult to resolve on the basis of empirical evidence, even though each side has made strong claims (Evans & Over, 1996a, 1997). However, it is becoming more and more apparent that the two camps share a common agenda – which I term *logicism* – that is rejected by a number of contemporary researchers, including myself. They assume that deduction is the primary mode of inference and that both logical errors and the massive influence of pragmatic factors (as I shall refer to the effects of problem content and context) interfere with this underlying deductive mechanism. Mental logicians, for example, faced with a mass of evidence of nonlogical influences on deductive reasoning tasks have argued that there is no singular mechanism of reasoning, and that mental logic is supplemented by a whole range of mechanisms discussed by other authors, including pragmatic implicature, pragmatic reasoning schemas (both discussed in Chapter 4) and even mental models (Braine & O'Brien, 1998a). Johnson-Laird and his colleagues have from the start tried to build in some principles to explain why reasoning is competent in principle but defective in practice. For example, it is claimed that working memory limits constrain the construction of the multiple mental models needed to avoid fallacious inference, or that beliefs may bias the process of searching for counterexample models (Johnson-Laird & Byrne, 1991).

Later in this chapter, a dual-process theory of hypothetical thinking will be described that is applied to a range of cognitive tasks, including the deduction paradigm. It will be argued that reasoning is by habit and default pragmatic and not deductive and that only conscious reasoning effort induced by special instructions can result in an effort at deduction. "Logicism" is rejected both as a normative standard (the idea that people ought to be reasoning logically) and as a descriptive approach (describing reasoning as deductively competent in principle). This will also imply, as we shall see, a non-normative definition of cognitive bias. If the brain is not designed as a logical reasoning machine, then it cannot be regarded as malfunctioning when reasoning does not conform to a logical standard. Before introducing this framework, however, some introduction is needed to the other main research paradigm with which this book is concerned.

THE PSYCHOLOGY OF JUDGEMENT AND DECISION MAKING

Decision making is of enormous theoretical interest and practical importance. We actually make thousands of decisions every day in the sense that we (or, at an automatic level, our brains) choose one course of action from among alternatives. How many "decisions" in this sense are involved, say, in a

20-minute drive from home to work? Traffic and weather conditions are never identical even in this most routine and boring of tasks. Most of these decisions (shifting gears, adjusting steering, modifying speed by use of brakes or accelerator) are automatic, but some may be conscious – for example, deciding whether to stop at traffic lights that annoyingly start to change just as we approach them.

Just as the psychology of reasoning has focused on formal and explicit reasoning problems, rather than the huge number of automatic conversational and pragmatic inferences that we make every day, so the academic study of decision making has tended to focus on formally defined decisions of a particular kind. These decision problems tend to be explicit and well defined. There is enormous interdisciplinary interest in economic, business and governmental decision making. Psychologists working in this field have, however, tended to focus on cognitive and social psychological accounts of individuals engaged in decision processes (Hastie, 2001; Koehler & Harvey, 2004). Typically, psychological experiments in this area consist of presenting people with hypothetical scenarios in which they are required to make choices between proposed alternatives, often imagining themselves to be in a role or situation described to them.

Like the psychology of reasoning, the psychology of decision making has a normative theory and a rationality debate. The normative theory, originally introduced from economics by Ward Edwards (1961), is that of expected utility. Most real-world decisions (certainly most that psychologists are interested in studying) are *risky*. They involve consideration of uncertain prospects. The central normative principle of economic decision theory is that people should estimate both the probability (p) of various outcomes and the utility (U, subjective value) to them. They should then calculate the expected utility (EU) of the n outcomes of a decision as follows:

$$EU = \sum_{i=1}^{n} p_i U_i \qquad 1.4$$

Finally, people should act so as to maximize expected utility – that is, choose the action (or inaction) that has the greatest expected utility among the choices present. This model of decision making assumes that people are essentially selfish and that it is optimal to maximize the gain (or minimize the loss) to yourself.

As with logic, it is apparently easy to demonstrate violations of normative decision theory. Consider the case of buying a ticket for the national lottery or buying insurance against your house burning down. From the viewpoint of objective probabilities and monetary values each of these everyday activities involves an expected loss. The lottery collects more in stakes than it gives out in prizes; similarly the insurance company collects more in premiums than it pays out on losses. Their expected gain is an expected loss to the customer, so why do people persist in these behaviours? Actually, there are many explanations that can be given, showing just how weak the normative theory of decision making really is (see Evans & Over, 1996a, chap. 2). For example, we can argue that people buy lottery tickets because they overestimate the chance of winning (subjective probability) or because their utility function for money undervalues the stake relative to the winnings. Or it can be argued that they have a utility for gambling based on its intrinsic pleasures and so on.

Decision theory even allows us another decision rule (maximin) in which we can prefer an option that has the better security level (least bad outcome). Hence, we buy fire insurance to avoid the worst outcome of losing our house even though it gives us an expected loss financially. Then there is the problem of how far ahead we project the consequences of a decision. Is it rational for a school leaver to choose a university course on the grounds of: (a) how much she will enjoy the course, (b) the first job that it will enable her to get or (c) her career and salary prospects in twenty years' time? Each analysis could lead to widely differing expected utility calculations. All of this means that establishing what constitutes a *bias* in decision making by reference to such an elastic and subjective normative framework is far from easy.

From the viewpoint of hypothetical thinking theory, however, decision making is very interesting. As already indicated, many decisions are made automatically, perhaps in response to past learning. *Consequential* decision making, however, requires hypothetical thinking about future events. We need somehow to imagine the world (in relevant respects) as it might be following a particular choice or action under our control and decide how much we would like to be living in it. Moreover, we need to conduct a set of thought experiments for each possible action and compare their evaluations. Alleged biases in decision making will be discussed in Chapter 5.

An important aspect of the mental simulations required for decision making is the assessment of probability and uncertainty, so much so that the study of judgement under uncertainty has become a large psychological field of study in its own right (Gilovich, Griffin, & Kahneman, 2002; Kahneman, Slovic, & Tversky, 1982). The dominant paradigm has become known as "heuristics and biases", originally introduced by Amos Tversky and Danny Kahneman (1974) over thirty years ago. In this case, the normative theory that applies is probability theory, with deviations from its prescriptions being regarded as biases. While biases are observed behaviours, heuristics are theoretical constructs. Two of the most famous of these are *representativeness* (Kahneman & Tversky, 1972; Teigen, 2004) and *availability* (Reber, 2004; Tversky & Kahneman, 1973).

The availability heuristic applies when we try to estimate the likelihood or frequency of some particular event. The claim is that we do this by calling to mind examples of the event. The more easily we can generate such examples, the more frequent we judge the event to be. While this seems reasonable, it can easily be biased, for example by media coverage. Hence, tourists might be deterred from visiting a city due to well-publicized acts of terrorism but not by road traffic accidents, which are a much more probable cause of death and injury that receive little media attention. The representativeness heuristic is applied to judging the probability of a sample given a population or an event given a hypothesis and is based on similarity. Given a thumbnail description of John, for example, we might judge him likely to be an engineer if the description fits our stereotype. However, this could lead to a bias if we ignored the base rate frequency of engineers in the population we are considering. Examples of biases in this literature will be discussed in Chapter 6.

There is another tradition within the psychology of judgement and decision making known as *social judgement theory* or SJT for short. This derives from the psychology of Egon Brunswick who put great stress on the interaction between people and the environment (for a special journal issue on this topic, see Doherty, 1996). Research in this area normally involves multicue judgement when people have to make a single holistic judgement in response to a number of potentially relevant cues. For example, a doctor making a diagnostic judgement might have to take into account a number of pieces of information such as patient symptoms, clinical interview, medical history, demographic variables such as age, gender and occupation, results of diagnostic tests and so on. Of course, some of these cues may be more diagnostic than others.

SJT uses a methodology known as the "lens model" (Cooksey, 1996) in which multiple regression analysis is used to assess the relationship between available cues to the criterion that is being judged on one side of the lens, and the judgements made by individual people on the other side of the lens. This is a clever technique about which I will have more to say later in the book. From the viewpoint of research on biases, it is a powerful method since it allows us to distinguish three different explanations of why people fail to make accurate judgements about the world. It could be that the world lacks predictability or that the judgements lack consistency. If neither of these things is true, but judgements are still poor, then it must be the case that there is a mismatch between the judge's model and the "world's" model. For example, if a personnel manager consistently prefers to select young males for positions in which neither age nor gender are relevant to performance, this will reduce his performance. Bias of this kind is easily detected with the methods of SJT.

DUAL-PROCESS THEORIES OF THINKING

The general framework for considering explanations of cognitive biases in this book is that of dual-process or dual-system theories. As mentioned earlier, dual-process accounts are springing up everywhere in the study of cognition these days. Within the psychology of reasoning, such accounts have a relatively long history, dating from the 1970s (see Evans, 2004). The contemporary dual-process theory of reasoning (Evans, 2003; Evans & Over, 1996a; Klaczynski, 2000; Osman, 2005; Sloman, 1996; Stanovich, 1999) has been influenced by dual-process accounts of learning (Berry & Dienes, 1993; Dienes & Perner, 1999; Reber, 1993) and is currently subject to some challenging arguments based on neural-imaging techniques (Goel, 2005).

Rather than detail the history of this theory or the precise variants suggested by different authors, I will describe here a generic version. Strictly speaking there is a distinction between dual-process and dual-system theories. Dual-process accounts simply emphasize the idea that two different kinds of cognitive processing affect inferences and judgements. Thus in my earlier heuristic–analytic theory (Evans, 1984, 1989) I suggested that we distinguish between (a) heuristic processes that are preattentive and pragmatic and form selective representations of problems, and (b) analytic reasoning processes that are applied to such representations in order to generate inferences or judgements. Other dual-process notions include the idea that there are associative and rule-based processes in reasoning (Sloman, 1996) or that we should distinguish between automatic and controlled processing, as is popular in dual-process accounts of social judgement (see Chaiken & Trope, 1999; Hassin, Uleman, & Bargh, 2005).

Stronger versions of the theory propose that such attributes and others reflect the presence of two distinct cognitive systems in the brain with sharply differing evolutionary histories (Evans & Over, 1996a; Reber, 1993; Stanovich, 1999, 2004). These have been given various names, but for now I will use the terms System 1 and System 2, following Stanovich (1999), corresponding with the broad distinction between intuitive and deliberative thinking. According to this view, System 1 is the older system with ancient origins, sharing many of its features with other animals. Among the attributes identified for System 1 cognition are the following:

- Unconscious, automatic
- Rapid, computationally powerful, massively parallel
- Associative
- Pragmatic (contextualizing problems in the light of prior knowledge and belief)
- Does not require the resources of central working memory
- Functioning not related to individual differences in general intelligence
- Low effort.

System 2, described as unique to humans (perhaps anatomically modern humans, see below), has a number of contrasting attributes including:

- Linked with language and reflective consciousness
- Slow and sequential
- Linked to working memory and general intelligence
- Capable of abstract and hypothetical thinking
- Volitional or controlled – responsive to instructions and stated intentions
- High effort.

If System 2 is indeed evolutionarily recent and unique to humans (a somewhat contentious claim) then it is interesting to consider when it may have evolved. Evidence from cognitive archaeology identifies a qualitative change in human thinking *c.* 60–50,000 years ago, a "big bang" of human culture that saw the emergence of art, religious imagery and the ability rapidly to adapt the design of artifacts, hunting methods and so on to changes in the environment (Mithen, 1996). This seems to have given modern humans a big advantage over early humans with their relatively "modular" minds and may explain why we are the only hominids that survive to the present day. Was this the birth of System 2? It certainly seems to have coincided with a period of major brain development and the evolution of language. It is also difficult to see how reflective consciousness – a central construct in the theory of System 2 – could be possible without language.

Dual-system theories are coming under some pressure from neuropsychological research, which shows, for example, that some cognitive biases – normally attributed to System 1 – are associated with frontal brain areas, indicating a modern human evolution (Goel & Dolan, 2003). I believe the problem stems from treating System 1 as though it were a single system with a single evolutionary history. This is almost certainly wrong. We know that some forms of implicit cognition are indeed ancient and shared with other animals, especially associative learning and conditioning. Pragmatic processes on the other hand – which serve to contextualize problems with relevant knowledge – require access to a human belief system, which unsurprisingly resides in the modern areas of the human brain. Perhaps, as evolutionary psychologists argue (Cosmides & Tooby, 1992; Pinker, 1997), there are also domain-specific cognitive modules that evolved to perform specific kinds of reasoning and continue to influence modern humans. According to Mithen (1996) these would have evolved at some intermediate stage – much more recent than the general learning system, but prior to the development of modern flexible intelligence.

Interesting though these broader dual system issues are, the present book is not the place to explore them. I will focus in this book on a revised version of the heuristic–analytic theory (Evans, 2006b) that deliberately minimizes reference to the controversial aspects of dual-system theories concerning such matters as consciousness and evolution. (Links with other dual-process theories will be considered in Chapter 7.) Essentially it is a theory of hypothetical thinking designed to give dual-processing accounts of the kinds of reasoning and judgement tasks that have been studied by psychologists. Such tasks always involve analytic thought processes to some degree (if only to interpret and apply the experimental instructions) but are subject to a variety of heuristic processes. It does not address the question of whether there are multiple sources of implicit processes, but in practice the heuristic processes I discuss will be largely *pragmatic* related to language, context and relevant prior belief. In contrast with much previous writing by myself and others, I will show in this book that the source of cognitive biases is not exclusive to heuristic processes but can arise from analytic processing as well.

HYPOTHETICAL THINKING THEORY AND THE REVISED HEURISTIC–ANALYTIC MODEL

In my 1989 book on biases, I used a rather simple form of dual-process account in which I distinguished between heuristic and analytic processes (corresponding to Systems 1 and 2 in more recent accounts). Heuristic processes, according to this account, were essentially pragmatic and pre-conscious, and they acted to form selective mental representations of the problems presented to participants in a laboratory. This happened in two ways: (a) by selective representation of problem features, and (b) by con-textualization – that is, by retrieval and application of relevant prior know-ledge from long-term memory. What was represented was what was perceived as *relevant*. Analytic thought processes, assumed to be capable of abstract hypothetical thinking and logic reasoning, were then applied to these selective representations.

In this theory, cognitive biases were explained on the basis of heuristic processes. It was argued that if logically relevant features were excluded at the heuristic stage, or normatively irrelevant features included, then biases would inevitably result, no matter how good the analytic reasoning. In this way, people could be shown to understand a logical principle on one task and then completely fail to apply it on another. It is important to understand that although heuristic processes are associated with biases in this account, these proposals did not fall within the mainstream "heuristics and biases" research programme of Kahneman and Tversky. Their use of the term "heuristic" was as a rule of thumb, a short cut that could often work in everyday life but also lead to error. They did not specify at that time that heuristics operated unconsciously or that they might compete with analytic reasoning applied to the same task. It is only recently that Kahneman has brought the discussion of heuristics and biases within the dual-process framework (Kahneman & Frederick, 2002).

There is a potential confusion in using the adjective *heuristic* to describe such processes in a somewhat different manner from the notion of a heuristic, as popularized by Kahneman and Tversky. However, many authors interested in the dual-processing approach to reasoning seem to like the heuristic–analytic terminology (for recent examples, see Ball, Lucas, Miles, & Gale, 2003; Klaczynski, 2001; Kokis, MacPherson, Toplak, West, & Stanovich, 2002; Roberts & Newton, 2002; Schroyens, Schaeken, Fias, & d'Ydewalle, 2000), and so it will be retained in the present book. The heuristic–analytic theory to be used here, however, is considerably revised and extended from that of Evans (1989) and incorporates much of the new thinking about dual processes that has developed since that work was written (see also Evans, 2006b). Although I believe that some cognitive biases can still be correctly accounted for in terms of the earlier theory, it has too many limitations. Most importantly, in the present book it is now proposed that *both* heuristic and analytic processes are involved in the production of cognitive biases.

This book is concerned with hypothetical thinking – that is, thought that requires imagination of possible states of the world. Examples include hypothesis testing, forecasting, decision making, counterfactual thinking, deductive reasoning and suppositional reasoning. By definition, hypothetical thinking always involves a supposition or hypothesis of some kind (for example, an action available to us as a choice) although the evaluation process may be shallow or deep, the latter often involving a mental simulation (see also Kahneman & Tversky, 1982b). The relevant literatures are discussed within a theoretical framework that I shall call *hypothetical thinking theory*. The theory comes in three parts: (a) a set of three principles that aim to describe the general characteristics of hypothetical thought; (b) a proposal that thinking involves manipulation of mental representations in the form of epistemic mental models; and (c) a processing model that extends and revises my earlier heuristic–analytic theory of reasoning. The three principles were originally described by Evans, Over, and Handley (2003c), and the rest of the theory that has been recently developed by Evans (2006b) will be further elaborated in this book.

We start with consideration of the three principles – see Table 1.1. The *singularity principle* claims that when we think hypothetically we consider only one possibility or mental model at a time. This is due to the fact that hypothetical thinking requires use of the analytic system (System 2), which is sharply limited in working memory capacity and inherently sequential in nature. This idea is not novel in itself as related ideas have been proposed by other authors. For example, it has been argued that people can consider only one hypothesis at a time (Mynatt, Doherty, & Dragan, 1993) and that people focus on only one explicit option when engaged in decision making (Legrenzi, Girotto, & Johnson-Laird, 1993). Note the qualifying phrase "at a time". People may of course consider more than one possibility but can only

Table 1.1
The three principles of hypothetical thinking proposed by Evans
et al. (2003c)

The singularity principle	People consider a single hypothetical possibility, or mental model, at one time
The relevance principle	People consider the model that is most relevant (generally the most plausible or probable) in the current context
The satisficing principle	Models are evaluated with reference to the current goals and accepted if satisfactory

Note: This table was previously published in *Psychonomic Bulletin and Review* (Evans, 2006b) and is reproduced by permission of the Psychonomic Society.

evaluate or simulate them singly, needing to store results in memory for comparison. Due to its combination with the satisficing principle (see below), people will rarely give full consideration to alternatives, however, and may never process more than the first that comes to mind.

The *relevance principle* uses the term "relevance" in much the same way as Evans (1989). It is not the famous (communicative) principle of relevance advanced by Sperber and Wilson (1995) but more akin to their *cognitive* principle of relevance. Basically, it asserts that mental models are generated by heuristic or pragmatic processes that are designed to maximize relevance in a particular context, given the current goals of the reasoner. By default, what is most relevant is what is most probable or plausible but this default can easily be reset. Thus when we consider a risky prospect we will normally focus first on the most likely outcome. However, a good insurance salesperson can easily get us to focus on an improbable but costly outcome such as our house burning down by setting a context and activating goals that ensure its relevance.

The *satisficing principle* is derived from the bounded rationality tradition of Herb Simon (see, for example, Simon, 1982). Satisficing is a term that is contrasted with optimizing: it is settling for what is good enough. What I mean by it here is that the (single) mental model that we consider in our hypothetical thinking is evaluated by the analytic system and is accepted unless there is good reason to reject, modify or replace it. This evaluation may be either casual or more effortful, involving active reasoning or mental simulation. Only if the first hypothesis (possible action etc.) is considered unsatisfactory will another be considered. True "rational" decision making, with full deliberation of alternatives, requires a conscious effort to accept no single model without consideration of others. This may sometimes occur in everyday decision making, but is probably rare unless required by a formal operating procedure (see Klein, 1999). Much more common is a process by which possibilities are considered in turn until one is found that satisfies.

We can imagine a relevance hierarchy of prospects that occur to us in a particular order. For example, I take a day working at home. It occurs to me first to work on the final draft of a journal article, but then I recall that I am waiting for comments on the previous draft by one of my co-authors. The prospect does not satisfy, so I (or my heuristic system) generate(s) another. I then recall that there is a paper that I promised to review for a journal that is well overdue and decide to work on this. Unfortunately, a search of my briefcase reveals that I left the manuscript at work. I sit at my desk and notice another paper that I was meaning to review poking out of the mess. So I work on that one.

Readers may wonder at my use of the term "mental model". Is this some variant of the famous theory of Johnson-Laird and colleagues? Not so, in fact. As pointed out earlier, his models are largely described as semantic devices. This means that they can only represent possible states of the world. The term here refers to *epistemic* mental models that encode not just possibilities but our beliefs about them and attitudes towards them. In decision making, for example, when we consider a possible action we may construct a mental model by mentally simulating the consequences of that action. Such a model (if it is epistemic) can incorporate any relevant beliefs such as how likely this consequence is to occur and how much we would like it if it did. With this kind of representation we could use our analytic processes to estimate its expected utility. The distinction between epistemic and semantic mental models is at the core of our theory of conditional sentences and its fundamental incompatibility with the model theory of Johnson-Laird and Byrne (2002) – see Evans and Over (2004; Evans, Over, & Handley, 2005b) and Chapter 3 of the present book.

Hypothetical thinking theory needs a processing model, and this is what the revised heuristic–analytic theory provides (Figure 1.1). This revised theory helps to resolve an apparent conflict between the original, sequential stage model of Evans (1989) and a critical feature of dual-process research: heuristic and analytic processes often seem to *compete* for control of our behaviour. For example, when people assess the logical validity of syllogisms whose conclusions conform to or conflict with prior belief, logic and belief bias set up an apparent with-participant conflict, with sometimes one and sometimes the other determining the judgement made (see Evans, Barston, & Pollard, 1983, and Chapter 4 of this book). How could this be if heuristic processes precede analytic ones?

It would be a mistake to think of heuristic and analytic systems as competitors of equal standing and a still worse mistake to think of them as thinking styles under strategic control (as implied by some dual-process theorists, such as Epstein, 1994). In the revised dual-processing model (Evans, 2006b) it is specifically proposed that heuristic processes set up *default* responses that will occur unless the analytic system intervenes to alter them. In common with the theory of Kahneman and Frederick (2002, see

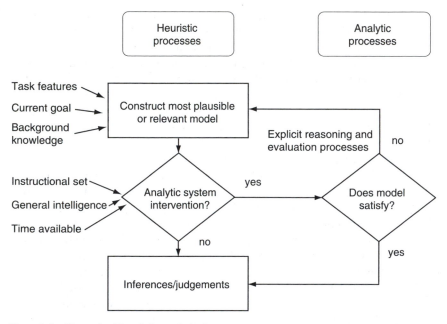

Figure 1.1   The revised heuristic–analytic theory.

Note: This figure was previously published in *Psychonomic Bulletin and Review* (Evans, 2006b) and is reproduced by permission of the Psychonomic Society.

Chapter 5), however, these analytic processes are said always to have at least a minimal involvement, if only to approve (perhaps without reflection) the default response suggested by heuristically derived mental models. As an example, consider *belief bias*, which is a tendency to accept or reject an argument on the basis of whether you agree with its conclusions (see Chapter 4). Suppose that heuristic processes prompt the belief based response by default, and that this will be given unless analytic reasoning overrides it. Under what circumstances will the analytic system intervene and change this default? The main factors (as much research to be reviewed in this book will indicate) are shown in Figure 1.1. First, the use of strong deductive reasoning instructions (assume the premises are true, draw necessary conclusions) will increase logical responding and reduce belief bias as people are less satisfied with the default, unreflective response. Second, people with high IQ or working memory capacity may be more able to inhibit belief biases. Finally, a requirement to respond very quickly (or when working memory is occupied by another task) will increase belief bias and reduce the opportunity for analytic system intervention. Note that these methods imply several of the key constructs of System 2 thinking described earlier.

In terms of the three principles, what is happening here is that the heuristic system is cueing as most relevant a model of the problem that favours prior belief. Shallow processing by the analytic system will allow this to be converted into a validity judgement that is belief based (belief bias). Under strong deductive reasoning instructions, however, people of higher ability may reject this model since with this motivation it does not satisfy. These instructions motivate a deeper and more effortful evaluation of the default model. What is generally thought of by dual-process theorists as *no* intervention of the analytic system is strictly incorrect. The analytic system is always involved to some degree in that the experimental tasks use verbal instructions. Some analytic processing of epistemic mental models is required to generate a response that is appropriate to these instructions. What is normally meant by analytic system intervention, however, is rejecting or revising the default model generated by the heuristic system. Many examples of such heuristic–analytic interactions will be discussed in this book.

The heuristic system operates in this revised theory in much the same way as proposed in the original (Evans, 1984, 1989). Its function is to deliver relevant content into consciousness on a continuous basis. What is relevant depends upon the attentional characteristics of the problem presented, the current goals that are being pursued and relevant prior knowledge evoked by the context. The analytic system – or System 2 – has, however, functions that go beyond what can be captured in the simple diagram of Figure 1.1. It adds a capacity for strategic and abstract thinking that is not possible at the heuristic level, and it has a major role in confabulation, rationalization and self-deception that I will discuss in Chapter 7. It is sequential and constrained by working memory capacity. It is not, however, a form of thinking that can operate without the heuristic system. The locus of attention and the content of analytic thinking are subject to continuous influence of rapid and parallel processing within the heuristic system.

This revised framework allows for cognitive biases to operate in two main ways. First, the heuristic system may bias reasoning through selective representation and contextualization as argued by Evans (1989) and Stanovich (1999). Second, however, singularity and satisficing principles imply that biases will arise in analytic processing also. This is because essentially one model is considered and accepted if there is no good reason to reject it. The evaluation process may be inadequate due to low processing effort, low cognitive capacity or lack of appropriate cognitive tools (see also Stanovich, 2004, 2006). The singularity principle also ensures that any kind of disjunctive thinking will be difficult, where alternative possibilities need to be compared. It will also interfere with deductive reasoning, as satisficing on a single model of the premise of an argument can easily lead to acceptance of fallacies – conclusions that are not logically necessary. I will illustrate in this book that each of these cognitive constraints plays a significant part in generating what are observed as cognitive biases on a wide range of tasks.

Table 1.2
Fundamental biases of the heuristic and analytic systems

Fundamental heuristic bias	People focus selectively on information that is preconsciously cued as relevant
Fundamental analytic bias	People maintain the current mental model with insufficient evaluation and/or consideration of alternatives

Stanovich (1999) argues for a "fundamental computational bias" being the tendency to contextualize all problems in the light of prior knowledge and belief. This will lead to cognitive biases, such as belief bias, when such contextualization is irrelevant to a formal or abstract problem. I will refer here instead to a more broadly defined *fundamental heuristic bias* (in System 1), which is essentially that on which the Evans (1989) account was based. The definition shown in Table 1.2 allows for influence of linguistic and attentional factors, as well as contextualization effects. Essentially, we tend to focus selectively on information that is preconsciously cued as "relevant" (relevance principle). The second bias in System 2 I shall call *the fundamental analytic bias* (see Table 1.2). This is the tendency to accept the current model (hypothesis, possibility) as the basis of inference, decision or action without either sufficient evaluation or consideration of alternatives (singularity and satisficing principles).

Both of these are biases only in the sense of the disposition of our cognitive systems to operate in particular ways, rather than in a pejorative sense implying irrationality. Nevertheless, I will show in this book that these *two* fundamental biases in the way our cognitive systems work account for very many of the cognitive biases demonstrated in the literatures on reasoning and judgement.

FORM OF THE BOOK

Chapters 2 to 6 of this book review a range of experimental evidence on how people reason and make judgements and attempt to show in the process how these provide evidence for the distinction between heuristic and analytic processing and the three principles of hypothetical thinking described above. The chapters are organized thematically and correspond roughly (but by no means precisely) to distinct research traditions and their associated literatures. Chapter 2, for example, focuses on the issue of hypothesis testing drawing on several research traditions. This chapter also introduces the Wason selection task, which requires hypothesis testing but is traditionally studied by researchers in the deductive reasoning area. Chapters 3 and 4 also draw heavily on the reasoning literature but are distinguished by their focus on issues concerning suppositional thinking and mental simulation

(Chapter 3) and on the role of knowledge and belief in reasoning processes (Chapter 4). Chapters 5 and 6 draw largely on the literatures on judgement and decision making, including the rather separate tradition of work on social judgement theory. Chapter 5 is focused primarily on decision making and Chapter 6 on studies of how people think about statistical information and make judgements under uncertainty. While best kept in pairs, the ordering of these four chapters is somewhat arbitrary. Hence Chapters 5 and 6 could be read prior to 3 and 4 without loss of continuity. The final chapter (7) is focused on several broader theoretical issues arising from these literatures and bearing closely upon the more general concerns of dual-process theory.

CHAPTER TWO

Hypothesis testing

This book is concerned with hypothetical thinking, which involves the imagination of possibilities and the simulation of their consequences. It is evident that hypothesis-testing behaviour must be of direct relevance to this enterprise. However, hypothesis-testing tasks differ from others considered in this book (for example, decision making) in that evaluation of imagined possibilities does not rest simply on the ability to simulate mentally their characteristics and consequences, although this may be involved in generating predictions. Hypothesis testing also involves observation of and frequently experimentation with the actual world, gathering evidence relevant to the hypothesis under consideration. As a result, hypotheses may be supported or refuted, and retained, revised or abandoned by the hypothesis tester. What I will attempt to demonstrate in this chapter is that this interactive process conforms with the same principles that describe other kinds of hypothetical thinking. In particular, hypothesis-testing behaviour is subject to the fundamental analytic bias (Table 1.2) in that there is a tendency to consider just one hypothesis at a time (singularity principle) and to retain it unless evidence is discovered that provides a strong reason to give it up (satisficing principle).

The tasks that psychologists have used to study how people test hypotheses fall somewhat outside the two main research paradigms introduced in Chapter 1, although they are closely related. While most research on human reasoning has used the deduction paradigm, hypothesis testing is normally associated with inductive reasoning tasks. Such tasks involve trying to discover a general rule or concept from specific forms of evidence. In contrast with deductive reasoning, inductive reasoning is not logically valid because the conclusions add information to the premises. Thus inductive inferences sometimes take the form of inductive generalizations, such as:

> All the psychology books I have read are boring; therefore, all psychology books are boring.

Clearly, the next psychology book you read (or hopefully this one) may not be boring, so this inference can never be valid. What makes this particularly interesting is that a traditional view of science is that empirical observations are undertaken in order to discover general scientific laws. How could this be achieved? A solution might be an inductive generalization such as:

> All electrons that have been observed carry a negative charge; therefore all electrons carry a negative charge.

If science does consist of such inferences then it is logically unsound, hardly a satisfactory state of affairs. This is known to philosophers of science as the *problem of induction* (Howson & Urbach, 1993). I will come shortly to some proposed solutions to this problem. Now, where does hypothesis testing come in? Whether you are an empirical scientist working in cutting-edge research, or a child trying to understand the world it is growing up in, or anyone exposed to new and unfamiliar circumstances, you are likely to hypothesize. Suppose, for example, that an American sports fan unfamiliar with the precise laws of cricket finds himself watching a cricket game on a holiday in England. He knows that a batsman can be given out in various ways, one of which is "leg before wicket" or LBW. This rule is there to prevent batsmen blocking the ball from hitting the stumps (or wickets) with their legs or any other part of the body. As he watches the game, the American fan sees the fielding team appeal to the umpires in a number of cases where the ball strikes the batsman's body without appearing to hit his bat. Some are given out, but many are not. Why? The actual rule is quite complex – see Figure 2.1.

With no one to explain the rules, he hypothesizes initially that if the umpire judges that the ball will hit the stumps then he is given out. However, it becomes clear that this is not always the case: in fact there are many counterexamples in the game watched. After a while, he notices that appeals are never successful if the ball pitches wide of the leg stump (the right-hand side of the wickets as seen by the bowler for a right-handed batsman). He decides this cannot be due to careless umpiring and there must be a rule, so he refines his hypothesis: the batsman is LBW if the ball pitches in line with the wickets and will hit them. This new hypothesis is confirmed by the observation that on several occasions a batsman struck outside the line of the off stump was also not given out. Content that he understands the rule

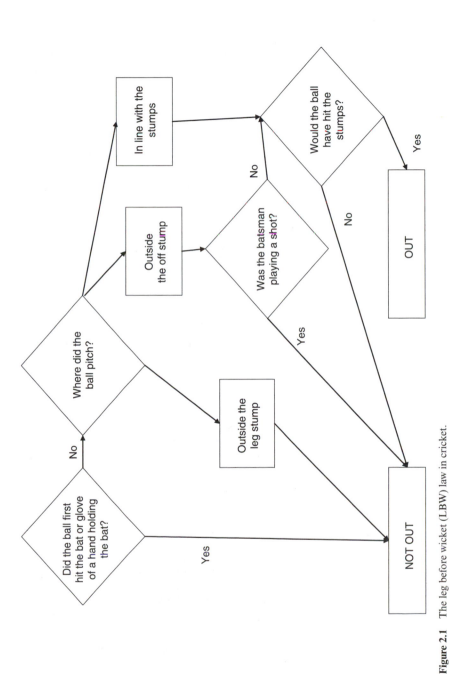

Figure 2.1 The leg before wicket (LBW) law in cricket.

Note: The batsman defends three stumps (or wickets). The off stump for a right-handed batsman is to his left as viewed by the bowler and the leg stump to his right. The reverse relationships hold for a left-handed batsman.

he settles down to enjoy the game. Several hours later a batsman is struck by a ball well outside the off stump, but which looks as though it will hit the wickets. Much to his surprise, the umpire gives the batsman out.

What does our confused American sports fan now do? His repeatedly confirmed LBW hypothesis is suddenly falsified. He may or may not observe what was different in this particular case: the batsman stuck his leg in the way of the ball *without attempting to play a shot*. The LBW rule is actually rather more complex than it might at first appear. The thought process described in this example is one of *passive* hypothesis testing. The observer here has no control over the events but nonetheless can observe and reason about them. Forming a hypothesis that is then abandoned or revised when disconfirmed is a pretty natural way of doing this. In fact, a tradition of study of concept learning or concept identification in the psychological laboratory has shown that with such passive tasks most people will form a particular hypothesis and stick with it unless there is a reason to give it up (disconfirming evidence). Then they will form a new hypothesis that they try to make consistent with evidence that they have already encountered (Bruner, Goodnow, & Austin, 1956; Levine, 1966).

Note that the evidence from such passive rule-learning tasks is entirely consistent with the principles of hypothetical thinking theory set out in Chapter 1. According to the singularity principle, we generally consider one mental model at a time, in this case representing a hypothesis. According to the satisficing principle we will maintain this model unless it fails to satisfy. Hence, maintaining the current hypothesis unless it is disproved is what we would expect people to do from the viewpoint of this theory. It conforms also with the general principle of bounded rationality. Constructing all possible hypotheses and keeping them in mind simultaneously would exceed our computational capacity. Proving a hypothesis to be true is a logical impossibility as indicated earlier, so keeping it until there is good reason to change it seems pretty sensible. Any hypothesis that avoids refutation for a long period of time is likely to be at least a useful approximation of the truth for practical purposes.

In this chapter, I will mostly consider tasks that involve *active* hypothesis testing. In this case, the individual is in charge of the procedure by which evidence is gathered. This is the type of task where *confirmation bias* (Klayman, 1995; Oswald & Grosjean, 2004; Wason, 1960) becomes an issue. To start with a real-world example, consider the case of police investigating a criminal offence. Where miscarriages of justice occur, or are believed to have occurred, a common accusation is that the police identified a suspect, often early in the investigation, and formed a strong belief that he or she was the perpetrator. From that point on, it may be argued, they looked only for evidence that could help to convict the suspect and ignored other lines of enquiry. This is what confirmation bias is: bias in the way in which we go about gathering evidence to test a favoured – sometime referred to as *focal* – hypothesis. It is distinct from biased evaluation of evidence, which is more akin to belief bias (see Chapter 4).

Psychologists' interest in active hypothesis testing and whether or not it involves a confirmation bias has mostly been based on the implications for the practice of science (Evans, 2002c). In the experimental sciences, including psychology, scientists can design true experiments to test hypotheses of the form: A causes B. Such experiments ideally involve controlled comparisons of situations in which A is present or absent, with no other variables differing, and allowing observation of whether or not B occurs. The question is whether or not their thinking about the design of such experiments is constrained by belief in a focal hypothesis and a desire to prove it true. This concern about confirmation bias in science arises from issues in the philosophy of science, which requires some discussion prior to examination of the empirical evidence.

POPPERIAN VERSUS BAYESIAN SOLUTIONS TO THE PROBLEM OF INDUCTION

The philosopher Karl Popper (Popper, 1959, 1962) proposed a famous solution to the problem of induction. The following argument is not logically valid:

> If the theory is correct then the predicted effect should occur   2.1
> The predicted effect occurs
> Therefore the theory is correct.

However, this argument is logically valid:

> If the theory is correct then the predicted effect should occur   2.2
> The predicted effect does not occur
> Therefore the theory is incorrect.

In the study of conditional reasoning (Evans & Over, 2004), 2.1 has a form known as Affirmation of the Consequent and is a fallacy: that is, the premises can be true and the conclusion false. The theory might be wrong even though it generates a correct prediction in some particular experiment. Example 2.2, however, is a valid argument known as Modus Tollens. Hence, we cannot logically confirm a theory but we can logically disconfirm or falsify it. On this basis, essentially, Popper built his philosophy of science and his solution to the problem of induction. The purpose of science is to falsify, not verify. This philosophy prescribes consequences such as: (a) theories, if they are to be called scientific, must be capable of falsification; they achieve this by assuming little and predicting much; and (b) scientists must devise ways of testing their theory that maximize the possibility of falsification: for example, they should make "risky predictions" that would not normally be made for reasons *other* than holding the theory.

Popper's falsificationism was unequivocally adopted as a normative standard by Peter Wason in his pioneering studies of human hypothesis testing and reasoning (Wason, 1960, 1966; Wason & Johnson-Laird, 1972). Wason was convinced by his own research that people have a confirmation bias (or verification bias as he preferred to call it) and that they were consequently irrational. He wrote of this research on the 2 4 6 problem, described below, that "the fixated, obsessional behaviour of some of the subjects would be analogous to that of a person who is thinking within a closed system – a system which defies refutation, e.g. existentialism and the majority of religions. These experiments demonstrate . . . how dogmatic thinking and the refusal to entertain the possibility of alternatives can easily result in error" (Wason, 1968, p. 174). Popperian philosophy continues to be popular among psychologists and other experimental scientists, with the widespread notion that falsification is the correct strategy of science.

In fact, as is the case with many of the biases to be discussed in this book, confirmation bias is set relative to a highly questionable normative standard. The logical argument (2.2) on which Popper's philosophy is based is fraught with difficulty (Howson & Urbach, 1993). Two major problems are those of probability and evidence. Let us return to the concept of experimentation in a statistical science such as psychology. We do indeed set up experiments to test hypotheses of the form A causes B, by checking for B under conditions where A is present and absent. However, we could not paraphrase the major premise 2.2 in the following way:

If the theory is correct, then we should observe B in the presence   2.3
of A and not in the absence of A.

The reason is simply that ours is statistical science and that our notion of causation is probabilistic, as are most contemporary normative accounts of causality (Pearl, 2000; Sloman, 2005). Our statistical methodology means that we are really testing claims of the following form:

If the theory is correct, then the probability of B will be greater in   2.4
the presence of A than in the absence of A.

Statistical significance testing, itself a highly dubious methodology (Evans, 2005; Gigerenzer & Murray, 1987), is designed to deal with this kind of question. We confirm our hypotheses in psychology by showing statistically significant differences between measures taken under experimental and control conditions. So do many other sciences. Statistical evaluations are used, for example, to test the effectiveness of medical interventions – new drugs or other kinds of treatments – in controlling diseases and symptoms. But what constitutes confirmation or disconfirmation in such a case? For example, if the predicted effect is not statistically significant then the theory is not confirmed, but it can hardly be argued that it is *logically* falsified as Popperianism requires. The effect may have been present but insufficient statistical power was available to detect it.

This brings us to the problem of evidence. Logical falsification of a hypothesis requires that the evidence is certain. A theory can be assumed true for the sake of a logical argument (that might disprove it) but can the evidence of a failed prediction be accorded the same epistemic status? How can evidence be certain when errors are possible in the conceptual design of experiments, in the recording and transcription of data, in the computer software that is used for data analysis? All of these have nonzero probabilities in addition to other less likely possibilities, such as dishonest experimenters faking their data. Theoretical physicists, for example, are not in the habit of revising their theories in the light of inconsistent experimental findings, until those findings have been thoroughly checked for possible experimental error (Feynman, 1985). The same has been shown for molecular biologists in a study I will describe later (Fugelsang, Stein, Green, & Dunbar, 2004).

Poletiek (2001) has demonstrated some paradoxical aspects of Popperian theory that seem to undermine the notion of confirmation bias. As mentioned earlier, Popper claimed that scientists should test risky predictions: formally these are predictions whose probability given the hypothesis plus background beliefs is much higher than those given background beliefs alone. In other words, the hypothesis must substantially *raise* the probability of the event. Formally, the severity of the test is given by the ratio:

$$\frac{P(x \mid H + b)}{P(x \mid b)} \qquad 2.5$$

where H is the focal hypothesis, b background beliefs, and x the predicted observation. When the prediction is unlikely to occur for reasons other than the hypothesis, Popper argued that this made the test more severe, more open to falsification. What is paradoxical about this, as Poletiek (2001, chap. 1) demonstrates is that exactly the same kind of test maximizes relevance from the viewpoint of confirmation. In other words, a disconfirmatory attitude, as recommended by Popper, leads to the same kind of testing behaviour as a confirmatory attitude!

The reason for this can be seen intuitively. Consider the case of Einstein's general theory of relativity. Some of the predictions made were very severe in Popper's sense: for example, rays of light should bend in the region of the sun's massive gravitational field, and atomic clocks should run faster at the north pole than at the equator. What background beliefs, held without the theory, would lead to such predictions? However, the eventual confirmation of these predictions strongly increased belief in the theory: the findings were seen as very strong confirmatory evidence precisely because there was no other basis for making these predictions. But if a confirmatory attitude can produce severe tests, is there any such thing as a confirmation bias?

Popper held the classical objectivist theory of probability, which can only represent relative frequencies and is hence inapplicable to events that do not form part of frequency distributions. This includes scientific theories and hypotheses, which therefore cannot be assigned a probability. In his view, positive results could only "corroborate" and not confirm a theory – that is, their probability was not raised by such results, as it was meaningless to talk of a probability in this sense. This view stands in stark contrast to the Bayesian approach, which has been developed from a theory of subjective probability and belief revision into a full-blown philosophy of science (Howson & Urbach, 1993). To a Bayesian, probability – while conforming to the mathematics of the probability calculus – is subjective. A probability is a degree of belief – no more, no less. Hence, probability can be assigned to any object of belief, including a scientific hypothesis or theory.

The Bayesian method prescribes that belief change is a gradual process. We hold a degree of belief in some hypothesis that is subject to revision when new evidence is encountered. The posterior belief we have – that is, what we believe after viewing the evidence – is a multiplicative function of our prior belief in the hypothesis and the diagnosticity of the evidence. Evidence (D) is diagnostic to the extent that it distinguishes the focal hypothesis from alternatives. In the "odds" form of Bayes theorem, in which two alternative hypothesis H_1 and H_2 are compared, the formula can be written as:

$$\frac{P(H_1/D)}{P(H_2/D)} = \frac{P(H_1)}{P(H_2)} \times \frac{P(D/H_1)}{P(D/H_2)}. \tag{2.6}$$

This formula can be read verbally as

Posterior odds = Prior odds × Likelihood ratio.

The mathematics of Bayesian revision are simple. The extent to which you believe in a hypothesis after viewing some evidence will depend both on your degree of prior belief in it and on the strength (or diagnosticity) of the evidence. The likelihood ratio expresses the probability of the evidence given the one hypothesis to its probability given the other. This is also known as the diagnosticity of the evidence. Note that in the case where H_1 and H_2 exhaust the possibilities – that is, when H_1 is some specific hypothesis and H_2 is any alternative to it – the diagnosticity of the test becomes equivalent to Popper's severity measure (2.5). Thus a *good* test of a hypothesis is the same from a confirmatory, disconfirmatory or Bayesian perspective!

What is very different in the Bayesian philosophy of science is that belief in theories can be raised or lowered in a gradual manner as evidence is encountered for and against them. This idea naturally maps on to the notion that people represent hypotheses in epistemic mental models that include the current degree of belief in them. Naturally, when this belief falls below a satisfactory level, the analytic system will reject the hypotheses, and another will be generated. Because Bayesian theory is intrinsically probabilistic, rather than logical, it does not fall prey to the problems for the Popperian approach mentioned earlier. The probabilistic nature of data in many sciences creates no difficulties. Bayesian revision can also be extended quite naturally to deal with the probability of evidence, rather than treating it as certain. The Bayesian philosophy does not require scientists to display either a confirmatory or disconfirmatory attitude – it merely recommends the use of diagnostic hypothesis testing. In my view, it also provides a much more credible descriptive model for how scientists – and for that matter ordinary people – behave when testing hypotheses and revising theoretical beliefs.

What do real scientists do when they encounter disconfirmation? A recent study by Fugelsang et al. (2004) involved observation of a number of research groups in the field of molecular biology. Of 417 original experiments covered by the study more than half (223) failed to conform to theoretical expectations! However, in only 31 per cent of these cases did the scientists concerned blame the theory; in other cases they questioned the experimentation. Subsequently, 154 new experiments were designed to follow up these discrepant results, with improved methodology. The majority of these (84) replicated the unexpected finding. In the majority of these cases (58 per cent), the scientists questioned their theoretical assumptions, although a substantial minority did not. This extensive and thorough study is of great interest. It shows first that experimental evidence is uncertain in the minds of the scientists, even in a relatively hard science. They clearly are not behaving like Popperians as they mostly hold on to their theory in the light of single disconfirmation. They are also more likely to give up their theory when a second disconfirmation is observed. The tendency to hold on to hypotheses is consistent with the fundamental analytic bias but that is not to say that they are wrong to behave as they do. Theories and hypotheses are expensive in time and effort to develop, and experiments can be flawed and misleading. Thus, while the less charitable view of these findings is that the scientists are bad Popperians, I prefer the interpretation that they are behaving like good Bayesians.

WASON'S 2 4 6 PROBLEM

One of the main reasons that confirmation bias became an issue in the psychology of reasoning was the results of a simple and elegant experiment presented by Wason (1960). Participants were told that the experimenter had a rule in mind which classifies sets of three integers (whole numbers). I will refer to such groups of three numbers as "triples" in this discussion. In the original form of the task, subjects were told that the triple "2 4 6" conformed to the rule. They were then asked to try to discover the rule by generating triples of their own. For each triple, the experimenter told the participant whether or not it conformed to his rule. They were required to keep a written record of their triples, the experimenter's responses and their current hypotheses about the rule. They were also told not to announce the rule until they were sure of its correctness. If they announced a wrong rule then they were told so and were asked to continue testing triples.

The example "2 4 6" was deliberately chosen by Wason to suggest a specific sort of rule to the subject such as "Ascending with equal intervals", whereas the actual rule held by the experimenter was "Any ascending sequence". Participants found the task surprisingly difficult. The majority announced at least one incorrect hypothesis, and a substantial minority failed to solve it at all. What created particular interest in this task, however, was the pattern of hypothesis-testing behaviour that emerged. In general, participants tested their hypotheses by generating only positive examples, with the consequence that they failed to receive disconfirming evidence. If, for example, they held the hypothesis that the rule was "Ascending with equal intervals" and tested triples such as 10 12 14, 10 20 30, 1 2 3, and 100 500 900, the experimenter would, of course, in each case respond that the triple conformed to his rule. Participants thus received consistent evidence for their hypothesis, became convinced of its correctness and were very puzzled when told that it was wrong. What they generally did *not* do was to test examples such as 100 200 500 that did not conform to the hypothesis. Such negative predictions could lead to falsification of the hypothesis since the experimenter would still say that they conformed to his rule.

On the basis of this experiment, Wason claimed that people have a verification or confirmation bias. In other words, contrary to Popperian dogma, they were attempting to find evidence that could confirm rather than falsify their current hypothesis. This claim was subject to immediate criticism by Wetherick (1962) on very good grounds but with little impact at the time. Based on both the 2 4 6 task and early findings on his other famous problem, the selection task (Wason, 1966), Wason spread the view that people were bad Popperians in possession of an irrational and damaging confirmation bias (Wason & Johnson-Laird, 1972). While the verification bias account of the selection task was effectively challenged soon after (Evans & Lynch, 1973), support for Wason's view of the 2 4 6 problem was built in a series of replication studies reviewed by Evans (1989). Only after the criticisms published by Klayman and Ha (1987) and Evans (1989) did psychologists seriously question Wason's original conclusions. Recent reviewers now generally agree that it is very hard to interpret the 2 4 6 tasks and related experimental problems as indicating any intentional attitude of confirmation on the part of the participants (Oswald & Grosjean, 2004; Poletiek, 2001).

There is no question that participants on the 2 4 6 task are demonstrating confirmatory behaviour, in the sense that they hold on to an incorrect hypothesis in the light of repeated confirmations. What is at issue is whether they are *trying* to confirm their hypotheses. What they clearly *are* doing is repeatedly testing positive cases of their hypotheses and rarely generating negative tests. The difficulty for Wason's argument is that both positive and negative testing can lead – in principle – to either confirming or disconfirming results. Suppose a pharmaceutical company devises an experimental drug X. It is similar to one tested and discarded earlier – an effective appetite depressant – that was discovered in clinical trials to have the unfortunate side effect of raising blood pressure. This time the researchers are confident that the new drug will work without side effects, but they need clinical trials to prove this. They have thus devised both a positive and a negative hypothesis:

A. Drug X will suppress appetite
B. Drug X will not raise blood pressure

In the research, they follow both a positive test strategy for Hypothesis A and a negative strategy for Hypothesis B. But, of course, each hypothesis may be confirmed or disconfirmed by the results as follows:

Hypothesis A
Predict suppression of appetite

Appetite suppressed
(positive confirmation)
Appetite not suppressed
(positive disconfirmation)

Hypothesis B
Predict blood pressure not raised

No rise in blood pressure
(negative confirmation)
Rise in blood pressure
(negative disconfirmation)

Wason's participants made only positive predictions (what should happen if their hypothesis was true) and not negative predictions (what should *not* happen if their hypothesis was true). Thus in principle they were open to positive confirmation or disconfirmation. What Wetherick (1962) was the first to point out was that the fact that they could not receive positive disconfirmation was, in effect, a trick of the experiment. Because they were induced to adopt a hypothesis that was more specific than the actual rule (in fact a subset of it), any positive test of their hypothesis would always conform to the experimenter's rule. However, does this mean that positive testing would normally lead to confirmation in science and other real-world settings? The general view is that this is not the case and that there is good reason to think that a positive test strategy would normally be effective (Klayman & Ha, 1987). My example above also shows that where negative testing is pragmatically cued as relevant (in this case concerns about side effects on similar drugs) it should quite naturally be adopted.

In view of the earlier general discussion, it is of interest to see whether inducing a falsificationist attitude in participants, by use of experimental instructions, actually changes the hypothesis-testing behaviour. Results of relevant studies are somewhat equivocal depending mostly on the tasks used, which are in some cases the 2 4 6 problem and in others minor or major variants on Wason's original task (Gorman & Gorman, 1984; Gorman, Stafford, & Gorman, 1987; Mynatt, Doherty, & Tweney, 1977, 1978; Poletiek, 1996; Tweney et al., 1980). In general, simply exhorting people to falsify their hypotheses has not been very successful. However, it has been claimed both to modify expectations of falsification without improving performance (Tweney et al., 1980) and conversely to induce more negative testing on the 2 4 6 problem, but without any greater expectation among the participants that these would lead to a falsifying outcome (Poletiek, 1996, Exp. 1). In a variant on the 2 4 6 problem (using number triples but different rules and more example triples) Poletiek (1996, Exp. 2) found that the main determinant of falsifications being obtained was whether or not the correct hypothesis was guessed initially, rather than an attitude of falsification.

A recent study by Spellman, Lopez, and Smith (1999) did succeed in inducing negative testing, albeit with substantially modified methodology. They did this by cueing participants to think of the task as either generaliz-ing or restricting a hypothesis. Here is an example (p. 76) of two of their problems:

> Suppose you know for a fact that:
> The ordered triad of numbers 2–4–6 conforms to an unknown rule about number triads called alpha.
> What triad would you examine to test whether or not:
> *(All condition)* All triads ascending by two conform to the alpha rule
> *(Only condition)* Only triads ascending by two conform to the alpha rule
>
> Choose one of the following triads (circle to answer)

(a) 8–10–12 *(positive test – similar triad)*
(b) 9–11–13 *(positive test – dissimilar triad)*
(c) 1–2–3 *(negative test)*.

In the "all" condition, only 10 per cent of participants chose the negative test option, but in the "only" condition this rose dramatically to 68 per cent (data from their Experiment 1). This finding was generalized to different content and replicated in a second experiment. This suggests that participants under standard instructions assume by default that they are to try to generalize the hypothesis rather than restrict it. I will return to this study shortly.

What do all these findings imply for hypothetical thinking theory? As pointed out earlier, the fact that people stick with a hypothesis until it is disconfirmed is entirely to be expected. Testing multiple hypotheses is not consistent with the singularity principle. However, positive testing bias, if I can call it that, needs to be accounted for. Is it a bias in the heuristic or analytic system? The arguments of Evans (1989) imply the former, a general *positivity* bias that is also manifest as a "matching bias" on other reasoning tasks (see next section). On the other hand the description of the effect as a positive test *strategy* (Klayman & Ha, 1987) might suggest a role for the analytic thinking system. I personally reserve the term "strategy" for conscious, volitional processes that involve the analytic system, although I have noticed that not all other authors do the same (see the collection of essays edited by Schaeken, DeVooght, Vandierendonck, & d'Ydewalle, 2000).

In principle, we are capable of following conscious hypothesis-testing strategies; otherwise we would not bother teaching research methods to our students. However, I think it is very likely that the positive testing bias observed in Wason's 2 4 6 problem and related tasks is a heuristic relevance effect. We tend to form singular mental models filled with relevant content, which by default is what is most plausible or probable. So once we have simulated a possibility it will be natural to model the consequences that are likely to follow. We would not normally think about what will *not* be the case, as that would involve simulating a different possibility. Thus the production of positive tests to the exclusion of negative ones is a manifestation of the fundamental heuristic bias. However, the confirmatory behaviour that is observed on the 2 4 6 and related tasks is also a function of the fundamental analytic bias. That is to say, having generated positive tests that are repeatedly confirmed (given the task structure), people will develop strong belief in the focal hypothesis and fail to consider alternatives to it. The reason that this should not be considered an intentional-level confirmation bias is simply that people are not generating positive tests *in order* to confirm their hypotheses.

In general, our analytic thinking system will naturally focus on the (heuristically delivered) positive consequences of hypotheses and construct tests around them. A natural exception to this, however, arises when we wish to deny a presupposition. In the case of the drug research example, the possibility of a side effect increasing blood pressure would come to mind as this had been associated with research on a related drug. Hence, there is a specific reason to test that this will *not* be the case with the new drug. We should also recall that the analytic system is responsive to verbal instructions and not always satisfied by default mental models. In the study of Spellman et al. (1999), described above, the use of the quantifiers "all" and "only" introduce significant changes to the logic of the task. In fact, neither correspond to Wason's original task in which people had to discover what the experimenter's rule was. The "all" rule can *only* be falsified by a positive test now. The hypothesis "All triads ascending by two conform to the alpha rule" is *not* the same as the hypothesis "The alpha rule is all triads ascending by two", although it may be that people are pragmatically cued to think about the standard task as though they were equivalent. The "only rule": "Only triads ascending by two conform to the alpha rule" can similarly only be falsified by the negative test. It is not surprising that university students are able to distinguish the logic of these two problems. The presentation of a negative test item for evaluation (as opposed to the standard request to generate all items) probably helps as well.

From a dual-process point of view, the protocols published by Wason are extremely interesting. Consider the following, from Wason (1960, rule announcements shown in italics):

No. 4. Female, aged 19, 1st year undergraduate
8 10 12: two added each time; 14 16 18: even numbers in order of magnitude; 20 22 24: same reason; 1 3 5: two added to preceding number.
The rule is that by starting with any number two is added each time to form the next number.
2 6 10: middle number is the arithmetic mean of the other two; 1 50 99: same reason.
The rule is that the middle number is the arithmetic mean of the other two.
3 10 17: same number, seven, added each time; 0 3 6: three added each time.
The rule is that the difference between two numbers next to each other is the same.
12 8 4: the same number subtracted each time to form the next number.
The rule is adding a number, always the same one, to form the next number.
1 4 9: any three numbers in order of magnitude.
The rule is any three numbers in order of magnitude.
(17 minutes)

What is remarkable about this case (far from unique, according to Wason) is that the middle three rules announced are logically exactly the same, just formulated in different words. This participant (in common with others) becomes fixated on a hypothesis that is repeatedly confirmed and never falsified by the tests made. As we might expect from the viewpoint of the Bayesian model, this induces strong belief in the hypothesis. This is then contradicted by verbal instruction as the experimenter tells her that the rule she has announced is wrong. As we shall see in Chapter 3, when experience-based belief conflicts with verbal instructions, belief often dominates people's inferences. A major role of the analytic system seems also to be that of rationalization and confabulation (see Chapter 7). The repeated verbalization of the same hypothesis seems to be a dramatic example of this.

THE WASON SELECTION TASK

Wason (1966) presented a new reasoning problem that has since become one of the most investigated tasks in the history of research into human reasoning (for a recent review, see Evans & Over, 2004, chap. 5). It is the main task used in the psychology of reasoning that falls outside the strict definition of the deduction paradigm as given in Chapter 1, although it tends to be investigated by researchers within the deductive reasoning tradition. The task is deceptively simple, for in its standard form the great majority of participants fail to give the correct solution to it. In a typical version of the task the participant will be told that the problem concerns cards that have capital letters on one side and single-figure numbers on the other. Sometimes they are given a pack of such cards to inspect. Originally, they were shown four cards lying on a table whose exposed sides showed two letters and two numbers. Most recent research has used a representation of this situation presented either on a sheet of paper or on a computer screen. A typical version is shown in Figure 2.2.

The problem is to decide which cards would logically need to be turned over in order to find out whether the stated rule "If there is an A on one side of the card then there is a 3 on the other side of the card" is true or false. The great majority of participants tested say either that the A card would be sufficient or else that the A and the 3 need to be turned over (Evans et al., 1993; Wason & Johnson-Laird, 1972). It is generally agreed (but see Oaksford & Chater, 1994) that one should turn over the A and the 7 or else all four cards if the statement is interpreted as a biconditional. Like the 2 4 6 problem, the four-card selection task requires people to seek evidence actively rather than simply to evaluate it. The task differs in that the hypothesis to be tested (the rule) is supplied by the experimenter. The participants can, however, choose to examine evidence that could confirm or disconfirm the rule according to the cards that they specify for turning over. Let us consider each of the cards in turn:

There are four cards lying on a table. Each has a capital letter on one side and a single-digit number on the other side. The exposed sides are shown below:

The rule shown below applies to these four cards and may be true or false:

If there is an A on one side of the card, then there is a 3 on the other side of the card

Your task is to decide those cards, and only those cards, that need to be turned over in order to discover whether the rule is true or false.

Figure 2.2   A standard abstract version of the Wason selection task.

1.   The A card. If this were turned over there could be either a number that is a 3 or a number that is not a 3 on the back. The former would be consistent with the rule but the latter would clearly violate the rule – that is, show it to be false.
2.   The D card. The rule does not specify any condition about letters that are not As so whatever number is discovered on the back could not disprove the rule.
3.   The 3 card. The 3 could have a letter that is an A or that is not an A on the back. Either would be consistent with the rule since it is required only that As have 3s on the back and not vice versa.
4.   The 7 card. If this were turned over and there were not an A on the back it would be consistent with the rule. However, if an A were found on the back the card would have an A on one side and a number that is not a 3 on the other, thus violating the rule.

In order to solve this task one needs apparently to appreciate only: (a) that the rule would be false if an A were paired with a number other than 3; and (b) that it is logically necessary to turn over any card that could reveal such a falsifying condition. On this basis clearly the A and the 7 must be chosen while the D and the 3 should not, since whatever they have on the other side cannot disprove the rule. In more general terms, for a statement of the form "if p then q", the common erroneous choices are p alone or p and q, and the correct response is the p and not-q cards, actually made by about 10–20 per cent of university students in typical experiments.

Why is the selection task so difficult? One explanation that we should dismiss straight away is that it is due to ambiguity of the conditional statement. Although the conditional states that an A must have a 3 on the back, the participant might well read it to mean that a 3 must also have an A on the back. In this case they would be reading the statements as an equivalence or biconditional. Would that not justify the selection of A and 3? The answer is no. If the rule is taken to read both ways then the correct solution is to choose *all four cards*, which people rarely do. The A and 7 must be chosen for the reasons already given. Since it is now assumed that a 3 must have an A on the back, then one must choose 3 and D as well since either could lead to the falsifying combination of a 3 on one side without an A on the other.

Another explanation that is sometimes proposed is that it shows a failure of Modus Tollens reasoning – that is, that people do not understand that a card without a 3 on one side must not have an A on the other. However, if we present an argument like this:

If there is an A on one side of the card, then there is a 3 on the other side of the card; there is not a 3 on the other side; what follows?

Most people (around 60–70 per cent in typical experiments) will say that there is not an A on the card. Competence in Modus Tollens reasoning appears much higher than the ability to pick out the 7 (not-3) card on this task. However, an explanation for this discrepancy has emerged in recent research, which I will describe below.

Wason's (1966) original explanation was that participants were exhibiting a verification or confirmation bias. Together with the 2 4 6 problem, this was the main foundation for the claim of a general confirmation bias in human reasoning (Wason & Johnson-Laird, 1972). As with the 2 4 6 problem it was assumed that people were motivated to find confirming evidence and therefore only looked at the cards that had A and 3 that could lead to the confirming combination of A3. Also as with the 2 4 6 problem, we have good reason to doubt that this explanation is correct. The main reason was discovery in 1973 of an effect called *matching bias* (Evans, 1998; Evans & Lynch, 1973), which we now consider in some detail.

Matching bias and the heuristic–analytic account of the selection task

Matching bias is a tendency to focus on (or perceive as relevant) cases that match the lexical content in the conditional statement. The effect can be demonstrated by using the *negations paradigm*, in which negated components are introduced into either component of the conditional statement. As an example, consider the variant on the standard abstract task shown in Figure 2.3. Apart from the actual letters and numbers used it differs from the version in Figure 2.2 by the addition of a negative consequent, so that the rule to be tested is: "If there is a G on one side of the card, then there is NOT a 4 on the other side of the card." For this rule, the matching choice is G and 4, but, because of the addition of the negation, this is now also the logically correct choice. This version is strongly facilitatory, as a majority of participants give the correct (and matching answer) – a finding first shown by Evans and Lynch (1973) and replicated many times since (see Evans, 1998).

By varying the presence of negations in both antecedent and consequent parts of the rule, it is possible to determine the impact of both the logical and the matching status of each card independently. If we define cards on the task by their logical status as follows:

True Antecedent (TA)
False Antecedent (FA)
True Consequent (TC)
False Consequent (FC)

There are four cards lying on a table. Each has a capital letter on one side and a single-digit number on the other side. The exposed sides are shown below:

The rule shown below applies to these four cards and may be true or false:

If there is a G on one side of the card, then
there is NOT a 4 on the other side of the card

Your task is to decide those cards, and only those cards, that need to be turned over in order to discover whether the rule is true or false.

Figure 2.3 A variant on the standard abstract version of the Wason selection task with a negated consequent.

then we can see that on the standard affirmative rule these correspond to p, not-p, q and not-q: the matching cases are also the true cases. The negations paradigm allows us to separate these out with the result shown in Figure 2.4. Note first that for all four logical choices, TA, FA, TC and FC, cards are chosen more often if they match than if they mismatch. Second, it can be seen that there is no verification bias, because, with matching controlled, TC and FC cards are chosen with roughly equal frequency. Third, with matching controlled, there is still a strong preference for TA over FA selections.

The dual-process account of the selection task (Evans, 1995; Evans & Over, 2004) proposes that on the standard abstract selection task described here, card choices are dominated by heuristic processes. It is not that analytic reasoning is not engaged, it is just that it (mostly) accepts the default selection of cards that are cued by heuristic processes. There seem to be two attentional heuristics that influence the perceived relevance of cards on the selection task: the if- and matching-heuristics (Evans, 1998). These account for the two trends that are evident in Figure 2.4. The if-heuristic, which we now link to our suppositional theory of conditionals (see Evans & Over, 2004, and Chapter 3), makes cases where the antecedent is true appear much more relevant than those where it is false. This seems to combine in additive fashion with the matching-heuristic, which cues matching over mismatching cards.

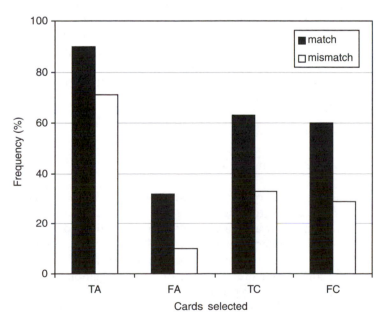

Figure 2.4   Frequency of card selections on the selection task in four experiments employing the negations paradigm (from Evans et al., 1993).

How can we relate this analysis to the hypothetical thinking theory? First, it indicates that attention is probably restricted to the cards cued as relevant by the if- and matching-heuristics, an example of the fundamental heuristic bias. Second, it implies that cards that are considered are generally chosen and not rejected by the analytic system, a manifestation of the fundamental analytic bias. It will be recalled that analytic system failures occur due to lack of appropriate motivation or cognitive resources, which cause people to be satisfied when they should not be. One reason that the selection task appears so much more difficult than most reasoning tasks studied in the literature is that analytic intervention either does not occur or is ineffective. (I will argue below that the latter explanation is correct.) If asked to point the mouse at cards they are "thinking of choosing", people spend very little time considering cards that they will not end up selecting (Evans, 1996), confirming the importance of preconscious attentional cueing on the selection task. Although this methodology has been criticized (Roberts, 1998), all of the predictions of Evans (1996) have been confirmed in a recent study using the improved method of eye-movement tracking (Ball et al., 2003). So that leaves us with two further questions: (a) why do people focus attention on matching cards; and (b) why does analytic reasoning fail to reject cards selected by the heuristic system? I will answer each in turn.

The cause of matching bias, in my view, is linked directly to the problem of implicit negation. Let us return to an issue discussed earlier, the discrepancy between rates of selection of the not-q card and rates of Modus Tollens inference in studies of conditional reasoning. A critical difference is that selection task research has traditionally used implicit negation while conditional inference research has used explicit negation. Thus Modus Tollens is normally presented like this:

If there is an A then there is a 3   2.7
There is not a 3
Therefore, there is not an A.

In this case the negation of 3 is explicitly not 3. But in the selection task example discussed earlier the negation of 3 is 7. People have to process the instruction that cards always have a letter on one side and a number on the other in order to infer that if a 7 is visible that card cannot have an A. Now what happens if we change the normal practice and use implicit negation in the conditional inference task, or explicit negation in the selection task? Happily, the relevant experiments have been run and the results are decisive. We can slightly amend the wording of the conditional inference task to produce implicit negation versions of inference such as Modus Tollens:

If the letter is an A then the number is a 3
The number is 7 (Implicit negation condition)
The number is not 3 (Explicit negation condition)
Therefore, the letter is not an A.

The results of experiments on this are very clear (Evans & Handley, 1999; Schroyens, Schaeken, Verschueren, & d'Ydewalle, 1999). When the minor premise of a conditional argument depends upon the processing of an implicit negation for its logical effect, there is a large and significant drop in rates of endorsement of the inference concerned. In effect, we have matching bias on the inference task once implicit negations are used. Conversely, we can introduce explicit negations into the selection task (Evans, Clibbens, & Rood, 1996a). The cards can bear descriptions of a letter–number pair, rather than the letters and numbers directly. In this case the four cards can read:

Implicit negation condition
The letter A   The letter D   The number 3   The number 7

Explicit negation condition
The letter A   A letter that is   The number 3   A number
                      not A   that is not 3

When this is done, matching bias *disappears completely* in the explicit negation condition (Evans et al., 1996a). However, logical performance does not improve! When matching bias is released, so that all cards are seen as equally relevant, people simply select more cards of all kinds, regardless of logical status. In spite of this strong evidence that matching bias reflects difficulty with implicit negation, however, there is a rival account of the phenomenon (Oaksford, 2002). Oaksford's account (first presented by Oaksford & Stenning, 1992) is based on the idea that negated propositions generally refer to contrast classes (what the proposition is not) that are very much bigger than the class of objects referred to by an affirmative proposition and hence much less informative. Recently, Yama (2001; see also a discussion of this paper by Evans, 2002b) designed experiments to separate these two accounts of matching bias and found evidence supportive of both. The debate continues, but will not detain us any further here.

Whatever the exact cause of the effect, it does seem clear that participants' attention becomes focused on the matching cards and on the true antecedent cards. The if-heuristic reflects the fact that conditional statements appear only relevant to situations where their antecedents hold in line with what is called the "defective truth table" (see Chapter 3 for discussion of this and the suppositional theory of conditionals). However, this does not explain why analytic reasoning seems to have so little effect on the selection task and contrasts with the general finding in the deductive reasoning literature that logical reasoning competes quite strongly with biases (see Chapters 3 and 4). The key to understanding this is to realize that analytic reasoning is not the same thing as logical reasoning. It is a conscious and deliberative attempt to reason according to the instructions, but in the case of the abstract selection task, only those of very high cognitive ability have the key insight that allows them to find the logically correct solution (Stanovich & West, 1998). Others simply end up *rationalizing* choice of the cards that appear relevant, just as Wason and Evans (1975) proposed many years ago.

The standard instructions on the task ask people to choose cards that help to decide whether the rule is true or false. We know from verbal protocol evidence that participants do in fact reason about the hidden sides of cards before making their selections (Evans, 1995; Lucas & Ball, 2005) and that selected cards are considered for some time before being chosen (Ball et al., 2003; Evans, 1996). Most people will, however, happily justify their card choices in terms of *either* verification or falsification (Wason & Evans, 1975). With the exception of participants of very high cognitive ability, people simply do not appreciate the asymmetry between the two concepts: namely that statements can be proved false but not proved true. And why should they, if they are not students of logic? If anything, the standard instructions suggest that the rule could be proved true as well as false. Finally, even though analytic reasoning does not normally inhibit card choices on the selection task there is evidence that it *can* do so. Feeney and Handley (2000; Handley, Feeney, & Harper, 2002) have found a manipulation that suppresses q card choices that can only be plausibly explained in terms of analytic reasoning (see Evans & Over, 2004, p. 79).

There has been extensive discussion of the selection task as a hypothesis-testing or decision-making task in the literature, which is beyond the scope of the present volume to consider in any detail (Evans & Over, 1996a; Kirby, 1994; Nickerson, 1996; Oaksford & Chater, 1994; Over & Manktelow, 1993; Poletiek, 2001). Some of these discussions relate to forms of the selection task that involve realistic content, which will be considered later in the book (Chapter 4). In such cases, people may be considered to be choosing cards in order to maximize expected utility. With abstract forms of the selection task, however, any such analysis can be framed only in terms of what people could expect to learn, the expected information gain (Oaksford & Chater, 1994) or "epistemic utility" (Evans & Over, 1996b) of card choices. Some analyses also assume effectively that the conditional statement applies more generally than to the four cards presented (Nickerson, 1996; Oaksford & Chater, 1994) in spite of the standard instruction introduced by Wason to explicitly restrict the scope of the rule. In my mind, it is allowable to assume that people's responses are insensitive to such instructional details, provided that the account given is in terms of default heuristics rather than explicit analytic reasoning processes.

CONCLUSIONS

This chapter has introduced the topic of hypothesis testing – a key type of hypothetical thinking. The major cognitive bias that is claimed in this area is that of "confirmation bias", the tendency to seek evidence to support rather than refute one's current hypothesis. However, we have seen that the normative system that originally inspired talk of such a bias – Popperian philosophy of science – is questionable for a number of reasons. For example, it relies on a form of logical argument that makes it inapplicable to any science dealing in uncertainty and probability, and it also assumes the certainty of evidence. Moreover, a falsificationist attitude will not in general lead to search for a different kind of evidence than will an approach based upon confirmation or Bayesian principles. Evidence from studies of real scientists suggests that they do not behave like Popperians: when experimental results conflict with theoretical expectations, scientists first question and check the methodology before revising or abandoning theory.

The principles of hypothetical thinking introduced in Chapter 1 support some aspects of the notion of confirmation bias. For example, we would expect people to consider one hypothesis at a time and maintain it until evidence against it is encountered. However, there is nothing in this theory that implies the *attitude* of confirmation implied by Wason and other writers in this area. The claim, especially based on Wason's famous 2 4 6 problem, that people are *trying* to confirm their hypotheses is one that no recent reviewer of this field has been able to support in the light of the evidence. Even in social psychological studies where people may have strong emotional commitment to a favoured hypothesis, confirmatory behaviour seems to occur only when the cost of maintaining a false belief is low (Oswald & Grosjean, 2004).

All in all, I see no reason to change my earlier assessment (Evans, 1989) that any bias observed in hypothesis-testing behaviour is cognitive rather than motivational. In general, people will test positive predictions but if such predictions fail then they will abandon or revise the hypotheses on which they are based. It is questionable whether positive testing should be viewed as "bias" at all from a normative standpoint, even though it will fail to solve Wason's particular task. From the viewpoint of the hypothetical thinking theory it is a natural consequence of the relevance principle. When we mentally simulate a possibility, we naturally fill out our mental model with plausible content: what is likely to be the case if the supposition holds. This leads to positive expectations of what should occur and the formulation of positive predictions.

In this chapter, I have also introduced the Wason selection task, originally claimed also by Wason to show evidence of confirmation bias. I have discussed only the abstract form of the selection task here and will return to realistic versions later. This task is mostly of interest for the cognitive bias that it does reliably demonstrate – matching bias. With abstract conditional statements, people have a strong tendency to focus on the named lexical items, regardless of the presence of negations. This powerful pragmatic influence of negation is generally restricted to tasks lacking any realistic materials that evoke real-world beliefs (Evans, 1998) and illustrates that the relevance principle in the revised heuristic–analytic account can operate linguistically as well as through the belief system. Figure 2.2 clearly shows that, in the case of the abstract selection task, it is not the true consequent cases but the *matching* consequent cases that appear relevant to participants. Thus people represent what is relevant rather than what is true. The preference for plausible or probable cases is only a default that can be overridden – in this case by matching bias.

I will have more to say about hypothesis testing in this book, especially in relation to the "pseudodiagnosticity" effect (Doherty, Mynatt, Tweney, & Schiavo, 1979) reviewed in Chapter 6, which has also been claimed as evidence of confirmation bias. Apart from the collection of evidence, all that really distinguish hypothesis testing from other kinds of hypothetical thinking are the goals pursued by the analytic system. In decision making, for example, we simulate the relevant consequences of some action, and in hypothesis testing we model the likely consequences of some hypothesis. In both cases epistemic mental models are formed, filled with relevant content generating plausible consequences. If the explicit goal is decision making, then the analytic system evaluates the expected utility of the outcome; if hypothesis testing, then the analytic system derives a relevant prediction. If it is a reasoning task, in which we are asked whether a conclusion follows from some premises, then we attempt to build a mental model linking premises to conclusion in some plausible arrangement. And so on. I will attempt to show throughout this book that broadly the same principles of thinking underlie all these tasks and can account for most of the cognitive biases that are claimed to be associated with them.

CHAPTER THREE

Suppositional reasoning: if and or

Hypothetical thinking involves the imagination of possibilities and, according to the theory advanced here, typically consists of singular mental simulations. In this chapter, I will focus on the thinking in which a person introduces a temporary belief or supposition as the foundation of such a mental simulation. Such suppositional reasoning is most often stimulated in natural language exchanges by conditional statements (or conditionals for short) that have the form "if p then q". For example, a statement such as "if you want to impress the boss you should arrive early in the mornings" is intended to make the listener reflect upon their behaviour and consider the benefits (and costs) of changing it. Such conditional thinking based on a single supposition is very natural, according to hypothetical thinking theory. Much more difficult are tasks requiring more than one simulation based upon different suppositions as some use of the disjunctive form "p or q" require. Hence, psychological studies of reasoning with both "if" and "or" will be examined in this chapter.

Conditional thinking, in a basic form, is perhaps not unique to human beings. In studies of discrimination learning, for example, pigeons can learn to peck at red keys but not green ones if only red keys lead to the reinforcement of a food pellet. There is no reason, however, to suppose the language-less pigeon could formulate a thought equivalent to "if the key is red then pecking will produce food". The ancient learning system is still part of our System 1 cognition, and so we can also acquire automatic and implicit conditional responses. For example, even though we have explicit knowledge that we need to stop at red traffic lights and not green ones, this is almost certainly encoded at an implicit level as well, so that we will react to traffic lights even if our conscious thought and attention are elsewhere.

What I think must be unique to human (System 2) cognition is the ability to think and reason in a suppositional manner. Humans have explicit knowledge organized in a belief system, which is distinct from knowledge acquired implicitly through associative learning and conditioning. The latter may be encoded simply as weightings in neural networks, while the former have some sort of propositional format. Explicit knowledge is not the tiny amount that we are aware of at a given time, but that which can potentially reach awareness. In the heuristic–analytic theory, a major function of rapid and automatic heuristic processes is to retrieve relevant knowledge and belief and deliver it for conscious analytic processing. What makes this process particularly complex is the role of supposition.

On the face of it, all reasoning about our beliefs involves supposition. For example, following the 2004 US Presidential election, one might have asked an American friend: "Now that Bush has been elected, what chance is there that the US budget deficit will be reduced?" At this point, Bush has been elected so no supposition of possibilities is apparently required. Had one asked him, prior to the elections, "If Bush is elected, what chance is there that the US budget deficit will be reduced?" he would have had to introduce the supposition that Bush was elected to add to other relevant beliefs in order to answer my question. However, a complex process of reasoning about his existing beliefs may be required for our American friend to give a reply even to the question asked after the result is known. He would still need to run mental simulations of possible events (calculating, for example, whether Bush is likely to increase taxes or reduce expenditure) that would themselves introduce suppositions. In fact, any act of hypothetical thinking will need to do so.

Suppositional thinking and reasoning is a fairly extraordinary facility that human beings have developed. However, the scope for cognitive biases to enter into such thinking is apparent. Mental simulations will almost certainly be selective in their nature and subject to heuristics that will prune out many branches (Kahneman & Tversky, 1982b). From a dual-process standpoint, suppositional reasoning requires the involvement of the explicit analytic system (System 2) as it is essential that we know that we are simulating a hypothetical possibility so as not to confuse it with reality (Evans & Over, 1999). However, this system is highly constrained by working memory capacity and subject to both satisficing and the singularity principles. Thus we will try to construct a single mental simulation of the given supposition that is good enough for our purposes. For example, it is well known that people tend to fall into the "planning fallacy" when imagining complex projects (Bueler, Griffin, & Ross, 2002) in which they chronically underestimate the time that a future task will take to complete, despite their experience of previous projects. This seems to be due to the use of idealized mental simulations that fail to anticipate the many problems that can impede progress with a task.

As indicated above, two little words in our everyday language, "if" and "or", are critically linked to suppositional reasoning. As we shall see, in standard logic, "if" and "or" can be used to express equivalent logical relationships but I believe that this shows the failure of standard logic to capture the everyday meaning of these terms. "If" is the primary linguistic device that we use as speakers to try to engage our listeners in acts of hypothetical thinking. Like "if", "or" can be used in various ways, but generally conveys to listeners that they need to consider alternative possibilities, often requiring them to perform not one but two mental simulations. Both "if" and "or" are associated with cognitive biases, as we shall see.

THE MEANING OF "IF"

Psychologists studying human reasoning have for far too long based their normative theory of reasoning on the kind of standard formal logic to be found in elementary textbooks. In the case of conditional reasoning, they have looked for the meaning of "if" in what is called the propositional calculus. Propositional logic, as its names implies, deals in propositions, atomic statements that must always be true or false: a principle known as *bivalence*. It has been the unfortunate habit of the authors of textbooks on standard logic to associate the ordinary English statement of the form "if p then q" with an operator known as material implication, often written as "$p \supset q$" or "$p \rightarrow q$". A conditional that is interpreted in this way may be termed the material conditional. It has exactly the same meaning as "not p or q". This is because the material conditional is false only when we have the state of the world "p and not-q" and is otherwise true. This also is the only state of affairs that the assertion "not p or q" rules out.

Consider the following example:

If the cat is happy then she purrs.   3.1

If this statement is a material conditional, then it means exactly the same as:

Either the cat is not happy or she purrs.   3.2

Truth table analysis, a technique used in propositional logic, assigns a truth value for each logical case. In standard logic, with two propositions p and q there are four logical possibilities to consider in which each proposition is either true (T) or false (F), as follows:

TT (pq)   Cat is happy; cat purrs
TF (p¬q)   Cat is happy; cat does not purr
FT (¬pq)   Cat is not happy; cat purrs
FF (¬p¬q)   Cat is not happy; cat does not purr.

In the case of 3.1, if this is a material conditional, then the only false case (TF) is when we have a happy cat that does not purr. In all other situations, the material conditional is deemed to be true. Now consider the disjunctive statement 3.2. This is true if either or both its disjuncts are true – that is, when the cat is not happy and does not purr (FF), when she is happy and does purr (TT); or when she is not happy and purrs (FT) – and is only false when neither disjunct is true: the cat is happy and does not purr (TF). In other words, the truth tables for 3.1 and 3.2 are identical. Hence, in standard propositional logic 3.1 and 3.2 mean the same thing and support the same inferences.

The material conditional supports some paradoxical inferences that have led most contemporary philosophers to reject it as a representation of the ordinary conditional of everyday language (Bennett, 2003; Edgington, 1995). Because "if p then q" means the same thing as "either not p or q", it must be true whenever we know "not-p" or "q" to be true. As applied to our example, the paradoxes are:

P1   The cat is not happy, therefore if the cat is happy then she purrs.
P2   The cat purrs, therefore if the cat is happy then she purrs.

If these inferences seem odd, consider another example. It would follow as a valid inference from your belief that it is not raining today, that "if it is raining today then it is sunny". The same conditional could be inferred from your belief that today is sunny. Such inferences are evidently absurd. This leads to an alternative view that the ordinary conditional of everyday language is *not* the material conditional, so that "if p then q" does not mean the same as "either not p or q". The view that I favour is that the conditional is *suppositional* (Edgington, 2003; Evans & Over, 2004). In order for us to intro-duce an ordinary (suppositional) conditional into our belief system, we need to believe that there is some plausible link between p and q and that q is at least a probable consequence of supposing p. Conditionals are naturally introduced as result of hypothetical thinking. Hence, a school-leaver choos-ing a university after researching the options might say, "If I go to university X then the course is better. However, if I go to university Y the night-life will be better." Such conditionals may, of course, be used to support decision making.

The suppositional conditional is based on what philosophers call the Ramsey test (Ramsey, 1931). Ramsey suggested that in order to decide whether or not you believe a conditional statement you can add p hypothetically to your stock of beliefs and then evaluate q. Instead of introducing our own conditionals by an act of hypothetical thinking, we may assess those that are asserted to us in similar fashion. Thus a driver given some advice such as: "if you take this detour, then you will avoid most of the traffic lights and arrive earlier" might well perform a mental simulation based on her knowledge of the city to decide whether the advice is good. Perhaps she decides that while the suggested route has fewer traffic lights it also encounters a bottle-neck and hence she rejects the advice. What has happened here is that the ante-cedent (p) has been assumed for the sake of the thought experiment, and the likelihood of the consequent (q) assessed by mental simulation. In effect, the listener believes the conditional statement to the extent that she ends up believing the consequent (arriving earlier) given the antecedent (taking the detour). For this reason, the Ramsey test naturally suggests that belief in a conditional statement, if p then q, will be equal to the conditional prob-ability, $P(q|p)$.

There is, however, a difficulty with Ramsey's suggestion that this is done simply by adding p temporarily to one's stock of beliefs. The problem arises in the case of past-tense counterfactual conditionals referring to events that are no longer possible. Suppose someone said to the driver, "If you had taken this detour then you would have arrived earlier". How does she now evaluate the conditional? If she simply adds the belief that she took the detour (when she did not) then she will have a contradiction. This is a very bad thing for a logician, as you can infer anything at all from a contradiction! To deal with such cases, Stalnaker (1968) proposed an extended form of the Ramsey test in which people add the supposition of the antecedent while the *least possible change* is made to their belief systems to accommodate it. In the example given this may be quite straightforward but with other counterfactuals the need to change beliefs to accommodate a supposition might be much more complex. For example, to evaluate the conditional, "if terrorists had not attacked New York, the USA would not have invaded Iraq" requires mental undoing of the belief that the world-changing 9/11 attacks occurred and all that followed from it.

While the Ramsey test is in essence a psychological hypothesis, the psycho-logical nature of it has not been developed by philosophers (but see Evans & Over, 2004). It should be apparent that it can be viewed as an application of hypothetical thinking which in this case involves a mental simulation whose purpose is to test the connection between p and q. For example, we might suppose that establishing belief in a conditional could occur in one of two ways: (a) retrieval of a belief in the link between p and q from memory; or (b) mental simulation of the q possibility under the supposition of p. In the case of happy cats purring most people have relevant beliefs already stored in their memory. However, more novel conditionals such as "if Queen Elizabeth dies than Prince Charles will become King" (Over, Hadjichristidis, Evans,

Handley, & Sloman, in press) would require an active mental simulation or thought experiment in order to establish the likelihood of p leading to q. A person reflecting on this conditional will know that under the rules of succession, Charles – as heir to the throne – will succeed. However, as the question is posed, they will also consider possible ways in which this might not come about, the most likely of which is that Charles dies before Elizabeth. This is relatively unlikely, however, so participants are likely to assign a high (but not certain) subjective probability to this conditional. Such a belief relation can be represented in an epistemic mental model of the conditional of the following form:

Queen Elizabeth dies → .95 Prince Charles becomes King.

Note that the → symbol here represents a conditional belief relation (s) and not, of course, material implication. The .95 indicates a very high degree of subjective belief in this case, where 1 would represent certainty.

The notion that the ordinary conditional is suppositional is supported in the writings of advocates of the mental logic approach to reasoning (Braine & O'Brien, 1991; Rips & Marcus, 1977). However, there is much in both the broad approach and the fine detail of these theories with which my colleagues and I disagree (see Evans & Over, 2004). For example, we do not agree that different mental processes underlie logically valid and fallacious inferences. Nor do we believe that people have an inherent set of logical inference rules built in. However, our theory has brought us into direct conflict with authors of the mental model theory of conditionals (Johnson-Laird & Byrne, 2002) as addressed in some of our recent publications (Evans & Over, 2004; Evans et al., 2005b).

There is insufficient space here to re-run our debate with mental model theorists in any detail, However, the essence of the issue can be indicated. Johnson-Laird and Byrne (2002) argue that the core meaning of a conditional is that it "allows" three possibilities: pq (TT), ¬pq (FT) and ¬p¬q (FF). These are the same as those for "either not p or q", which immediately suggests that their conditional is material. However, if their argument is simply that these cases are compatible with the conditional statement, then this is a very weak claim that follows from the suppositional as well as the material conditional (and indeed all major theories of conditionals, as discussed by Edgington, 1995). Consider again:

If the cat is happy then she purrs.   (3.1)

All theories of the conditional agree that the only state of affairs that contradicts 3.1 is a happy cat not purring (TF), and so all other cases are possible. The key issue is whether these other cases are accorded the same epistemic status. The model theory accords special status to the TT case in one sense by proposing that only this is included in the initial representation of the conditional statement:

cat is happy   cat is purring
   . . .

Anyone reasoning with this representation will not be treating the conditional as material. For example, as it stands, they could not make the valid Modus Tollens inference: the cat is not purring, therefore the cat is not happy. However, the three dots ". . ." represent what is known as an implicit mental model or a mental footnote to the effect that there may be possible situations where the cat is not happy. According to Johnson-Laird and Byrne (2002) people may also succeed in fleshing out a fully explicit set of models (possibilities) as follows:

cat is happy   cat is purring
cat is not happy   cat is purring
cat is not happy   cat is not purring.

These full possibilities are the TT, FT and FF cases. Anyone fleshing these out could make Modus Tollens, as the minor premise (cat is not purring) eliminates the first two possibilities and leaves only the last, thus licensing the conclusions that the cat is not happy. However, this still is not sufficient for us to tell whether the conditional is material. The suppositional theory agrees that these cases are possible and that Modus Tollens is a valid inference. The key issue is whether the last two possibilities (false antecedent cases) make the conditional statement *true* (material conditional) or have a *truth value gap* as advocates of the suppositional theory allow (Adams, 1975; Edgington, 2003).[1] The gap occurs for the suppositional theory because of the Ramsey test. This conditional is not truth-functional, meaning that you cannot tell whether it is true simply by knowing the truth value of p and q. Whenever the antecedent is not known to be true (future indicative conditionals) or known to be false (counterfactual conditionals), people perform the Ramsey test to determine its subjective probability as described above. Hence, the suppositional conditional has believability – or subjective probability – when the antecedent is false, but this is not the same thing as a logician's meaning of truth.

---

[1] Edgington (2003) and Evans and Over (2004) actually discuss two alternatives to the material conditional (T1), which are referred to as T2 (Stalnakaer conditional) and T3 (Adams conditional). In this book, I will use the logic of the T3 conditional as the basis for my discussion of the suppositional conditional. However, there may be psychological applications for which the T2 logic should be considered (see Evans & Over, 2004).

There is much potential for confusion about "truth" and "belief", especially since ordinary people may say of a statement "that's true" when all they mean is that it is believable (highly probable). As an example, Johnson-Laird (2005) argues against suppositional conditional on the mistaken view that it can only be asserted when true in the sense used by logicians. For example, he says that to assert that "if Phil gets his next grant application funded, Phil will be happy" implies that Phil has already got the grant because TT is the only true case in the truth table for this conditional. However, the assertability conditions for the suppositional conditional only require that the speaker finds it *believable*. I can assert the above conditional if in a mental simulation of Phil getting his grant funded, I can feel reasonably confident that it will make him happy. Pragmatically, in fact, I could *not* assert the conditional if I already knew that he had the grant, as the conditional nature of the assertion would violate Gricean principles.

So, is the Johnson-Laird and Byrne (2002) conditional material in its core meaning, even if it has to be fully fleshed out for this to be apparent? It seems to us that several arguments put forward by these authors support the material conditional while being incompatible with the suppositional conditional. First, a fundamental axiom of the theory is the principle of truth: "mental models represent *true* possibilities" (Johnson-Laird & Byrne, 2002, p. 654, italics mine). Second, they state that the paradoxes of the material conditional (discussed earlier) are valid inferences. They are valid only for the material conditional. Third, they deny the psychological reality of what is known as the "defective truth table" (Wason, 1966) in which people regard TT cases as true, but FT and FF cases as irrelevant (see next section). Describing false antecedent cases as irrelevant seems to correspond to the logical notion of a truth value gap and is a key finding for the suppositional conditional. Confusingly, however, Johnson-Laird and Byrne (2002) also say that the conditional is not "truth functional", which is logically equivalent to saying that it is not material (see also Schroyens & Schaeken, 2004, for a denial that mental model theory is committed to the material conditional).

Empirical evidence for the suppositional conditional

In our view, there are two main pieces of evidence in favour of the suppositional theory of conditionals, when abstract conditionals of the type discussed here so far are considered. First, and in spite of the arguments of Johnson-Laird and Byrne (2002, see below) it seems that people do have "defective" truth tables for the conditional statement. That is, they have a strong tendency to think that the conditional is neither true nor false when the antecedent is false. This links with the "if-heuristic" discussed in Chapter 2 with regard to the Wason selection task. It will be recalled that with the abstract

Table 3.1
An example of the conditional truth table task completed in accordance with the defective truth table

Below is shown a statement that applies to letter–number pairs, followed by four such pairings. In each case, you need to decide whether the pair makes the statement true, makes it false or is irrelevant to it.

If the letter is D then the number is 6

	T/F/?
D6	T
D9	F
B6	?
B1	?

selection task people are much more likely to select true than false antecedent cards, as well as being more likely to choose cards that match the lexical items in the rule.

The conditional truth table task involves asking people to judge whether the four truth table cases (TT, TF, FT and FF) make the conditional statement true or false or are irrelevant to it. An example of the task for an affirmative conditional is shown in Table 3.1, completed in accordance with the defective truth table. The first study to show evidence for this defective pattern was that of Johnson-Laird and Tagart (1969) and there have been many replications since (see Evans et al., 1993). However, the story is somewhat complicated since matching bias affects the truth table task in a similar manner to the Wason selection task (see Chapter 2). There are close parallels between the two tasks when the negations are introduced. Consistent with the if-heuristic (Chapter 2) is the defective truth table pattern: people are much more likely to see cases as relevant (true or false) when the antecedent is true. Consistent with the matching-heuristic, however, people are also more likely to classify cases as relevant if they match the items named in the conditional statement.

In discussing the selection task in Chapter 2, it was pointed out that matching bias could be inhibited by use of explicit negations in the cases presented, so that lexical content always matches. However, when this happens, people do not improve their logical performance on the selection task as a result (Evans et al., 1996a). The same study, however, showed that when matching bias is released from the *truth table* task by using explicit negations, a marked improvement in logical performance results. Inspection of Figure 3.1 reveals the reason why. Cards heuristically cued as relevant on the selection task will be selected unless people can find a logical reason to reject them. On the truth table task, the instructions require that any relevant case be classified as true or false, and this necessarily involves the analytic system.

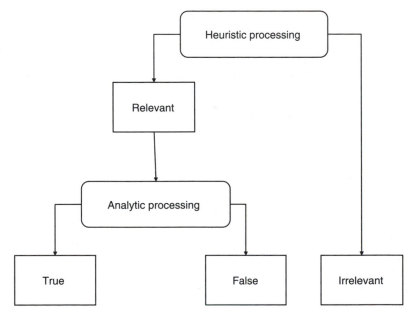

Figure 3.1   The heuristic–analytic model of the conditional truth table task.

When judged relevant, most people classify TT cases as true and TF cases as false, in line with logic. Hence, on this task, when there is less matching bias, more cases are seen as relevant, so more are correctly classified.

Johnson-Laird and Byrne (2002), as already indicated, claim that the meaning of the conditional statement cannot be captured by the defective truth table. They explain the experimental findings on the basis of the principle of implicit models. That is, participants who fail to flesh out the implicit not-p cases will describe them as irrelevant. Evans et al. (2005b) point out that the Modus Tollens inference requires this fleshing-out process in the theory (see above) and that this inference is typically made by about 60–70 per cent of participants in abstract conditional inference tasks. This seems inconsistent with the modal tendency to deny the relevance of these cases. A more difficult problem for their argument has arisen in recent research findings, which are discussed a little later. First, we need to consider the other key piece of evidence for the suppositional conditional.

As indicated above, the Ramsey test leads directly to a prediction that the people will equate the probability of "if p then q" with the conditional probability, $P(q|p)$. This is known as the conditional probability hypothesis (Evans, Handley, & Over, 2003b) or simply "the Equation" (Edgington, 1995). We can also link this with the defective truth table since people consider only p cases to be relevant when evaluating a conditional. They suppose p and evaluate their belief in q via mental simulation as described earlier. Experimental evidence of this hypothesis has only recently been collected (Evans, Ellis, & Newstead, 1996b; Evans et al., 2003b; Girotto & Johnson-Laird, 2004; Hadjichristidis, Stevenson, Over, Sloman, Evans, & Feeney, 2001; Oberauer & Wilhelm, 2003). With abstract conditionals, we can provide frequency distributions of the TT, TF, FT and FF cases. An example of a problem given by Evans and colleagues (Evans et al., 2003b) is the following:

A pack contains cards that are either yellow or red and have either a circle or a diamond printed on them. In total there are:

1 yellow circle
4 yellow diamonds
16 red circles
16 red diamonds.

How likely are the following claims to be true of a card drawn at random from the pack?

If the card is yellow then it has a circle printed on it
(0–100 per cent) _____
If the card has a diamond printed on it then it is red
(0–100 per cent) _____

According to the Equation, people should respond with the conditional probability, $P(q|p)$. For the first conditional above, this probability is $\frac{1}{5}$ as only one of the five yellow shapes is a circle. For the second conditional, the probability is $\frac{16}{20}$. However, if the conditional were material, these two conditionals would be equivalent (one is said to be the *contrapositive* of the other). They would both have a probability of $\frac{33}{37}$ as each is only falsified by yellow diamonds. In the experiments reported by Evans and colleagues (Evans et al., 2003b), there was in fact no correlation between ratings of the probability of conditionals and their contrapositive statements. The majority of participants, as predicted, based their judgements on the conditional probability $P(q|p)$, but a sizeable minority based it on the conjunctive probability $P(pq)$. For example, in the above case, they would give an estimate of around $\frac{1}{37}$. These appear to be qualitatively distinct groups, a finding confirmed in the independent study of Oberauer and Wilhelm (2003). As both Evans et al. and Oberauer and Wilhelm observe, the conjunctive probability response can be reconciled with the mental model theory (on the basis that initial representations only explicitly represent the pq case) but the majority conditional probability response cannot.

What could be the cause of these individual differences? Evans and colleagues (Evans et al., 2003b) suggested that conjunctive probability responders are superficial processors who fail to go beyond consideration of the pq frequency while conditional probability responders correctly compare it with the p¬q frequency. In a recent large study, we administered four tasks to the same 120 student participants: an AH4 test of general intelligence, the probability of conditionals task, the truth table task and the conditional inference task (Evans, Handley, Neilens, & Over, in press). As we predicted, the conditional probability responders – as identified from the probability of conditionals task – were higher in general intelligence and showed more clearly defective truth tables. Those who reason suppositionally on one task also do so on the other. These participants also showed better logical performance and were significantly less vulnerable to matching bias on the truth table task.

The three-way association between high ability, conditional probability responding and the defective truth table not only supports the suppositional theory but clearly falsifies some proposals within the mental model account of conditionals. Johnson-Laird and Byrne (2002) explain the defective truth table pattern, as already indicated, on the grounds that people neglect the implicit model. They provide the same explanation for the conjunctive probability response, P(pq), commonly given when people judge the probability of the conditional statement. So it is the conjunctive and not the conditional probability responders who should have the most defective truth table – the opposite to what is observed. The link with cognitive ability makes it worse. It is well known that measures of general intelligence and of working memory capacity are highly correlated (Colom, Rebollo, Palacios, Juan-Espinosa, & Kyllonen, 2004; Kyllonen & Christal, 1990). Those of higher working memory capacity should be more, not less, able to flesh-out implicit models and avoid the defective truth table.

BIAS IN CONDITIONAL INFERENCE[2]

There are two main biases known to be associated with people's reasoning about *abstract* conditional sentences (realistic conditionals are dealt with in Chapter 4). One that we have met already in the previous and current chapters is matching bias. Previous theoretical analyses (Evans, 1998) suggest strongly that matching bias arises from heuristic processes in System 1 that determine the perceived relevance of cases considered. At one time, it appeared that matching bias might be restricted to conditional statements that by their suppositional nature seem only sometimes to be relevant. However, we now

---

[2] This section contains arguments that should be of interest to researchers in the field of deductive reasoning. However, the more general reader may find it hard going. It may safely be skimmed or skipped without loss of continuity.

know that the effect is more general as it has been demonstrated with several connectives including "or" and "and" (Evans, Legrenzi, & Girotto, 1999b) but always with abstract problems. There is reason to think that the effect is weak or absent when realistic materials are used that introduce real-world knowledge and belief (Evans, 1998) but it is extremely strong in the case of abstract conditionals on both the truth table and the selection task. It can also be demonstrated on the third main paradigm in the psychology of conditionals: the conditional inference task, when the minor premise of the argument involves implicit negation (Evans & Handley, 1999).

Recent findings provide support for the idea that matching bias originates in the heuristic system. First, there is neuropsychological evidence suggesting that matching bias is associated with occipital lobes of the brain, suggesting a perceptual effect. Moreover, when matching bias is inhibited, there is a "frontal shift" with frontal brain areas more usually associated with logical reasoning and executive control being recruited (Houdé et al., 2000). Although matching bias has a different neurological location from belief bias (see Goel & Dolan, 2003, and Chapter 4), the fact that both effects can be inhibited by people high in cognitive ability, activating the prefrontal cortex in the process, is a striking parallel.

The other major bias associated with abstract conditional reasoning is manifest in the conditional inference task. Much research (for reviews, see Evans et al., 1993; Evans & Over, 2004) has focused on the willingness of participants to endorse each of four inferences associated with the conditional, as shown in Table 3.2. Two of these inferences are logically valid, meaning that their conclusion must be true if the premises are true. Modus Ponens (or MP for short) is readily apparent. Given, the conditional "If Paul is an athlete then he is fit" and the additional (minor) premise "Paul is an athlete", the conclusion that "Paul is fit" follows immediately. The other valid inference, Modus Tollens (MT), takes a little more thought. In this case, we are told that Paul is not fit. The major premise tells us that if he were an athlete he would be fit, so the only assumption consistent with him not being fit is that he is not an athlete.

The other two inferences that participants in psychological experiments are invited to consider are logical fallacies. Affirmation of the Consequent (AC) reasons from the fact that Paul is fit to infer that he is an athlete. However, this does not necessarily follow. He might be fit for some other reasons (perhaps he is a soldier or a dancer). For the same reason, Denial of the Antecedent (DA) is a fallacy: it does not necessarily follow that Paul is not fit, given that he is not an athlete. I have deliberately chosen here a conditional where counterexamples to these valid inferences are easy to find. Many real-world conditionals appear to be *biconditional*, in which q implies p as well as vice versa, for example: "If Pat is female, then Pat has ovaries", for which DA and AC would be strongly suggested inferences. Although logicians

Table 3.2
The four inferences associated with a conditional statement

Modus Ponens (MP)	If p then q; p therefore q
EXAMPLE:	
If Paul is an athlete, then he is fit; Paul is an athlete, therefore, Paul is fit	
Modus Tollens (MT)	If p then q; not-q therefore not-p
EXAMPLE:	
If Paul is an athlete, then he is fit; Paul is not fit, therefore, Paul is not an athlete	
Affirmation of the Consequent (AC)	If p then q; q therefore p
EXAMPLE:	
If Paul is an athlete, then he is fit; Paul is fit, therefore, Paul is an athlete	
Denial of the Antecedent (DA)	If p then q; not-p therefore not-q
EXAMPLE:	
If Paul is an athlete, then he is fit; Paul is not an athlete, therefore, Paul is not fit	

NOTE: MP and MT are valid inferences: their conclusions necessarily follow. DA and AC are fallacies: their conclusions do not necessarily follow.

use the form of words "if and only if p then q" to indicate biconditionals, ordinary people generally do not, so that conditionals may appear to be biconditional according to context (see Chapter 4). When conditional inference is studied with abstract problem materials, there is no context to signal clearly whether the statement should be taken as conditional or biconditional.

Studies of conditional inference using abstract materials typically present people with each of the four arguments shown in Table 3.2 and ask them to judge whether the conclusion necessarily follows. Abstract materials may relate colours and shapes (if it is a triangle then it is blue) or letters and numbers (if there is an A on the card, then there is a 4 on the card) and so on. When affirmative conditionals are used such studies show that MP is nearly always endorsed, but the valid MT inference is significantly less frequently endorsed, about 60–70 per cent of the time. The two fallacies, DA and AC, are also quite often endorsed as valid arguments (Evans et al., 1993). Different theories of these effects have been proposed in the literature. Both mental logic and mental model theorists (see Chapter 1) agree that more mental work is required to derive MT than MP but for different reasons. Fallacies may arise from a failure to consider the fully explicit set of models for the conditional (mental model theory) or by the introduction of pragmatic implicatures (mental logic theory). A detailed review of these theories and their application to conditional reasoning is provided by Evans and Over (2004, chap. 4).

A number of studies have applied the negations paradigm with the conditional inference task (see Table 3.3). Study of reasoning with all four kinds

Table 3.3
Logical form of the four conditional inferences for statements with use of the negations paradigm

	MP		DA		AC		MT	
Rule	*Given*	*Conclude*	*Given*	*Conclude*	*Given*	*Conclude*	*Given*	*Conclude*
If p then q	p	q	not-p	not-q	q	p	not-q	not-p
If p then not q	p	not-q	not-p	q	not-q	p	q	not-p
If not p then q	not-p	q	p	not-q	q	not-p	not-q	p
If not p then not q	not-p	not-q	p	q	not-q	not-p	q	p

of conditionals led some years ago to discovery of a phenomenon known as "negative conclusion bias" (Evans, 1982). Negative conclusion bias is a theoretically neutral term that describes a tendency for people to accept more conditional inferences as valid if the conclusion is negative rather than affirmative. If this were a universal response bias – for example, to accept negated conclusions due to caution (Evans, 1982) – then it would seem to be a heuristic effect. However, the bias is absent on MP, strongly marked on DA and MT and only weakly present for AC (see Schroyens, Schaeken, & d'Ydewalle, 2001, for a meta-analysis). The fact that it is strong for DA and MT suggests that it is mostly due to a difficulty with double negation.

Compare the following two MT arguments:

If the letter is G then the number is 7; the number is not 7,   3.3
therefore the letter is G.

If the letter is not A then the number is 8; the number is not 8,   3.4
therefore the letter is A.

And now the following two DA arguments:

If the letter is B then the number is 5; the letter is not B,   3.5
therefore the number is not 5.

If the letter is R then the number is not 1; the letter is not R,   3.6
therefore the number is 1.

There are strong and reliable findings in the literature (see, for example, Evans, Clibbens, & Rood, 1995a) that show that people make many more MT inferences like 3.3 than like 3.4 and many more DA inferences like 3.5 than like 3.6. The obvious account of this is a *double negation* effect. That is, in 3.4 people decide the letter cannot be a not A and in 3.6 that it cannot be a not 1, but that does not necessarily lead them to the conclusions given. Seeing that "not not an A" is the same as "A" requires what logicians call double negation elimination. This, in turn, depends upon a bivalent logic in which propositions are either true or false. We have already seen from the way people think about conditional statements that they do not necessarily embrace bivalence as such statements are classified as true, false or irrelevant.

The double negation effect on MT can be explained in terms of either mental logic or mental model theory (Evans et al., 1995a). In the mental logic account, MT is made by *reductio* reasoning. Taking 3.3 we suppose that there is a G and infer that there must be a 7. However, there is not a 7, so we have a contradiction. This implies that our supposition is false: there is not a G. The same line of reasoning with 3.4 leads one to the view that the supposition "the letter is not A" is false, but finding the conclusions "the letter is A" requires elimination of the double negation. While this account seems plausible, and we have suggested something similar ourselves (Evans & Over, 2004), it does not sit comfortably with other assumptions in the main mental logic systems. For example, Braine and O'Brien (1998b) propose a direct inference rule for double negation elimination. Although 3.2 would require an extra step of inference over 3.1, it should be as easy to make as Modus Ponens. Rips (1994) has a rule for indirect proof in his system, which allows negative suppositions to be reversed without even the need for an extra step of inference. Another difficulty for mental logic theorists is that the double negation effect is equally marked on DA as on MT. This makes little sense of their claim that different mental processes underlie valid and fallacious inferences.

The mental model theory can also account for the effect but has to be modified somewhat to do so. Recall that the model theory explanation of Modus Tollens is that it requires fleshing out of FF as a true possibility from among the implicit models. The psychological nature of this fleshing-out process has never been defined at all clearly in the writings of Johnson-Laird and Byrne. However, consider the model representation of problem 3.4:

If the letter is not A then the number is 8   (3.4)
    ¬A   8
    . . .

It might be argued that given the premise "not 8", which eliminates the explicit model, people try to flesh out a possible model by reversing the antecedent, leading to a double negation. However, this account is ad hoc, as the principles of fleshing out have never been specified at this level of detail. It also requires the idea that FF is understood as a true possibility that is contradicted by most of the truth table data as discussed earlier.

Developmental data show that the negative conclusion bias on denial inferences is absent in young children but grows steadily through adolescence (Lott, 1999). This rather strongly suggests that the bias lies in the analytic thinking system, which would make sense if MT and DA results from reductio reasoning. (In the case of DA, we would have to assume that people had added the converse "if q then p" and were giving an MT response for this reverse conditional.) Suppositional reasoning as required by reductio is exactly the kind of explicit hypothetical thinking that I have been associating with the analytic system. However, some recent findings of individual differences in adult participants are puzzling in this regard. In a large quantitative study Newstead, Handley, Harley, Wright, and Farelly (2004) found that while MP rates were correlated positively with general intelligence, DA, AC and MT rates were all positively correlated with each other and *negatively* with general ability. Recent unpublished studies from our laboratory in Plymouth have shown similar trends.

The suppression of the DA and AC fallacies in higher ability groups is not surprising, as we know that such participants are better able to comply with deductive reasoning instructions and show much less evidence of biconditionality in their general reasoning with conditionals (Evans et al., in press). But why do they then find the valid MT so difficult, contrary to the general finding that high-ability participants find more normatively correct solutions to reasoning problems (Stanovich, 1999)? Perhaps this is because they do have a truly conditional representation and must solve MT by genuinely suppositional (reductio) reasoning in the manner proposed by mental logic theorists. We know that problems that can only be solved by reductio reasoning are very difficult for the great majority of participants (Handley & Evans, 2000). However, this implies that the majority are finding MT by an easier method, but one that still entails a double negation effect.

My suggestion is this. Most adults faced with abstract conditional sentences interpret them as biconditionals. This enables them to adopt a *simple equivalence* reasoning strategy: p goes with q; not p goes with not q. On this basis, people would tend to endorse all four inferences, MP, MT, AC, DA. They do in fact, endorse MP and AC at very high rates, which becomes especially obvious if you separate out the high-ability participants with their conditional (rather than biconditional) interpretations. These affirmation inferences are easy and also highly common in young children. Denial inferences are somewhat weaker and will also be affected by a double negation effect that is *symmetrical on DA and MT*. Consider again the four denial inference problems discussed earlier (3.3–3.6):

If the letter is G then the number is 7; the number is not 7,   (3.3)
therefore the letter is G.

If the letter is not A then the number is 8; the number is not 8,   (3.4)
therefore the letter is A.

If the letter is B then the number is 5; the letter is not B,   (3.5)
therefore the number is not 5.

If the letter is R then the number is not 1; the letter is not R,   (3.6)
therefore the number is 1.

Problems 3.3 and 3.5 are straightforward for the simple equivalence strategy. "I don't have a 7 so I can't have a G; I don't have a B so I can't have a 5". Look what happens, however, when the same approach is applied to 3.4 and 3.6. "I don't have an 8 so I can't have a not A; I don't have an R so I can't have a not 1." Double negation will tend strongly to block both MT and DA inferences for these participants on an equal basis, which is exactly what the data show. In support of this account, Evans et al. (in press) found that the double negation effect was universally observed and not restricted to participants of higher cognitive ability who might be expected to reason suppositionally.

So, is the double negation effect a bias of the heuristic or analytic system? The answer is analytic without any doubt, in my opinion. It is not like matching bias or belief bias. As yet, no relevant neuropsychological studies of this bias have been run although doubtless they will be in due course. I expect brain areas associated with abstract and deductive reasoning effort to be activated. The dual-process theory does not propose that the analytic reasoning system is any form of mental logic but only that it permits high-effort, low-capacity reasoning of an abstract and sequential nature that is generally responsive to the task instructions. Simple equivalence is a poor reasoning strategy from the viewpoint of logic and one most likely to be adopted by lower ability participants. However, it does meet the criteria for analytic thinking, reflecting an explicit attempt to derive a conclusion from the premises given.

DISJUNCTIVE THINKING

There is much less psychological and philosophical research on "or" than on "if". This is a pity, because "or" is also very interesting from the viewpoint of hypothetical thinking theory. According to our theory, people follow a singularity principle: they consider one hypothesis at a time. If the conversational effect of "if" is to induce a thought experiment in the listener's mind, is "or" used to provoke two such experiments? Can people in fact consider two possibilities simultaneously? In her recent book, mostly concerned with counterfactual thinking, Byrne (2005) frequently offers accounts of hypothetical thinking in terms of whether or not people "keep in mind" one or two possibilities. For example, she claims that a difference between causal and counterfactual conditionals is that with the former people only consider one possibility (cause and effect co-occurring) whereas with counterfactuals they consider two (what did happen and what might have happened). I will return to the topic of counterfactual thinking later in the chapter.

The logical use of "or" relates two propositions together as in "p or q". There is an inclusive reading of this, "p or q or both", which can always be expressed by an equivalent material conditional (because just one possibility, not-p and not-q, is ruled out), and an exclusive reading "p or q but not both", which can always be expressed as a material biconditional (because a second possibility, p and q, is also ruled out). Quite apart from the serious doubt over whether ordinary conditionals can ever be material, there are other reasons for thinking that "or" and "if" play very different roles in everyday discourse and communication. One is the relation that these two words have with "not". As Evans and Over (2004) observe, "if" and "not" combined very happily in everyday conditional statements. Not so with disjunctives.

Hypothetical thinking seems to be equally well equipped with the facility to imagine events and nonevents. For example, inducement and advice conditionals can easily be expressed with negations:

If you don't finish your homework, I won't let you out to play
If you don't hurry you will miss your train

as can causal conditionals:

If you brake quickly you will not run through the traffic lights
If you don't smoke you will live longer

as can counterfactuals:

If I had finished my degree I would not be unemployed now.
If the car had not swerved there would have been a nasty accident.

Although, as we have seen, the use of negations in abstract conditionals provokes more than one kind of cognitive bias, participants do not claim that they are incomprehensible. They tend, however, to be completely flummoxed by statements such as:

Either the letter is not an A or the number is not a 3
Either the letter is a G or the number is not a 4 but not both.

Some researchers even report that participants "drop" the negatives and reason as if they were not there at all (see Evans et al., 1993, chap. 5)! It is also much harder to think of natural everyday disjunctives that included negated components. A possible exception is an *imperative* disjunction such as:

Either finish your homework or I won't let you out to play

which does seem to mean the same thing as (and be much more naturally expressed as):

If you do not finish your homework then I won't let you out to play.

Just as conditionals can be interpreted in everyday language in a conditional or biconditional way, so disjunctives can be interpreted inclusively or exclusively. We have seen that with abstract conditionals the common interpretation is biconditional. Correspondingly, it turns out that with abstract disjunctives, lacking a modifier such as "or both" or "but not both" will be interpreted by the majority of participants as exclusive (Evans et al., 1999b; Evans & Newstead, 1980). However, in natural discourse, both conditionals and disjunctives tend to be interpreted according to context.

We do know that the use of the logical "or", particularly in an exclusive manner, can create enormous problems for people in abstract reasoning tasks. For example, trying to infer an experimenter's rule from exemplars classified as conforming or not conforming to it is especially difficult when the rule takes an exclusive disjunctive form (Bruner *et al.*, 1956). People tend to fall into a "common element fallacy" in which they assume (erroneously) that members of the same category must have features in common. To illustrate the difficulty, consider one of the most difficult reasoning problems ever invented, the notorious Wason THOG problem (Wason & Brooks, 1979). A standard THOG problem is shown in Figure 3.2.

This problem is doubly fiendish and all to do with exclusive disjunction. First, the experimenter's rule is an exclusive disjunction: if the design has a particular shape or else a particular colour, it is a THOG. It must have one *but only one* of these features. Next, it is impossible to infer what this rule is from the information given: there are two mutually exclusive hypotheses that are possible (another exclusive disjunction!). However, each of these rules classifies the figures in the same way, so the problem set is soluble. We know that the black diamond is a THOG. Therefore, it contains one, but only one, of the features with the experimenter's rule. That feature could be black or it could be diamond, but not both. If it is black, the rule must be:

A. Either the figure is black or else it is a circle

and if it is diamond, the rule must be:

B. Either the figure is white or else it is a diamond.

In front of you are four designs: a black diamond, a white diamond, a black circle and a white circle:

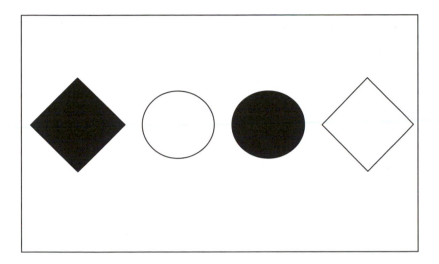

You are given a rule that allows an arbitrary name to be applied to the designs.

Rule: In the above designs there is a particular shape and a particular colour, such that any of the designs that has one, and only one, of these features is called a THOG.

The black diamond is called a THOG. What can you say if anything about whether each of the remaining designs is a THOG?

Figure 3.2 Wason's THOG problem.

If people get this far, the rest is fairly easy. Whichever rule applies, the white circle is a THOG, and both the black circle and white diamonds *cannot* be THOGs. Rule A excludes the black circle as it has both features and the white diamond as it has neither. Conversely, Rule B excludes the black circle as it has neither feature and the white circle as it has both. Wason and Brooks (1979) found that the majority of their participants, perhaps unsurprisingly, failed to give the logically correct answer. Of more interest was a very common intuitive error among the nonsolvers that more or less reverses the correct answer. Many are convinced that the white circle *cannot* be a THOG, while the other two figures may or must be THOGs. This appears to be another manifestation of the common element fallacy and can be seen as a kind of matching bias. Logically, the white circle must be a THOG because it shares no common features with the black diamond; intuitively this just seems wrong: there is no THOGness about it!

Subsequent research on the THOG problem has confirmed its extraordinary difficulty for most people (Newstead, Girotto, & Legrenzi, 1995). Unlike with the Wason selection task (see Chapter 4), introducing realistic content generally does not help people to solve it. I believe that the difficulty of the THOG problem results directly from the use of exclusive disjunction. To solve this problem by analytic reasoning requires simultaneous consideration of mutually exclusive possibilities: something that we expect to be very difficult due to the singularity principle of hypothetical thinking. The intuitive error is a form of matching bias: heuristic processes are cueing both black and diamond as relevant features from the example figure given, and by default both will be encoded into a single mental model of the hypothesis. This default model must be rejected by explicit analytic reasoning in order for people to have any chance of finding the correct solution.

The difficulty of exclusive disjunction is manifest in other tasks in the literature, even when the authors of these papers do not necessarily focus on this aspect in their framing of the research. Two good examples are the studies of "illusions" in reasoning by Johnson-Laird and his colleagues (Goldvarg & Johnson-Laird, 2000; Johnson-Laird & Savary, 1999) and the study of meta-deduction using Knights and Knaves problems (Byrne & Handley, 1996; Elqayam, 2006; Johnson-Laird & Byrne, 1990). An example of one of the reasoning illusions is the following:

> Only one of the following premises is true about a particular hand of cards:
> If there is a King in the hand then there is an Ace in the hand
> If there is not a King in the hand then there is an Ace in the hand.
> What follows?

Most people say that it follows that there is an Ace in the hand. According to Johnson-Laird this is the opposite of the correct answer. Logically, people should infer that there is not an Ace in the hand. The argument is this: if the first conditional is false, then there is a King and not an Ace; if the second conditional is false, then there is a not a King and not an Ace. Either way there is not an Ace. Johnson-Laird believes that the illusions result from their principle of truth – people model true but not false possibilities – and from their principle of implicit models. Hence, they think that if the first rule is true they have a King and an Ace, and if the second rule is true they have no King and an Ace, so either way they have an Ace.

The normative analysis showing "not an Ace" to be correct is highly debatable as it relies on the material conditional. With the suppositional conditional, people might well interpret the claim that "if p then q" is false to mean that "if p then not q", and strong evidence that they do so has recently been produced by Handley, Evans, and Thompson (2006). On this basis you could rewrite the premises as one of the following two conjunctions:

If there is a King in the hand then there is an Ace in the hand
If there is not a King in the hand then there is not an Ace in the hand

OR ELSE

If there is a King in the hand then there is not an Ace in the hand
If there is not a King in the hand then there is an Ace in the hand.

Since people know neither which rule set applies nor whether there is a King in the hand, the problem is indeterminate – that is, nothing follows. On this analysis, the typical answer that there is an Ace in the hand is still illusory. In some versions, participants are additionally told that there is a King in the hand, from which they still infer an Ace. On the above analysis, this would still be indeterminate. However, the phenomenon may not be to do with conditionals *per se*, since similar effects have been reported with disjunctives.

What do these problems have in common with THOG? The instruction that one and only one of the following premises is true: an exclusive disjunction. The singularity principle does not prevent people from running more than one mental simulation in sequence but we normally think in terms of alternative suppositions rather than alternative complex connectives like conditionals and disjunctives. In fact, it is quite common to use a disjunction of conditionals to argue for an inevitable outcome, as in the case of an employee who has received an offer to move to another company and a counter-offer to stay where she is. She might well say in this situation:

If I take the offer, then I get a pay rise or if I stay where I am I get a pay rise. Either way, I am better off.

It is almost impossible to imagine anyone using such a sentence structure to imply that they would not get a pay rise! Of course, the "or" here does not have the logical effect of disjoining the two conditional statements as a whole. What it disjoins are two different mental simulations, or, if you prefer, the antecedents of these conditionals. On the supposition that I move, I get a pay rise. On the supposition that I stay, I also get a pay rise.

Meta-deduction problems are set on the island of Knights and Knaves (Smullyan, 1978). Knights and Knaves look the same, but the former always tell the truth and the latter always lie. This is exclusive disjunction in yet another guise: people are either Knights *or else* they are Knaves; their statements are true *or else* they are false. A set of rich reasoning problems can be devised in these scenarios and were first introduced into the psychology of reasoning by Rips (1989). They are called meta-deductive because you have to reason about truth and falsity. People tend to struggle with these problems because they fail to keep track of alternative hypotheses: in particular they may not consider the Knave hypothesis if a Knight hypothesis will fit the available information. Elqayam (2006) calls this the "collapse" illusion. Consider the following claim:

I am a Knave.

This is a version of the famous liar paradox and most participants can see that this statement has indeterminate truth value. If the speaker is a Knight then he must be a Knave, which is a contradiction. If the speaker is a Knave, then since Knaves always lie, he must be a Knight, which is also a contradiction. Now consider:

I am a Knight.

This statement too is indeterminate: a Knight could say it, but so too could a Knave. In this case, many people assume, however, that the speaker is a Knight, "collapsing" indeterminate to true. As Elqayam (2006) also points out, the collapse illusion and reasoning with Knights and Knaves problems generally are consistent with hypothetical thinking theory. One of the general proposals in this theory is that people adopt a hypothesis and maintain it until there is reason to give it up. We saw in Chapter 2 that there is much evidence from the hypothesis testing literature that supports this proposal. What seems to happen in Knights and Knaves problems is that people try the Knight hypothesis first and only give it up if it fails to satisfy, as with the paradoxical "I am a Knave" claim. Where it works, as in "I am a Knight", they tend to stick with it.

COUNTERFACTUAL THINKING

The discussion of conditionals given so far has concerned so-called indicative conditional statements. These are often contrasted with counterfactual conditionals that have false antecedents. There is a close – but not one-to-one – linkage between counterfactuals and use of the subjunctive mood. Counterfactuals can be used in the present tense, for example, "If I were president, I would pull the troops out of Iraq", but they are most commonly used in the past tense, to refer to actions or events that were once but are no longer possible, as in our earlier example: "If terrorists had not attacked New York, then the USA would not have invaded Iraq."

Counterfactual conditionals have been subject to much philosophical investigation (see Bennett, 2003; Evans & Over, 2004). Past-tense counter-factuals are particularly interesting because they posit consequences for antecedents known to be false and events that cannot be changed. Terrorists did attack New York in 2001, so what is the point in speculating about what might or might not have happened had history failed to deliver this event? It might seem that this statement is a roundabout way of stating a causal relation. The speaker is implying that the attack on New York somehow caused (or perhaps enabled) the war with Iraq that followed. However, although counterfactual and causal claims are related, the psychological evidence suggests that they are not equivalent and do not stimulate the same processes of hypothetical thinking (Byrne, 2005).

A different question we can ask is whether counterfactual and indicative conditionals are fundamentally different. A present-tense subjunctive and a future-tense indicative can seem to mean the same thing, as in:

If Paul were to win the lottery then he would buy a Ferrari.   3.7

If Paul wins the lottery then he will buy a Ferrari.   3.8

The believability (or subjective probability) of these two statements would certainly be the same under the suppositional theory of conditionals. We would use our knowledge of Paul to perform a mental simulation of a possible world in which he wins the lottery. Our knowledge of relevant facts such as his age, personality and driving style might leads us to assign a (similarly) high or low degree of belief in 3.7 and 3.8. We might also perform similar mental simulation with similar results for the past-tense counterfactual:

If Paul had won the lottery then he would have bought a Ferrari.   3.9

Of course, we might evaluate 3.9 differently if relevant beliefs had been updated in the passage of time. Suppose the counterfactual applies to a period of time since when Paul had a serious accident while speeding in his more modest road car. We might have believed 3.7 or 3.8 if uttered at the time, but not believe 3.9 now. It is not the nature of the conditional or its mental processing that has changed, just our database of relevant beliefs.

Mental model theorists (Johnson-Laird & Byrne, 2002) propose that the mental representation of indicative and counterfactual conditionals is fundamentally different. Instead of representing just one explicit possibility (the TT case) as with an indicative conditional, people represent two possibilities. Thus 3.6 would be represented as:

Paul wins the lottery   Paul buys a Ferrari
                . . .

whereas 3.7 would be represented as:

FACT
Paul did not win the lottery   Paul did not buy a Ferrari
COUNTERFACTUAL POSSIBILITY
Paul did win the lottery   Paul did buy a Ferrari.

In our suppositional theory, we disagree with this account (Evans & Over, 2004; Evans et al., 2005b). First, the actual state of the world should not be described as "fact" because it is only pragmatically and not logically implied. Suppose the speaker of 3.9 learns that Paul did in fact win the lottery and did buy a Ferrari. They would hardly declare their statement to have been *false*; more likely, they would say "I told you so". Second, we do not believe that there is a fundamental difference in the mental representation of indicatives and counterfactuals. Recall that our mental models are epistemic, not semantic (Chapter 1). That is, they represent not factual possibilities but beliefs. They can be also supplemented by pragmatic implicatures. Hence, 3.7 might be represented as follows:

Paul wins the lottery → .8 Paul buys a Ferrari
[Paul does not win the lottery → .001 Paul buys a Ferrari].

Recall that the notation "→ s" represents a conditional belief strength s (a subjective probability) that one event leads to the other. The arrow does not represent an embedded conditional or (worse) a material implication. This conditional also carries a very strong pragmatic implicature that Paul will not buy a Ferrari unless he wins the lottery as we know that such a purchase is totally beyond his current means. This implicature is represented by the square brackets. In our system this is one mental model not two, and we are representing beliefs, and not logical possibilities. We might represent 3.9 as follows:

Paul had won the lottery → .8 Paul would have bought a Ferrari
[Paul did not win the lottery (.999); Paul did not buy a Ferrari (.999)].

What people do with this model depends upon what question is asked. Within the heuristic–analytic theory, heuristic (or pragmatic) processes generate such epistemic mental models in an automatic and effortless way, but only the analytic system can interpret, process or modify such models with respect to verbal instructions and the task set. Establishing the degree of conditional belief in such a model may involve active participation of the analytic system in order to simulate the likelihood of q in the supposition of p, if people are asked to consider a novel conditional sentence, for example. It may also be retrieved directly from memory if the relation is one with which people are familiar. The implicature part, however, would be added automatically or as a by-product of the main mental simulation.

If the question asked of a counterfactual conditional is whether one can infer not-p or not-q as a consequence, then I would expect such an inference to be much more commonly endorsed than with indicative conditionals as has been observed (Thompson & Byrne, 2002). This would reflect the pragmatic implication of real-world events that goes with the counterfactual form as shown in the model for 3.7. The same implicature can account for the higher rates of DA and MT inferences observed with counterfactual conditionals (Byrne & Tasso, 1999; Quelhas & Byrne, 2003; Thompson & Byrne, 2002). On the other hand, if the question asked is the extent to which the counterfactual conditional is probable or believable then I would expect this to depend only on the conditional belief between p and q, which can be determined by a single relevant mental simulation based on the supposition of p. Again, this is what the data show. When asked to judge the probability of either causal or conditional statements, people predominantly base this on the conditional probability, $P(q|p)$, in line with the extended Ramsey test (Over et al., in press). On this task, data for indicative and counterfactual conditionals are indistinguishable as predicted by the suppositional theory.

Are there biases in counterfactual thinking? This is hard to decide in the normal sense, as we would need an agreed normative theory of what is "correct" counterfactual reasoning. However, there are a number of factors established by psychological research that affect the likelihood that people will engage in counterfactual thinking (see Byrne, 2005; Mandel, Hilton, & Catellani, 2005). A lot of these involve mental "undoing" (Kahneman & Tversky, 1982b) in the form of "if only" thoughts, which commonly occur when outcomes of some scenarios are seen as negative and undesirable. For example, people will more often mentally undo (or regret) an action than an inaction, unusual rather than common actions, actions that violate social obligations and more recent rather than older events. Counterfactual thoughts do not necessarily reflect perceived causes. If you change your route home from work, skid on a patch of oil and crash your car, you are more likely to think "if only I had not changed my route" than "if only the patch of oil had been cleaned up" even though you perceive the oil and not your choice of route as the *cause* of the accident (see Byrne, 2005).

One of the most interesting things about counterfactual thinking is that we do so much of it. Our mental life (in the conscious System 2) is rich in hypothetical thinking about past as well as uncertain and future possibilities. We simulate the future in order to try to make good decisions and the past – presumably – in order to learn from experience. Of course, this is a very different concept of experiential learning from that which operates at the

System 1 level, in the associative learning subsystem. Many of our choices and intuitive judgements may be based on implicit and associative learning from our repeated past interactions with events in the world. This kind of learning is "automatic" and does not require reflective consciousness. Hypothetical thought does, however, require such reflection. We theorize constantly about the world and our own actions within it. Counterfactual thoughts help us to learn from mistakes and formulate better rules for our future behaviour – or so it seems. Analytic thinking also serves to confabulate and rationalize explanations for our own behaviour, as we shall see in Chapter 7.

CONCLUSIONS

In this chapter, I have discussed both conditional and disjunctive forms of suppositional reasoning. Studies of abstract conditional reasoning have strongly identified two major biases: matching bias and the double negation effect. As explained, there is good reason to think that these originate in the heuristic and analytic systems, respectively. Matching bias strongly influences perceptions of what is relevant and can only be inhibited by quite a small group of high-ability participants (the top 20 per cent of a university student population in the study discussed). When allowance for this is made, the main determinant of relevance lies with the suppositional nature of the ordinary conditionals: they concern only possibilities in which the antecedent condition holds. The double negation effect arises in analytic reasoning when people try to draw conditional inferences that deny either the antecedent or the consequent.

According to the principles of hypothetical thinking laid out in Chapter 1, people think about only one possibility or hypothesis at a time. Research on conditionals is consistent with this, as "if" strongly appears to trigger a mental simulation based on the supposition of p. This is why the most common response to a request to judge the probability of a conditional statement is the conditional probability, $P(q|p)$. There is also evidence that disjunctive thinking is very difficult, especially when it requires consideration of mutually exclusive possibilities. Exclusive disjunction lies at the heart of several notorious difficult problems including Wason's THOG problem, Johnson-Laird's illusory inferences and reasoning about Knights and Knaves.

I have also given some brief discussion in this chapter of counterfactual thinking. According to Byrne (2005) counterfactual thinking arises when people consider two possibilities rather than one, in apparent conflict with the singularity principle. However, our notion of mental models is epistemic and allows the idea that such models are embellished with pragmatic implicatures. In the case of counterfactuals, the pragmatic implication is that neither antecedent nor consequent is held in the actual world. The idea that people are considering two possibilities is a direct consequence of a system based on semantic mental models. I suggest instead that counterfactual conditionals, like indicatives, evoke only a single thought experiment or mental simulation. We evaluate belief in a counterfactual in exactly the same way as we do for an indicative conditional (Over et al., 2005). We suppose that p were (is, will be, had been) true and, using all relevant belief that can be retrieved, try to decide whether q would follow, leading to a judgement based on $P(q|p)$.

What has not been addressed in this chapter is the extraordinarily strong effect of prior belief and knowledge on human reasoning processes, once problems are presented with realistic content and context. I will consider this issue in the chapter that follows.

CHAPTER FOUR

The role of knowledge and belief in reasoning

One of the strongest findings in the psychology of reasoning is that people's thinking about inferential problems is profoundly influenced by the content and context in which the problems are framed, even though logical form is held constant. Such findings have progressively undermined the view that human reasoning is based on any kind of mental logic and have also provided fertile ground for the development of dual-processing accounts. A widespread view is that since System 1 or heuristic processes are responsible for contextualization (automatic retrieval and application of relevant prior knowledge) then they are the major cause of any content effects observed. By contrast, it has been widely assumed, System 2 analytic reasoning is responsible for the ability to solve problems by decontextualized reasoning that is also manifest in these experiments (Evans, 1989; Stanovich, 1999).

The equation of the heuristic system with domain-specific processes responsible for biases and of the analytic system with providing domain-general processes that support good reasoning is now seen to be oversimplified and misleading (Evans, 2006a; Stanovich, 2006). It is true that the fundamental heuristic bias is responsible for a number of the content effects observed, as the following review will demonstrate. However, the analytic system can also be responsible for biases as has already been demonstrated in the preceding chapters. Moreover, as will become evident in this chapter, analytic thinking is not by its nature abstract and decontextualized, let alone logical. Analytic thinking is slow, sequential, conscious and reflective but it is not a mental logic. This kind of thinking can as well be applied to content-rich problems as to abstract ones, and the subject of reflection may be explicit knowledge and belief evoked by the context. Thus the nature of dual-process accounts of contextualized reasoning is undergoing radical revision in recent accounts, as I will show in this chapter.

Another important issue in the study of content effects is that of whether influences of prior belief on reasoning should necessarily be perceived as biases. Both science and society seem to be divided on the issue of whether prior belief is necessarily prejudicial. The very term "prejudice" implies pre-judging a person or an issue on the basis of our prior belief as when we attribute characteristics to an individual person based on some kind of stereotype that we hold. Thus when a colleague tells you that her husband is an accountant you may assume that he is dull and introverted, but when another describes her husband as a sales executive you might assume that he is outgoing and extroverted. In dual-process theories of social psychology (Chaiken & Trope, 1999) the application of such stereotypes is generally regarded as rapid and automatic, whereas the identification of the individual's actual attributes requires more conscious processing effort. It can be argued that stereotypes serve a useful purpose in the absence of any other information about an individual, providing better than chance information about the social world. However, it can also be argued that the application of stereotypes is the foundation for prejudice and discrimination.

The rational case for prior belief derives from the Bayesian framework, which has already been introduced earlier in this book. To apply Bayes' theorem (see Equation 1.4), you need to combine your prior belief in a hypothesis with some current evidence in order to produce a revised belief. Hence, in this system it is rational to take account of prior belief. Consider the criminal justice system. When police investigate a crime, they consult a database of known offenders and compare methods of operation. Increasingly, criminal investigators working on serious crimes rely on psychological or geographical profiling of offenders (Canter & Alison, 2000), which increases their probability of identifying suspects. This is clearly a rational use of prior belief. However, criminal justice procedures do not regard Bayesian prior probabilities as *evidence* that can be used in a court of law, and in fact the rules of evidence in Western courts normally prevent the prosecution from telling juries about a defendant's prior criminal record for fear that it will prejudice their judgement. The principle here, apparently, is that people should be tried on the facts of the case alone. This is far from self-evidently correct. The criminal justice system does require juries to make judgements of probability. In civil cases they are required to find in favour of one party of another on the "balance of probability", while in criminal cases they traditionally must find that the prosecution has proved its case "beyond reasonable doubt". Is it right, then, to deny juries access to highly relevant prior probabilities?

In my view, as discussed in Chapter 2, real science is a Bayesian process (Evans, 2005; Howson & Urbach, 1993) in which new evidence is always contextualized in the light of prior belief and knowledge. I also believe that ordinary people are broadly Bayesian in their everyday lives. The reason that *belief bias* has been such an issue in psychological research on reasoning derives from the conventions of the "deduction paradigm" that has been largely used in this field. Standard instructions require that people should (a) assume that the premises are true and (b) endorse only conclusions that necessarily follow from these assumptions (Evans, 2002a). These instructions constrain what might naturally be a probabilistic form of inference to one that is logical and deductive and exclude the relevance of prior belief in the process. If we let P represent a set of premises and C a conclusion that may be derived from them, then the following total rule of probability is a simple consequence of the probability calculus (see Evans & Over, 1996a):

$$\text{Prob(C)} = \text{Prob (P)} \cdot \text{Prob(C}|\text{P)} + \text{Prob(}\neg\text{P)} \cdot \text{Prob(C}|\neg\text{P)}. \qquad 4.1$$

In other words, Equation 4.1 means that the probability of a conclusion (or our belief in it, if you take a subjective view of probability) is the sum of two factors: (a) the extent to which the conclusion follows from the premises weighted by the likelihood of those premises; and (b) the extent to which the conclusion follows if the premises do not hold, weighted by the probability that they do not. In real life, it is likely that people at least focus on (a), although they may neglect (b) in light of the singularity principle of hypothetical thinking. That is, given some salient evidence to think about, people may neglect to consider the likelihood of the conclusion in the absence of the evidence, a problem related to *base-rate neglect* (see Chapter 6). However, they may well take into account both the uncertainty in the evidence itself and any uncertainty in the process of drawing the conclusion from the evidence in establishing their overall confidence in the conclusion of an argument.

To take a real-world example, suppose a right-wing politician wants to convince you that uncontrolled immigration will be a cause of crime. She might argue that current government policy will allow immigration to rise steeply in the next four years and that this will lead to an increase in crime due to pressures on housing and employment, as well as to tensions between different ethnic groups. She wants you to conclude that crime rates will soar. In evaluating this argument, you will consider the likelihood of the premise that current policy will increase immigration, or Prob(P), and the likelihood that this will cause an increase in crime, or Prob(C|P). If you are very sophisticated you may also consider whether crime will also rise in the absence of increased immigration – Prob(C|¬P). It seems to me that this kind of probabilistic evaluation of arguments is not only habitual but also *rational*, given the uncertainty of real-world propositions.

Now consider the effect of deductive reasoning instructions. You are to remove all uncertainty from your thinking. Assume the premises are true and so set Prob (P) = 1. Decide whether the argument is valid, meaning that you must decide whether $P(C|P) = 1$. Strictly speaking, you do need to assume the premises are true to evaluate a logical argument as you only need to decide whether the conclusion follows necessarily from them. However, this instruction is commonly given because it makes the task equivalent to that of deciding whether the conclusion is certain. If the premises are true and the argument is valid then the conclusion must be true, a case known in logic as a sound argument. There is evidence that ordinary people confuse the notions of validity and soundness – that is, they are reluctant to endorse an argument whose premises they disbelieve (Thompson, 1996). However, the major claim in the literature on belief bias, as we shall see, is that people are strongly influenced by whether or not they believe the *conclusion* of an argument. As Evans and Over (1996a) have argued, one can make a case that such belief bias is rational in one sense and irrational in another, depending on whether you think in terms of what habitually works in ordinary life, or whether you take into account the precise experimental instructions.

From the perspective of dual-process theory, it is to be expected that prior belief will have a strong influence on reasoning as one of the main functions of heuristic processes is to contextualize problems in the light of prior belief, retrieving and applying relevant knowledge from long-term memory. What I have been calling the fundamental heuristic bias is the consequential restriction of focus in any reasoning that follows. However, it turns out that beliefs may directly influence the analytic reasoning processes as well. The remainder of this chapter is taken up with a detailed examination of the psychological literatures that bear on these issues.

THE BELIEF BIAS EFFECT IN SYLLOGISTIC REASONING

Before examining the specific evidence on belief bias, I will introduce a paradigm that has been extensively used in the study of human reasoning – categorical syllogisms. Psychologists working in this area have largely confined themselves to a limited logical system devised by Aristotle. In this system there are always two premises and a single conclusion that relate together three terms often known as the subject (S) and predicate (P) of the conclusion, linked together by a middle term (M). A complete syllogism might look like this:

All M are P   4.2
Some S are not M
Therefore, some S are not P.

We already saw some examples of syllogisms in Chapter 1, when reasoning about the colour of books. Whether or not the above syllogism is valid depends only on its form and not on its content. It makes no difference at all what particular terms are substituted for S, M and P. Presented in this abstract form, you may think the above argument is valid, as many people do. However, our perception of whether an argument is valid can be strongly influenced by the content chosen. Consider, this instantiation of the above syllogistic form:

All cats are carnivores   4.3
Some pets are cats
Therefore, some pets are not carnivores.

Let us suppose that people try to integrate this information into a mental model. Despite the criticism of the mental model theory of conditionals in the previous chapter, the theory is quite plausible when applied to syllogisms, with an important caveat that will be given later. Johnson-Laird proposes that syllogisms are represented by mental models that have tokens, rather than a diagrammatic form, but the format is not important for the present purposes. The above syllogisms, based on real-world knowledge, suggest relationships between the three sets S, M and P like the one shown as Model A in Figure 4.1 There is a large set of carnivores (P), a subset of which is cats (M). Some cats are pets (S) and some are not (for example, feral cats). Some pets are carnivores and some are not. In Model A, both premises hold and so does the conclusion: it is true that all M are P, some S are not M and some S are not P. However, this does not mean that the conclusion is *necessarily* true for all arrangements of S, M and P consistent with the premises.

The fallacy becomes apparent when we modify the wording of 4.3 as follows:

All cats are carnivores   4.4
Some *meat-eating* pets are cats
Therefore, some *meat-eating* pets are not carnivores.

Something is wrong here, since it is evident that while both premises are true for 4.4 the conclusion is patently false. What this reveals is that the premises are compatible with another mental model (Model B of Figure 4.1) that provides a *counterexample* to the argument, since the set of meat-eating pets is by definition entirely contained within the sets of carnivorous animals. When presented with this content, few people would endorse the logically fallacious conclusion.

Johnson-Laird's mental model theory of deductive reasoning was first applied to syllogisms (see Johnson-Laird & Bara, 1984, for a detailed formal

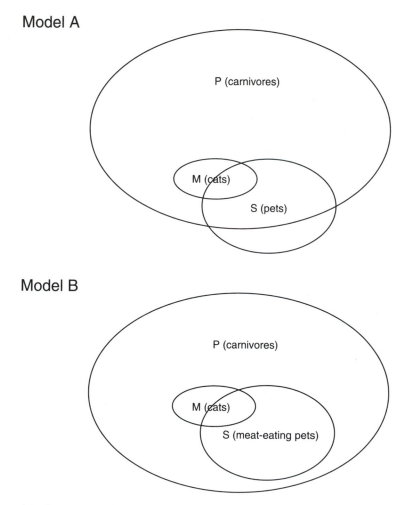

Figure 4.1   Set representations of syllogistic statements.

model and empirical test). The idea was that people start by forming a mental model that integrates the two premises and then try to form a conclusion, linking the end terms that hold in this model. They then attempt to search for counterexamples: models that are consistent with the premises but not the putative conclusion. If they fail to find such a counterexample, they declare the inference to be valid. Due to working memory constraints, however, people make many mistakes when reasoning with syllogisms, like the example above, that are consistent with multiple models. The theory was originally applied to a syllogistic production task, in which people are given the premises without a conclusion and are asked to generate their own. Say they were given, in abstract form, the premises of the above syllogism:

All M are P
Some S are not M.

and were asked what conclusion followed. If they formulated Model A (Figure 4.1) then they might well form the fallacious conclusion, Some S are not P. However, they should then search for a counterexample case. If they succeed in finding Model B, then they would withdraw this conclusion. Johnson-Laird and Bara (1984) found that people made many mistakes with syllogisms of this kind, often giving a conclusion that does not necessarily follow and also being biased by the order in which the terms S, M and P are mentioned. (More conclusions of the form S–P are generated for premises that mention S before P, an effect known as *figural bias*.) Mental model theorists also produced an explanation of how belief bias could affect syllogistic reasoning (Oakhill, Johnson-Laird, & Garnham, 1989). In essence, if the provisional conclusion generated is compatible with prior belief, people would be less motivated to search for counterexamples than if it were incompatible with belief.

Many experiments on syllogistic reasoning, including most of those on belief bias, have used the syllogistic evaluation task in which a complete syllogism is presented, and people have to say whether or not the conclusion follows. There are actually 256 possible syllogisms of a standard kind, assuming a fixed order of premises. These are formed as follows. Each statement is one of four types, known classically as A, E, I and O:

A	All A are B	Affirmative universal
E	No A are B	Negative universal
I	Some A are B	Affirmative particular
O	Some A are not B	Negative particular.

Since there are three statements (two premises and one conclusion) in a standard syllogism and four forms for each statement, that makes $4^3 = 64$ possible *moods* in which a syllogism can appear. However, we must multiply this number by four, as there are four ways of arranging the order of terms in syllogisms (known as *Figures*). Adopting the convention that the conclusion is always S–P, the premises can be M–P; S–M or M–P; M–S or P–M; S–M or P–M; M–S. Although there have been many experimental studies of syllogistic reasoning (for reviews, see Evans *et al.*, 1993; Manktelow, 1999), to my knowledge the only study to have presented participants with all 256 syllogisms to evaluate is that of Evans, Handley, Harper, and Johnson-Laird (1999a). In this study, we used computer presentation, and all syllogisms were in an abstract form, using randomly chosen capital letters to represent the three terms.

Of the 256 syllogisms, a mere 24 are logically valid. However, it has been known for many years that people will endorse many invalid syllogisms, where the conclusion is *possible* given the premises but not necessitated by them. In fact, this is the most prevalent finding in all studies of deductive reasoning and clearly supports the satisficing principle of hypothetical thinking. It seems that if people can find a model that supports the conclusion presented, they will satisfice on this model and endorse the conclusion. This is a clear example of the fundamental analytic bias that allows us to link theoretically phenomena as diverse as confirmation bias in hypothesis testing (Chapter 2) and the endorsement of fallacies in deductive reasoning as well as many phenomena in the psychology of judgement and decision making to be discussed in subsequent chapters.

If people chronically satisfice on models that are merely consistent with the premises presented, how can this be resolved with the "search for counterexamples" principle of the model theory? The findings of Evans et al. (1999a) bear directly on this issue. They discovered that although many fallacies are endorsed in syllogistic reasoning, not all fallacies are. First, few participants endorsed syllogisms whose conclusion were *impossible* given the premises. In such cases, there is no mental model of the premises to be found that supports the conclusion given. Technically, these are classed as fallacies, but the great majority of syllogisms have conclusions that are possible but not necessary. Evans et al. (1999a) found that these broke down into two groups, which they called Possible Strong and Possible Weak. Possible Strong syllogisms were consistently endorsed as valid by most participants, whereas Possible Weak syllogisms were usually rejected as invalid. In fact, endorsement rates corresponded closely to those for syllogisms that were actually valid in the case of Possible Strong, or which were impossible (conclusion cannot be true given the premises) in the case of Possible Weak.

What these data strongly suggest is that people do *not* search for counterexamples in syllogistic reasoning, but generally only form one mental model of the premises (but see Newstead, Thompson, & Handley, 2002, for evidence that some participants may do so). This is the caveat in my support for the mental model theory of syllogistic reasoning to which I alluded earlier. In the case of valid syllogisms, conclusions are usually endorsed because there is no counterexample model to be found. Similarly, impossible syllogisms are rejected because there is no model that supports the conclusion. In case of syllogisms with *possible* conclusions, people endorse them if the model that comes to mind includes the conclusion, and otherwise they reject them. In the paper, we showed that two different theories can account for the reason that Possible Strong syllogisms are the ones endorsed. In nearly all cases, they conform to what Chater and Oaksford (1999) call the *min*-heuristic. This means that people prefer conclusions that are weaker in information-theory terms than the premises. Johnson-Laird's computational model of syllogistic reasoning also shows that when premises yield more than one conclusion, the one generated *first* corresponds to that given in a Possible Strong syllogism.

It is clear that the findings of Evans et al. (1999a) provide a strong fit to the principles of hypothetical thinking theory. People form a single mental model of the premises and stick with it unless there is reason to give it up. If the conclusion presented is consistent with the model then it satisfies. Only when the conclusion cannot be reconciled with the model of the premises do people reject it. These findings are also significant for the interpretation of the belief bias effect in syllogistic reasoning, to which I now turn.

Belief bias in syllogistic reasoning

Realistic content was introduced into syllogisms in one of the earliest reported studies of deductive reasoning (Wilkins, 1928). Her findings led to two apparently contrary hypotheses that have since been thoroughly explored in the psychology of reasoning: (a) that realistic content can *facilitate* logical reasoning relative to artificial problem content; and (b) that the existence of prior beliefs and attitudes can *bias* reasoning. The former hypothesis will be discussed later in the chapter. Belief bias, which she was the first to demonstrate, is normally described as a tendency to accept conclusions that are a priori believable and to reject those that are unbelievable, regardless of their logical validity. This early study was followed sporadically by replications in the social psychological literature while interest in the effect in the cognitive literature dates from the early 1980s (Evans et al., 1983; Revlin, Leirer, Yopp, & Yopp, 1980).

Evans et al. (1983) introduced all relevant controls and established the main phenomena to be explained (Table 4.1). Using the syllogistic evaluation task they examined people's willingness to accept the conclusions of four types of syllogism as valid. There are two cases with no conflict between logic and belief: valid syllogisms with believable conclusions and invalid arguments with unbelievable conclusions. As shown in Table 4.1, acceptance rates were high (89 per cent) for the former and very low (just 10 per cent) for the latter. There are two cases, however, in which belief and logic conflict: valid-unbelievable (56 per cent) and invalid-believable (71 per cent). Statistically, these data reveal *three* significant effects to be explained: a main effect of logical validity, a main effect of belief, and a belief-by-logic interaction. Each of these has been replicated many times in the subsequent literature (see, for example, Klauer, Musch, & Naumer, 2000; Morley, Evans, & Handley, 2004; Newstead, Pollard, Evans, & Allen, 1992).

Table 4.1
Examples of the four types of syllogism used by Evans et al. (1983)
together with acceptance rates combined over three experiments

Valid-believable	
No police dogs are vicious	
Some highly trained dogs are vicious	
Therefore, some highly trained dogs are not police dogs	89%
Valid-unbelievable	
No nutritional things are inexpensive	
Some vitamin tablets are inexpensive	
Therefore, some vitamin tablets are not nutritional	56%
Invalid-believable	
No addictive things are inexpensive	
Some cigarettes are inexpensive	
Therefore, some addictive things are not cigarettes	71%
Invalid-unbelievable	
No millionaires are hard workers	
Some rich people are hard workers	
Therefore, some millionaires are not rich people	10%

Evans et al. (1983) also conducted a number of protocol analyses, mostly based on concurrent "think aloud" protocols. One of these analyses involved scoring the presence and absence of mentions of the premises and of irrelevant information. These were correlated with the decisions made. For example, on valid-unbelievable problems – where logic and belief conflict – participants making (logical) "yes" decisions made significantly more references to the premises and fewer to irrelevant information than did those making (belief-based) "no" decisions. Another analysis based only on concurrent think-aloud protocols looked at the order in which people mentioned the premises and the conclusion. Some mentioned only the conclusion. Some mentioned the conclusion before the premises while some seemed to reason from premises to conclusion. The more conclusion-centred was the protocol, the stronger the observed influence of belief and the less the influence of logic. This is consistent with a dual-processing account in which sometimes logical reasoning (premise based) and sometimes belief (conclusion based) controls the decision made. Consistent with such an account also is the recent study of De Neys (2006b) who found that concurrent working memory load disrupted reasoning and increased belief bias only on those problems where logic and belief are in conflict. Individuals of high working-memory capacity also had an advantage only on the conflict problems. The point here is that when belief and logic are consistent, fast heuristic processes will deliver the correct answers.

From the viewpoint of dual-process theory, the belief bias effect is of great interest because of this apparent belief–logic (heuristic–analytic) conflict.

Evans et al. (1983) showed that the conflict was *within* participant: that is, that the same person might sometimes go with belief and sometimes with logic. It is important to understand exactly how the two influences combine, and for this reason there has been considerable interest in the belief-by-logic interaction (Table 4.1), which can be described by saying that belief bias is stronger on invalid arguments. Evans et al. (1983) proposed two rival accounts, which have since become known as Selective Scrutiny and Misinterpreted Necessity. You can also think of them as belief-first or logic-first accounts. Under the Selective Scrutiny model – which was designed to account for syllogistic evaluation tasks – it is assumed that the conclusion is read first and that, if believable, people tend to accept it without reasoning. When the conclusion is unbelievable, however, people are much more likely to check the logic of the argument. This explains why one conflict problem – invalid-believable – is generally accepted in line with belief, while the other – valid-unbelievable – is more evenly balanced. However, this is a simplification, as there is still a significant belief bias on valid arguments in the study of Evans et al. (1983) and in most replication studies.

The Misinterpreted Necessity model is not well supported in the literature and will not be discussed here (but see Evans et al., 1993). The notion of Selective Scrutiny is consistent with common sense as well as evidence from social psychological experiments (Lord, Ross, & Lepper, 1979) that people are much more likely to look critically at the evidence for propositions that they disbelieve. It also appears to fit the revised heuristic–analytic theory of Evans (2006b), which characterizes heuristics like belief as providing default responses that a slow analytic process or reasoning may or may not attempt to change. However, this account has been challenged by recent studies measuring latencies of evaluation of syllogisms. The claim that people do more reasoning on problems with unbelievable conclusions seems to imply that they should spend more time on such problems. Two recent studies show that this is not so. If anything, people spend rather more time on syllogisms with *believable* conclusions (Ball, Wade, & Quayle, 2006; Thompson, Striemer, Reikoff, Gunter, & Campbell, 2003). Ball et al. used an eye-movement tracking system that allowed them to differentiate locus of attention further. Fixations on the premises of arguments following inspection of the conclusions were higher for conflict than for nonconflict problems. This suggests that people are aware of the conflict on invalid-believable as well as valid-unbelievable arguments, another problematic finding for the dual-process theory.

A recent finding that clearly is consistent with dual-process theory is that of Evans and Curtis-Holmes (2005). They used the standard syllogistic evaluation paradigm with the same four categories of syllogisms as those studied by Evans et al. (1983). A control condition was compared with the performance of a group who were given a short time limit in which to respond – known as the speeded-task method. Under speeded-task conditions the belief bias effect was much stronger and the logic effect much weaker. More significantly, the belief-by-logic interaction disappeared (see Figure 4.2). If we imagine that the speeded condition allows insufficient time for slower analytic processing to operate, then the selective scrutiny of unbelievable conclusions will not take place, and the default belief heuristic will dominate. Note that of the two conflict problems, valid-unbelievable syllogisms increase in acceptance (according with logic) with free time responding much more sharply than the acceptances of invalid-unbelievable conclusions decline.

The most recent account of belief bias is the Selective Processing model (Evans, 2000; Evans, Handley, & Harper, 2001b; Klauer et al., 2000), an account that is specifically focused on the syllogistic evaluation task and linked to the conclusions of the study of Evans et al. (1999a) using abstract syllogisms, described earlier. It will be recalled that the data of this study suggested that most people considered only one mental model of the premises and rarely looked for another. On this assumption, how would belief bias work? The model posits both a heuristic and an analytic component to belief

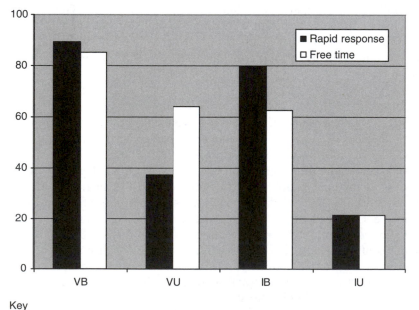

Key

VB   valid-believable
VU   valid-unbelievable
IB   invalid-believable
IU   invalid-unbelievable

Figure 4.2 Frequency of acceptance of syllogistic conclusions in the study of Evans and Curtis-Holmes (2005).

bias (see Figure 4.3). The default heuristic response is to accept believable and to reject unbelievable conclusions. This explains the fact that belief biases affect valid as well as invalid inferences and correspond to the assertion by mental model theorists that there is a response bias element to belief bias (Oakhill et al., 1989). If the analytic system intervenes, however, a single mental simulation is carried out, which attempts to build only one mental model of the premises. This process is *also* biased by the believability of the conclusion, delivering the analytic component of belief bias. When the conclusion is believable, a search is carried out for a model that supports the conclusion and if successful the conclusion is accepted. If the conclusion is unbelievable, a search is carried out for a model that refutes the conclusion (supports its negation). If successful, the conclusion is rejected (see Figure 4.3).

While the default heuristic responses can produce only a main effect of belief, the analytic process produces the interaction. When a conclusion is valid, there is only one model to be found that supports the conclusion. Hence, despite the motivated search, no further belief bias can occur. When it is invalid, however, there exist models that both support and refute the conclusion. This produces an enhanced belief bias effect on invalid-believable arguments, leading to the observed belief-by-logic interaction. This model is fully consistent with the heuristic–analytic theory and with the speeded-task results of Evans and Curtis-Holmes (2005). Under speeded-task conditions, there is little time for analytic intervention, and so the default heuristic belief

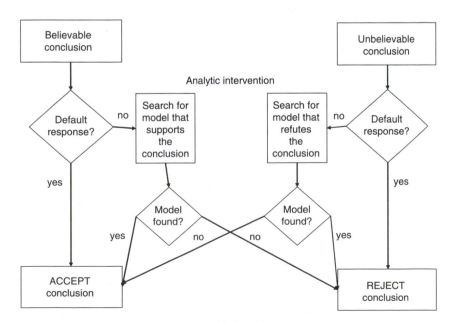

Figure 4.3   The selective processing model of belief bias.

bias dominates and the belief-by-logic interaction disappears. Unlike the Selective Scrutiny model, Selective Processing does not make the (falsified) prediction that people will think longer about unbelievable conclusions. The model works on the basis that analytic system intervention is equally likely for both believable and unbelievable conclusions.

The Selective Processing model specifically accounts for belief bias in the syllogistic evaluation paradigm where a conclusion is presented. The model implies that the mental processing of syllogisms in this paradigm should be substantially different from that in the production task, where there is no conclusion to bias the process of reasoning. While there is evidence of belief bias in the syllogistic production task (Markovits & Nantel, 1989; Oakhill & Johnson-Laird, 1985; Oakhill et al., 1989) the effect seems weaker and can be harder to demonstrate than on the evaluation task (Barston, 1986). The recent study of Morley et al. (2004) is especially relevant to this issue.

Morley *et al.* ran two experiments using the syllogistic evaluation task and two using the production task. In the evaluation task experiments they found the usual pattern of belief bias, but could find no evidence for *figural bias*. Figural bias was reported by Johnson-Laird and Bara (1984) using the syllogistic *production* task. When people spontaneously formulate conclusions to syllogistic premises, they are biased by the ordering of the terms S, M and P as mentioned earlier, so that they tend to produce conclusions compatible rather than incompatible with the Figure. In their production task experiments, Morley et al. replicated this effect, but in those experiments there was no significant effect of belief bias. This study hence suggests that the mental processing of syllogisms is strongly affected by the presence of a conclusion to be evaluated. In the absence of a conclusion, people reason forward from the premises. In its presence they start by inspecting the conclusion, and any attempt to reason is shaped by it. However, we still have to account for the fact that some studies show belief bias on the production task.

If people simply reason forward from the premises, it seems there should be no belief bias as they do not know in advance whether the model they generate will support a believable or unbelievable conclusion. However, any model that will support an unbelievable conclusion has to be built upon at least one unbelievable premise, and this may block the reasoning process, since people are reluctant to draw conclusions from syllogisms with unbelievable premises (Thompson, 1996). There are other possible explanations. For example, people might construct a model and find that it implies an unbelievable conclusion and think they have made a mistake. Such a model would not satisfy, so they may attempt to generate another. It is also possible that provisional conclusions spontaneously occur to people when thinking about the general content of the syllogisms and, as with the Selective Processing model, they try to generate models that include believable and exclude unbelievable conclusions generated in this way.

In this section, the literature on belief bias in syllogistic reasoning has been considered in some detail. However, it should be noted that there is also widespread evidence of belief bias effects in cognitive and social psychology on a range of cognitive tasks (Klayman, 1995), but this lies outside the scope of the current review. For example, people are biased by prior beliefs in statistical and scientific reasoning problems (Klaczynski, 2000) and in reasoning about causal relations (Fugelsang & Thompson, 2003). The latter authors actually propose a dual-processing account of belief bias in causal inference that has a very similar structure to the heuristic–analytic theory of Evans (2006b) as applied in the current book. They argue that beliefs are rapidly and automatically recruited and then shape and restrict efforts at analytic reasoning about the causal relations that follow. I now turn to consideration of how beliefs influence performance in another major paradigm in the psychology of reasoning: the inferences that people are willing to draw from conditional statements.

THE ROLE OF BELIEF IN CONDITIONAL REASONING

The great majority of studies of the belief bias effect have used syllogistic reasoning, manipulated belief in the conclusion and employed strong deductive reasoning instructions. Under these conditions, any effect of belief on reasoning is technically a normative bias, due to the use of the deduction paradigm. However, as stated earlier, it is not a bias in ordinary everyday reasoning to take account of beliefs when reasoning. In terms of achieving one's goals, it is highly adaptive to contextualize everyday problems with regard to prior belief. If we look at studies of how knowledge and belief affect conditional inference, the studies differ somewhat from those in the syllogistic reasoning literature. First, most relevant studies have manipulated the effect of belief in the major premise (the conditional statement) rather than in the conclusion given. Second, the kinds of instructions used have been varied quite a lot in these studies.

There are numerous studies of the way in which knowledge influences people's tendency to accept or reject each of the four conditional inferences MP, DA, AC and MT as defined in Chapter 3 (see Table 3.2). As with studies on the belief bias effect in syllogistic reasoning, content strongly influences conditional reasoning even when strict deductive reasoning instructions are applied (see Evans & Over, 2004, for a recent review). Thompson (1994, 2000) describes these effects in terms of sufficiency and necessity. When we assert that "if p then q" we may intend to mean that knowing p is sufficient to infer q (Modus Ponens), and we may also mean that p is *necessary* for q, in which case we can also infer q from p (Affirmation of the Consequent). If p is both sufficient and necessary for q then the statement is a *biconditional*, equivalent to "if and only if p then q".

The terms "sufficiency" and "necessity" are taken from a system known as modal logic, but are used in the psychological literature in a rather loose sense to refer to the *beliefs* that people hold about the terms p and q in a realistic conditional statement. In fact, it turns out that there are two different ways of thinking about this, one probabilistic and one all-or-none. I will take the all-or-none version first as this has a longer history of study and is also consistent with the popular mental model theory of conditionals. Recall that the model theory proposes that people will draw an inference unless they find a counterexample to it. The model theory also uses an extensional semantics, so that the meaning of a conditional is the set of possibilities that it allows, a set that can be modified by prior knowledge by the mechanism of pragmatic modulation (Evans et al., 2005b; Johnson-Laird & Byrne, 2002). Consider the sentences:

If the key is turned then the car's engine will start.   4.5

If it rains then the sky is cloudy.   4.6

In the model theory, by default people represent only one state of affairs in which the antecedent is true, the one where the consequent is true also. So they should make the MP inference form 4.5 from the assumption that the key is turned to the conclusion that the engine starts. However, someone asked to do this might call to mind a counterexample. Say they remember a time when they left their lights on and the battery went flat. On that occasion turning the key failed to start the engine. If they attend to such a counterexample they might refuse to make the MP inference, even though it is universally endorsed when abstract problems are used. What authors like Cummins et al. (Cummins, Lubart, Alksnis, & Rist, 1991) and Thompson (1994) mean by "low-sufficiency" conditionals are ones where these kinds of counterexamples – also know as disabling conditions – come readily to mind. High-sufficiency conditionals are ones like 4.6 where few disabling conditions can be generated. The method involves having one group of participants attempt to generate counterexamples for a particular set of sentences and then having another group draw inferences from them.

What the authors of these papers predict and observe is that MP rates drop when low sufficiency conditionals are used. MT rates drop also because these are valid inferences that require the conditional relation to hold, no matter what your theory of how MT is made. If the instructions to these experiments are strictly deductive, as they sometimes are, then we could consider this to be a form of belief bias. Beliefs are interfering with a person's ability to draw valid logical inferences. The only problem with this argument is that exactly similar effects can be observed on the invalid inferences, DA and AC. Whether or not these are endorsed depends on the perceived necessity of p for q. Consider the following conditionals:

If the tomato is red then it is edible.   4.7

If you take up running then you will lose weight.   4.8

Conditional 4.7 would be high-necessity conditional for most people (unless you like fried green tomatoes). So you would be inclined to infer that a tomato that is not red is inedible (DA) and that a tomato that is edible is red (AC). However, 4.8 is low necessity. Although taking up running probably would make you lose weight, we all know there is another way of doing it (eating less) even if we are not too keen on the idea. So in this case, you would likely refuse the DA and AC inferences. The reason that it is rather tricky to call this belief bias is that people tend to make DA and AC with abstract materials when there are no beliefs in play (Evans et al., 1995a). So the effect of a low-necessity conditional is more like a belief *de*bias. This is where we can see the problem of defining bias by normative standards such as logic. Adherents of mental logic (Braine & O'Brien, 1998a) argue that different mental processes underlie valid inferences, like MP and MT, than fallacies like DA and AC, but it is hard to justify this assertion on my reading of the psychological literature. Both seem receptive to the same kind of psychological factors, as in the examples discussed here.

In terms of what it means to *believe* a conditional statement, the sufficiency of p for q seems to be the critical factor. However, this is where the probabilistic view comes in. With an extensional semantics, like that of the model theory, we must either represent or not represent the counterexample case – p and not-q – as being a possibility. If we do not represent this case, we make MP; if we do, then we withhold MP. However, a view that is gaining popularity in the literature is that we can believe a conditional statement to a degree – in other words assign it a subjective probability of being true (Liu, Lo, & Wu, 1996; Oaksford, Chater, & Larkin, 2000; Over & Evans, 2003). If asked, people will give a rating on a scale from low to high belief/probability (using the full range), and this degree of belief in turn will predict their tendency to endorse the MP and MT inferences (Dieussaert, Schaeken, & d'Ydewalle, 2002; George, 1995, 1997, 1999; Liu et al., 1996; Stevenson & Over, 1995).

Only recently have we learnt what probability people use when deciding their belief in a real-world conditional statement. In Chapter 3, we saw that one consequence of the suppositional theory of conditionals (Evans & Over, 2004) is that people should assign the probability of "if p then q" as the conditional probability P(q|p) due to use of the Ramsey test (suppose p, evaluate q). I also referred to experiments on abstract conditional statements, where people were given frequency distributions. We have since developed a new paradigm for study of the probability of realistic, everyday conditionals. We call this the *probabilistic truth table task*, and the method has been applied to real-world causal conditionals by Over et al. (in press). In a typical experiment, participants are asked to consider conditional statements of a causal nature that describe events that may or may not occur in the next five years. As an example:

If Queen Elizabeth dies than Prince Charles will become King.   4.9

It is easy enough to ask people to rate the probability of a list of such statements. The tricky part is how to decide what underlying probabilities predict this, since they are all subjective. Clearly there is no frequency distribution that can be supplied for a conditional like 4.9. In the probabilistic truth table task what we do is ask people to rate the subjective probability of each of the four truth table cases – that is, the following four conjunctive statements:

pq   Queen Elizabeth dies and Prince Charles becomes King
p¬q   Queen Elizabeth dies and Prince Charles does not become King
¬pq   Queen Elizabeth does not die and Prince Charles becomes King
¬p¬q   Queen Elizabeth does not die and Prince Charles does not become King.

Participants are required to assign a percentage probability to each statement such that they total 100 per cent. From these four probabilities we can then compute any probabilities that may be relevant to belief in the conditional statement. What we actually did was to calculate three statistically independent predictor probabilities:

$$P(p) = P(pq) + P(p\neg q)$$
$$P(q|p) = P(pq)/[P(pq) + P(p\neg q)]$$
$$P(q|\neg p) = P(\neg pq)/[(P(\neg pq) + P(\neg p\neg q)].$$

We then performed multiple regression analyses across our sentences using the rated probability of the conditional statement (collected in a separate task) as the dependent variable. We found first that belief in the conditional statement is independent of P(p). For example, in the above case, the subjective probability that Queen Elizabeth would die in the next five years had no bearing at all on the rated probability of the conditional statement. (Note that if the conditional were a material conditional, it should be rated as more probable when p is less likely. This is because material conditionals are always true when their antecedents are false.) The main finding was that the regression weighting for conditional probability P(q|p) was very high, just as it should be according to the suppositional theory of conditionals described in Chapter 3. If people decide the truth of the conditional by a mental simulation in which the truth of its antecedent is supposed, then clearly belief in the first two statements of the probabilistic truth table task should be the main predictor. For example if people assign some probability to the case in which Charles does not succeed Elizabeth (say because he dies first) then this proportionately lowers their belief in the conditional.

So we know that belief in conditionals largely reflects the conditional probability P(q|p) and that this belief in turn strongly influences the tendency to draw MP and MT. The influence of belief on conditional reasoning can, however, be attenuated by the use of strong deductive reasoning instructions (George, 1995; Stevenson & Over, 1995), which makes sense in terms of dual-process theory, since people instructed to assume the truth of the premises may reset the default probabilities supplied by the belief system by conscious effort. How is this conditional belief related to retrieval of counterexamples? Do people judge P(q|¬p) simply on the basis of how many counterexample cases of ¬pq cases they can think of, in line with the measures used by Cummins, Thompson, and others? Not so, it appears. Recent studies have shown that conditional reasoning is sensitive to strength of association of counterexamples to both valid and fallacious conditional inferences (Quinn & Markovits, 1998, 2002).

Dual-process theories of reasoning have tended to put emphasis on the ability of the analytic system to perform abstract, decontextualized reasoning (Stanovich, 1999). However, evidence is accumulating from the studies of conditional reasoning that the analytic system is heavily involved in con-textualized reasoning. De Neys, Schaeken, and d'Ydewalle (2005a) have shown that the ease of retrieval of counterexamples to conditionals is dependent on working-memory resources, as measured both by individual differences in working-memory span and by the use of secondary tasks. The findings hold for counterexamples to both valid and invalid inferences. This leads to an intriguing question. Will participants with high working-memory spans suppress more valid as well as fallacious conditional inferences? The problem is that high working-memory capacity is very highly correlated with cognitive ability (Colom et al., 2004), and high-ability people have generally been shown to be better at finding logically correct answers to reasoning problems (Stanovich, 1999). De Neys et al. (2005b) hypothesized that as higher ability people are more likely to understand the instructions to make validity judgements, they will in fact use the executive aspect of their working-memory resources to *inhibit* counterexamples to valid inferences (see

Markovits & Barrouillet, 2002, for a similar hypothesis). Consistent with Stanovich's work they in fact found that participants with high working-memory span accepted more valid (MP, MT) and fewer invalid (DA, AC) inferences when reasoning with ordinary causal conditionals, implying active inhibition in the former cases.

From the discussion of the belief bias effect in syllogistic reasoning earlier, it appears that there is an influence of belief on both heuristic and analytic processing. Recent studies suggest that the same may be true in conditional reasoning. In this section, I have referred both to studies that predict conditional inferences from direct ratings of belief or probability in the relation between p and q (e.g., Dieussaert et al., 2002) and from studies that measure availability of counterexamples (e.g., Cummins et al., 1991). Are these two ways of measuring the same thing, or is there a heuristic-level intuition of belief strength on the one hand, and an analytic-system level of explicit consideration of counterexamples on the other? They are difficult to separate, but Verschueren, Schaeken, and d'Ydewalle (2005a) found that likelihood ratings better predicted reasoning on fast trials and counterexample ratings better on slow trials. Since heuristic processing is faster, they suggested that beliefs may operate through the heuristic system in a graduated manner, or through the analytic system in an all-or-none manner more consistent with the mental model theory (Evans et al., 2005b). They have also offered evidence from verbal protocol analysis for this hypothesis (Verschueren, Schaeken, & d'Ydewalle, 2005b).

It is clear that the way in which people reason about realistic conditional statements is very strongly influenced by the beliefs evoked by the content and context of the problem presented. There is also much evidence for dual processing in such tasks. It seems that heuristic-level processes retrieve belief relations that can be expressed as judgements of belief or probability in the relation between p and q and other relations (q to p, not-p to not-q, etc.) and that these beliefs affect reasoning. However, it is unlikely that the data can be explained by a single-level probabilistic treatment of conditionals of the kind proposed by Oaksford and Chater (2001). We know that deductive effort, leading to a differentiation between valid MP and MT inferences and falla-cious DA and AC inferences, can be induced both by use of strong deductive reasoning instructions and by participants of higher cognitive ability or working-memory capacity. There are also now a number of studies showing that analytic-level reasoning is involved in the processing of contextualized reasoning, as both the retrieval and application of counterexamples to conditional inferences is related to the capacity and inhibition properties of central working memory.

DOMAIN-SPECIFIC VERSUS DOMAIN-GENERAL
REASONING: THE SELECTION TASK DEBATE

The abstract Wason selection task was discussed in Chapter 2. Actually it should really be called the abstract, *indicative* selection task. Although authors commonly classify selection task research as involving either an abstract or a thematic form, the tasks really fall into four classes:

A. Abstract indicative
B. Abstract deontic
C. Thematic indicative
D. Thematic deontic.

The great majority of experiments on the selection task have been of either Type A or Type D, which means that any comparison between them is potentially confounded, something that went unrecognized for many years prior to the paper of Manktelow and Over (1991). The difference between indicative and deontic conditionals is that the former refer to relationships in the world that might or might not hold, while the latter refer to rules and regulations. Consider the following statements:

If you are hungry then you will eat that apple.   4.10

If you are hungry then you may eat that apple.   4.11

The example in 4.10 is an indicative conditional that effectively constitutes a prediction about your behaviour. Supposing that you are hungry; your eating behaviour will show whether the prediction was true or false. However, 4.11 – a deontic conditional – is a social rule that gives you permission to eat the apple. You cannot say that 4.11 is true or false. Deontic conditionals are either permissions or obligations, often (but not necessarily) containing the modal terms "may" and "must", respectively. An example of a deontic obligation is:

If you ride a motor bike then you must wear a crash helmet.   4.12

In the case of 4.12, you could not say that someone riding a bike and not wearing a helmet (the p¬q case) is proving the rule false; he is simply failing to obey it. Deontic obligations may or may not have legal force, as 4.12 does in many countries. In ones where it does not, 4.12 might still be a social obligation, for example, when this rule is given by a parent to a teenage child as a condition for being allowed a motor bike.

Ironically, the first demonstration that thematic content could facilitate performance on the Wason selection task used a thematic but *indicative* rule

(Wason & Shapiro, 1971). The rule concerned journeys made by the experimenter, who claimed that "Every time I go to Manchester I travel by train." The cards represented journeys with a destination on one side and means of transport on the other, with the exposed sides reading:

Manchester   Leeds   Train   Car

In this study, people did select p and not-q cards (Manchester and Car) more often than on the control letters and numbers task. However, subsequent research showed that these materials produce only a weak facilitation that later studies often failed to replicate (e.g., Griggs & Cox, 1982).

Much research on this problem has shown that strong and reliable facilitation of p and not-q card choices requires problems that are both deontic and thematic in nature (see Evans et al., 1993; Evans & Over, 2004; Manktelow, 1999, for reviews of this literature). A good example is the drinking-age problem (Griggs & Cox, 1982) in which people are told to imagine they are police officers checking people drinking in a bar. They are then given a rule such as, "if a person is drinking beer then they are over 18 years of age". The four cards represented drinkers, showing the beverage on one side and the age on the other: "beer", "coke", "22 years of age", "16 years of age". This problem really is easy: most people pick "beer" (p) and "16 years of age" (not-q). In this case, people may have direct experience of the rule, but research shows that permission rules can facilitate reasoning even in contexts with which people are unfamiliar (see Evans et al., 1993). On such deontic rules we can still say that the correct choices are the p and not-q cards where rules have the form "if p then (must) q", and the instruction is to find cards that *violate* (not falsify) the rule. However, the deontic and indicative selection tasks cannot be described as logically equivalent.

The striking content effects in the selection task have made it a testing ground for a debate about whether reasoning mechanisms are domain-specific or domain-general. The earliest theory claiming a domain-specific mechanism was the proposal of pragmatic reasoning schemas by Cheng and Holyoak (1985; see also Cheng, Holyoak, Nisbett, & Oliver, 1986; Holyoak & Cheng, 1995). They argued that people acquire schemas for reasoning about deontic rules – permission and obligations – and that these schemas facilitate logical performance. For example, the schemas would contain production rules such as "if you do not fulfil the precondition then you cannot take the action" that would cue choices of the not-q card such as a person in a bar who is under 18 years of age. This theory has been criticized on several grounds (see Evans & Over, 2004, pp. 83–85) but has attracted nothing like the storm of protest surrounding the claim that deontic selection tasks can be solved using innate Darwinian algorithms.

Evolutionary psychology entered into the psychology of reasoning with the paper of Cosmides (1989), with ideas that were swiftly popularized as their form of evolutionary psychology gained popularity (Barkow, Cosmides, & Tooby, 1992; Pinker, 1997) as well as notoriety in the 1990s. This school of work, which I will capitalize as Evolutionary Psychology, is a form of cognitive psychology that applies *a priori* evolutionary theory to paint a picture of the mind as "massively modular" (Cosmides & Tooby, 1992; Samuels, 1998; Tooby & Cosmides, 1992). In fact, it is quite a narrow part of the discipline more generally known as evolutionary psychology (Barrett, Dunbar, & Lycett, 2002; Caporael, 2001). The notion of a cognitive module seems to have been derived from Fodor's (1983) theory of mind, in that it is regarded as domain-specific with dedicated or "information encapsulated" cognitive processes. However, Fodor applied this concept only to input systems such as vision and language and not to higher order reasoning, which he regards as part of a *domain-general* system for higher cognition. Fodor, who effectively has a dual-process theory of mind, is hence one of the leading critics of massive modularity (Fodor, 2001).

Tooby and Cosmides (1992) argued on *a priori* grounds of evolutionary theory that domain-general cognition could not have evolved because it would be easily out competed by domain-specific mechanisms of thought. This extreme position was never likely to be sustainable in light of the widespread evidence of general systems of learning and reasoning and has been at least partially retracted in more recent writing (Cosmides & Tooby, 2000). However, it inspired a research programme seeking evidence of domain-specific mechanisms in higher human thought that introduced a particular methodology. The method is to find two forms of a problem, A and B, such that (a) each has the same logical form X, and (b) only A can be solved by application of an innate cognitive module. Performance on A should be greatly superior to that on B. This method has been applied in two main areas: facilitatory effects on the selection task and the use of frequency information in statistical reasoning (see Chapter 6).

Cosmides (1989) argued that all successful facilitatory contexts used in selection task research involved *social contracts* that imposed obligations. She further argued that people would have evolved innate Darwinian algorithms for reasoning about social contracts that would include a *search for cheaters* algorithm. In order to test this she constructed problems in unfamiliar scenarios. For example, a culture is described in which men crave cassava root (an aphrodisiac) but are only allowed to eat it if they are married, indicated by a tattoo on their face. The rule used was "if a man eats cassava root then he must have a tattoo on his face", leading to correct selections of cards showing cassava root (p) and no tattoo (not-q). However, there have been numerous critiques of these experiments published (see, for example, Buller, 2005; Cheng & Holyoak, 1989; Evans & Over, 1996a; Fodor, 2000; Over, 2003; Sperber & Girotto, 2002). One common objection is that the studies were poorly controlled in that comparisons were made to "control" selection tasks that were in fact indicative rather than deontic. Hence, A and B did not have the same logical form X.

The A, B, X method actually appears too weak to test the hypothesis for which it was designed. Suppose that the experiments were perfectly controlled and that A was better than B whenever people could search for cheaters. The problem is that detecting cheaters is adaptive in the modern social world as well as in the ancient environment of evolution, and so this behaviour could have been shaped by social learning within the lifetime of the individual. Hence, evidence for domain-specific reasoning is not evidence for *innateness*. It is also a fallacy to think that domain-specific cognition is necessarily generated by domain-specific mechanisms (Almor, 2003). For example, knowledge that is acquired experientially through implicit learning is known to be domain-specific (Berry & Dienes, 1993).

Some of the strongest criticisms of social contract theory have come from authors proposing that content effects on the selection task reflect domain-general mechanisms. There are two main theories of this type, one based on decision theory principles (Evans & Over, 1996a; Manktelow & Over, 1991; Oaksford & Chater, 1994) and one based on relevance theory (Oaksford & Chater, 1995; Sperber, Cara, & Girotto, 1995). In the decision theory approach, people are assumed to choose cards on the deontic selection task in a way that is rational according to the goals they are pursuing. Manktelow and Over (1991) were able to provide a counterexample to the claim of Cosmides that all facilitatory contexts involved cheater detection. They found that people chose correct cards on a rule such as "Every time I clean up spilt blood I wear rubber gloves." Evolutionary Psychologists responded by arguing that they had discovered a new module for hazard avoidance or precaution leading to a whole new line of experimentation (Fiddick, Cosmides, & Tooby, 2000). In support of this, Evolutionary Psychologists have recently claimed evidence for neurological differentiation of reasoning about precautions and social contracts (Fiddick, Spampinato, & Grafman, 2005; Stone, Cosmides, Tooby, Kroll, & Knight, 2002).

The relevance theory of Sperber et al. (1995) proposes that conditional statements can be processed superficially or deeply according to the context. The deepest level indicates the relevance of the not-q card, which is cued on the easy deontic versions. The proponents of this approach recently made a very strong criticism of social contract theory (Sperber & Girotto, 2002). They pointed out that successful forms involve an explicit cue in the scenario that people should be looking for cheaters. It is quite clear in a given context what a cheater is: say a person under 18 years of age who is drinking beer. Once this cue is given, Sperber and Girotto argue, the selection task is no longer a reasoning problem but reduces to a simple classification task, something they demonstrate with some new experiments. If you already know that you need to find all cards with an alcoholic drink and a person under 18 years of age, for example, no reasoning about the conditional statement is needed to pick out the cards that show these values.

Implications for dual-process theory

According to dual-process theory, reasoning has both domain-specific (heuristic) and domain-general (analytic) aspects. For example, in discussing the belief bias work earlier, logical success was attributed to deductive effort via the analytic system while the main effect of belief was due to direct cueing of believable conclusions by the heuristic system. Now there is no question that people think about selection tasks differently when the content and context are changed. On many of the successful deontic versions, the correct solution seems quite easy and obvious because, as Sperber and Girotto say, little if any analytic reasoning is required. Where knowledge strongly cues the correct choices, these selection tasks are rather like the no-conflict syllogisms: believable-valid and unbelievable-invalid. Performance on such syllogisms is consistently high. The problem cases are where belief and logic come into conflict. Is there an equivalent of this in the selection task research?

There are comparable versions of the selection task in which pragmatic cues and logical structure are put into conflict. For example, Cosmides (1989) used a switched social contract rule. Using a similar context to before, the rule "if a man has a tattoo on his face then he eats cassava root" will still generate selections of "cassava root" and "no tattoo" even though these are now the not-p and q cards. Similar findings have been demonstrated with perspective shifts (Gigerenzer & Hug, 1992; Manktelow & Over, 1991; Politzer & Nguyen-Xuan, 1992). For example, if a mother says to her son, "if you tidy up your room you may go out to play", the son is cheating on the rule if he goes out to play without tidying up his room, and these cards are chosen from the mother's perspective. If the son's perspective is given, however, the mother is cheating if he tidies his room and is not let out to play, and accordingly the card choices switch even though the conditional statement is unaltered (Manktelow & Over, 1991). Thus it seems that heuristic processes dominate on realistic deontic selection tasks with little evidence of analytic or logical reasoning.

On abstract selection tasks, there is evidence that the small minority who can solve it are much higher in cognitive ability than nonsolvers (Stanovich & West, 1998). In this large-scale study, the authors also showed that the relation between ability and performance on deontic selection tasks was very much weaker. This suggests that analytic reasoning is required for solution of the indicative but not the deontic selection task. Consistent with these conclusions are recent findings of De Neys (2006a), who used response latency as an indicator of reasoning process, on the basis that heuristic processes are quicker. De Neys showed that on abstract indicative versions of the selection task, correct card selections were associated with longer latencies than were matching responses, consistent with the assumption of analytic and heuristic process control, respectively. On the deontic selection, by contrast, correct selections were the quickest, as might be expected if these are cued by rapid pragmatic processes.

The findings of a more recent study of individual differences on the selection task by Newstead et al. (2004) were, however, somewhat different from those of Stanovich and West (1998). In two experiments, Newstead et al. found a correlation of ability with performance for deontic and not indicative selection tasks. However, it turned out that the samples of participants used in these experiments were of unusually low cognitive ability for university students. In a third experiment, using higher ability participants, the pattern was similar to that observed by Stanovich and West. It is possible that the population at large really has three groups: (a) low ability who are poor at both tasks; (b) medium ability who are good at the deontic task; and (c) high ability who are good at both tasks. The results make sense if Stanovich and West mostly sampled groups (b) and (c) while Newstead et al. (first two experiments) were mostly sampling (a) and (b).

The findings of Newstead et al. are somewhat at odds with the claim that System 1 is a universal cognitive system unrelated to heritable differences in intelligence (Evans, 2003). They are more consistent with the claims of some developmental psychologists that System 1 (heuristic, experiential, pragmatic) processes develop through childhood and are related to working memory capacity and cognitive ability (Klaczynski, Schuneman, & Daniel, 2004; Markovits & Barrouillet, 2002; Markovits, Fleury, Quinn, & Venet, 1998). What seems to be developing is the efficiency of retrieval of relevant prior knowledge. As developmental studies also make clear, however, the ability correctly to utilize such knowledge to block invalid inferences rather than to exhibit belief biases is related to analytic reasoning ability, which develops in parallel. There are clear links here with the studies of conditional inference discussed earlier in which we saw that the analytic system and working memory were involved in contextualized reasoning.

As indicated in Chapter 1, while the heuristic–analytic theory is a dual-process theory, it is not framed at the level of the more ambitious dual-system theories (Evans, 2003), which posit, for example, an evolutionarily old System 1 shared with animals and a uniquely human System 2. In fact, System 1 is not really one system at all, but a whole collection of implicit subsystems (Evans, 2006a; Stanovich, 2004). The heuristic processes with which this book is concerned are mostly *pragmatic*, relating to language and belief systems that are modern human developments rather than older learning systems of the kind discussed, for example, by Reber (1993). Although these pragmatic processes are unconscious and automatic in the selection and retrieval of knowledge, they deliver their outputs for conscious processing via working memory. It is not therefore surprising that the ability to reason about familiar as well as abstract content is linked to analytic reasoning and cognitive ability.

How does dual-process theory stand on the issue of whether reasoning is domain-specific or domain-general? I would argue that unless strong evidence to the contrary can be shown – for example, implying an innate cognitive module – both heuristic and analytic processes are domain-general mechanisms, with two caveats. Note first that the term "heuristic" is used here in a narrower sense than the catch-all "System 1", which might well include domain-specific modules. Second, while the heuristic processes responsible for selecting and retrieving relevant belief and knowledge may be dedicated to that function (and domain-specific in that very broad sense) they are general with regards to the content and contexts about which we learn and think. In this respect, I agree with much that has been written about relevance theory by Sperber and Wilson (1995). The fact that our knowledge may be "modular" in the sense of being context-bound does not mean that a content-specific mechanism (such as a cheater-detection module) was involved. As noted earlier, experiential learning tends to lead to context-specific knowledge (Berry & Dienes, 1993). However, the mechanism by which such knowledge is retrieved and applied to a current problem would seem to be equally general.

This having been said, it is clear that analytic processes are distinct from the heuristic processes that provide content. It would be a mistake to think of analytic reasoning as some kind of mental logic that is inherently abstract and decontextualized in nature, as it clearly is involved in contextualized reasoning. However, the evidence is also clear in showing that abstract and logical reasoning, when necessitated by the task given, requires the highest levels of analytic reasoning ability. That is why performance on such tasks takes the longest time to develop in children and is most marked in adults of the highest cognitive ability.

CONCLUSIONS

The studies reviewed in this chapter are consistent with the two fundamental cognitive biases that affect reasoning and judgement. The first bias (of the heuristic system) is that we rapidly and automatically contextualize problems in the light of prior knowledge and belief (see also, Stanovich, 1999). This prompts default belief-based responses and also restricts the scope of analytic reasoning by focusing attention on content that appears relevant in the light of prior knowledge. This chapter has been primarily about these belief-based heuristic processes, which underlie belief bias effects in syllogistic and conditional reasoning and are responsible for apparently domain-specific reasoning on the deontic selection task. The second fundamental bias (of the analytic system) to satisfice on a single mental model without consideration of alternatives has been in evidence also. For example, we can explain the main effect of belief bias in syllogistic reasoning in purely heuristic terms, but we need the notion of selective analytic processing to explain the belief-by-logic interaction. Similarly, recent research on contextualized conditional inference indicates that content effects operate at both the heuristic and analytic levels. The thematic and deontic selection task, as with the abstract version discussed in Chapter 2, is apparently dominated by heuristic processes that cue relevance of the cards that are typically chosen. This does not indicate an absence of analytic reasoning on this task, however, as has often been assumed. Rather it reflects the fundamental bias of the analytic system to accept what appears relevant unless there is good reason to reject it. People do attempt to reason on the selection task, but only those of very high cognitive ability appear to do so to much effect.

Dual-processing accounts of reasoning have been around since the 1970s but, as this chapter shows, are subject to continual revision and refinement. By contrast, dual-processing accounts of judgement and decision making – the topics of the following two chapters – are in their infancy. However, this book is predicated on the strong claim that all forms of hypothetical thinking are subject to the same basic principles. The following chapters will assess the degree to which theoretical ideas primarily developed in the psychology of reasoning can be generalized to other domains in which higher cognitive processes are studied.

CHAPTER FIVE

Dual processes in judgement and decision making

In this chapter, the main literature on the psychology of judgement and decision making (JDM) will be examined for evidence of dual processing and the principles of hypothetical thinking. Despite the obvious connections with the psychology of reasoning in terms of higher mental processes, this endeavour is not as straightforward as might be expected. Unlike the psychology of reasoning, the study of decision making is interdisciplinary and not firmly situated within cognitive psychology. Much research on decision making is conducted by psychologists and those trained in other disciplines within business schools where links to economics and applications in public policy are considered more important than the investigation of cognitive processes. Psychological studies in this area have also traditionally been linked very closely with questions about normative theory and rationality. For example, the rational theory of choice – subjective expected utility (see Chapter 1) – has dominated much of the huge literature on this topic, albeit as an ideal from which departures are regularly demonstrated (for recent reviews, see Hastie, 2001; Koehler & Harvey, 2004; LeBeouf & Shafir, 2005). The rational model involves the notions of consequentialism and optimization. That is to say, people should analyse a decision problem by calculating the consequences of alternative actions. They should also attempt to optimize choice by maximizing expected utility across all available choices, analysed to whatever depth is feasible (see Chapter 1).

If rational decision making is so defined, then people are irrational, as endless violations of the principles of decision theory are to be found in the psychological literature. Unfortunately, knowing what people do *not* do is not necessarily very informative about the cognitive processes that underlie their choices and decisions. One approach to this problem is to emphasize the limited cognitive capacity of human beings, the "bounded rationality" of Simon (1982) from which the satisficing principle of hypothetical thinking theory is defined. Advocates of the bounded rationality approach include Anderson (1990), Oaksford and Chater (1998), and Gigerenzer (1996). For example, the last has initiated a major research programme on the study of "fast and frugal" heuristics that people are said to employ in order to generate many effective (though less than optimal) decisions on the basis of simple rules that make minimal demands on cognitive resources (Gigerenzer & Todd, 1999). Such decision making would appear to lie in the heuristic system of the current framework and be intuitive (unreflective) in nature, but there are dual-process issues here that I will discuss later. Such heuristics can be "adaptive" if they have been shaped by evolution or experiential learning on the basis of past success and failure. While Gigerenzer and colleagues have emphasized the adaptive nature of heuristics, the "heuristics and biases" programme of Kahneman and Tversky (Gilovich et al., 2002; Kahneman et al., 1982) has, in contrast, more often emphasized the situations in which heuristics lead to biases, putting the two camps into apparent conflict.

The manner in which people make their judgements and decisions is a matter of central interest to the theory that motivates this book but I will focus on work that I believe illuminates the cognitive processes involved. Hence, although I will give some coverage of the major topics in this field, there is no attempt to balance this chapter to reflect the extent of published literature or the perceived importance of work within the field. After all, this volume is an essay and not a textbook, and its purpose is to develop understanding of the nature of hypothetical thinking. From this viewpoint and as heuristic–analytic theory would lead one to expect, decision making can and often is performed without conscious reflection on the consequences of choices (Baron, 1994). Involvement of the analytic system in real-world decision making is bound to be limited as this system is slow, capacity limited and essentially able to attend to only one thing at a time. However, we would also expect that while judgements can be made "intuitively", they can also reflect intervention of the analytic system, just as when belief biases are overcome by an effort at deductive reasoning. Recently, leading psychologists in the field of judgement and decision making have started to explore this idea.

DUAL-PROCESS THEORIES OF JUDGEMENT AND DECISION MAKING

In line with the lesser attention given to cognitive processes generally, the psychology of judgement and decision making (a tradition known for short as JDM) has included comparatively little discussion of dual processes compared with research in reasoning (Evans, 2003) and social cognition (Chaiken & Trope, 1999). For example, in the *Blackwell Handbook of Judgement and Decision Making* (Koehler & Harvey, 2004), which provides a recent and eclectic review of these topics, the subject index identifies only 9 of the 600-plus pages in which this approach is discussed. I find this extraordinary since it is fairly evident that if dual systems of cognition dominate our thought and judgement to the extent that reasoning and social cognition researchers have identified, they must be equally strongly implicated in the behaviour studied by JDM researchers. Fortunately, there are signs that the situation is changing, led by that most influential of figures, Daniel Kahneman, in his most recent writings.

Kahneman and Frederick (2002, 2005) endorse the generic dual-process framework as favoured by thinking and reasoning researchers (see Evans, 2003), adopting Stanovich's (1999) general labels of Systems 1 and 2. It is interesting that their application of dual-process theory is similar to that of the revised heuristic–analytic theory (Evans, 2006b) in that they emphasize the default nature of heuristic (System 1) processes with which analytic (System 2) processes may or may not intervene. For example, they state that "system 1 quickly proposes intuitive answers to judgement problems as they arise [while] system 2 monitors the quality of these proposals, which it may endorse, correct or override" (Kahneman & Frederick, 2005, p. 268). They go on to talk of the two processes competing for control of a judgement, with the probability of System 2 intervention being affected by its limited cognitive capacity and the ability to attend to only one task at a time.

Kahneman and Frederick developed a theory of biases based on the idea of attribute substitution: "a general feature of heuristic judgement [is that] whenever the aspect of a judgemental object that one intends to judge . . . is less readily assessed than a related property that yields a plausible answer . . . [the] individual may unwittingly substitute the simpler assessment" (Kahneman & Frederick, 2005, p. 269). This provides a link to the influential heuristics and biases research programme of Kahneman and Tversky (Gilovich et al., 2002; Kahneman et al., 1982) in which cognitive biases were regularly attributed to the use of heuristics such as *representativeness* or *availability*, which were simple short-cuts to judgements that could lead people into systematic error and bias. This kind of work is discussed in Chapter 6.

While all dual-process theorists envisage a distinction between processes that are fast and automatic on the one hand and slow and controlled on the other, they vary in the degree to which it is proposed that the systems are autonomous and independent. The default-interventionist approach of the heuristic–analytic theory, echoed by Kahneman and Frederick (2002) and by Stanovich (1999), is not the only approach (see also Evans, in press). Some theorists described the systems as two parallel styles of thinking that people may adopt. This is true of some of the theories that have been particularly influential in social psychology, including the rational–experiential theory (Epstein, 1994; Epstein & Pacini, 1999) and heuristic–systematic theory (Chaiken, 1980; Chen & Chaiken, 1999) discussed in Chapter 7. Epstein, for example, lists attributes for the experiential and rational systems that map on to those common in dual-process theories of reasoning, such as the idea that the experiential system evolved earlier and that the rational system is uniquely human. However, he also talks of rational and experiential processing styles that can be induced by experimental manipulations but that also correspond to stable personality characteristics that he measures by the rational–experiential inventory or REI (Epstein, Pacini, Denes-Raj, & Heier, 1996). If he is right, then some people will make decisions based on intuitions from past experience, whereas others will make them by rational analysis of alternative actions and their consequences.

There is an important confusion to be avoided here. In terms of quantity, the analytic system can meet very little of the cognitive demands on the brain but in terms of quality it can do things that the heuristic system cannot. The analytic system is required when we need to decontextualize problems and examine their formal structure; it is involved whenever we engage in hypothetical thinking, supposition or mental simulation; it is also needed when we apply explicitly learnt rules. By contrast the heuristic system is massively parallel and rapid, and its strength lies in identifying relevant prior knowledge and belief that are then activated and made available for conscious processing. This implies a cognitive architecture that *cannot* be conceived of in terms of parallel thinking styles. For example, the analytic system could not function at all unless pragmatic processes in the heuristic system were delivering content into consciousness on a continuous basis. At the same time, it is undeniable that there are differences in thinking style that sound as though they are related to Systems 1 and 2. Not only are these linked to individual differences in personality, but they also seem to be strongly culturally influenced. For example, there is considerable evidence that people in Western culture have a more "analytic" thinking style while those of Eastern culture are more "holistic" (Nisbett et al., 2001).

Dual-process theorists studying reasoning have become increasingly interested in the study of individual differences in the ability to solve cognitive tasks and have extended their research into the domain of judgement and decision making as well as that of deductive reasoning (for examples, see Klaczynski & Cottrell, 2004; Klaczynski & Lavallee, 2005; Kokis et al., 2002; Stanovich, 1999; Stanovich & West, 2000). These researchers have examined both cognitive ability and cognitive style measures. In general (there are some exceptions) those who are high in cognitive ability show greater normative accuracy and less susceptibility to cognitive biases on tasks drawn from both the reasoning and JDM literatures. This has been taken as evidence for dual processing on the grounds that System 2 (but not System 1) processes are related to heritable individual differences in general intelligence. However, the same researchers have also shown that when residual variance is examined (not attributable to ability) there is also evidence for dispositional factors related to cognitive style. Some people are more able to reason analytically than others, but independently of this, some people are also more *inclined* to reason analytically.

The resolution of the apparent conflict between asymmetric cognitive architecture for the two systems with evidence of parallel thinking styles is actually quite straightforward. In essence, intuitive thinkers are people who like to go with their "gut" feelings, while analytic thinkers are people who like to engage in conscious reflection before making a decision. First, most theorists identify a *volitional* or controlled aspect to System 2 that contrasts with the automaticity of System 1 processes (although this does not necessarily imply "free will", as what we apparently choose to do is also causally related to variables manipulated by experimenters – see Bargh & Ferguson, 2000). Second, within the current dual-process framework, analytic thinking may or may not intervene for a variety of reasons. The disposition by personality (or culture) for a person to invest the cognitive resources of analytic processing to check intuitions prior to making a decision is just another of these factors.

Dijksterhuis and colleagues have recently developed a dual-process approach to decision making that implies parallel conscious and unconscious processes (Dijksterhuis, Bos, Nordgren, & von Baaren, 2006). In fact, they seem to be reviving the old "incubation" theory of problem solving that derives from the introspective recollections of the mathematician Poincaré (1927) on creativity in mathematics. According to Poincaré, he was able to find solutions to complex mathematical problems on which he was stuck by turning his mind to completely different subjects. Incubation theory proposes that unconscious thinking can solve problems when conscious thinking is absent, for example during sleep, or when conscious attention is distracted by other matters. Dijksterhuis et al. (2006) revive this idea under the new label of Unconscious Thinking Theory suggesting that people can engage in *deliberative* thought without attention and that in some circumstances this leads them to make better decisions than conscious thinking does. If they are right, then we would need a quite different form of dual-process theory to accommodate their proposals. However, incubation theory has long been controversial, with other explanations offered: for example, absence of conscious attention to a problem may clear unhelpful sets and assumptions that were inhibiting its solution (see Woodworth, 1938; for a recent critical treatment of the theory, see Segal, 2004). The evidence that Dijksterhuis et al. (2006) offer for their rather startling claim is considered a little later. Next, we consider some research paradigms in judgement and decision making and their relevance to dual-process theory.

RISKY CHOICE

As already noted, the psychology of decision making has long concerned itself with testing for violations of human choices from the prescriptions of formal decision theory, which was developed by economists and mathematicians in the 1940s and 1950s and first introduced into psychology in two famous review papers by Ward Edwards (1954, 1961). Decision theory is key to understanding this field because it provided via its normative framework the structure of the decision tasks that would dominate psychological research on the topic for the next fifty years. From economics, we get the notion of utility, which is the subjective value of an outcome to a decision maker that should be reflected in his or her choices. Decision making may occur under uncertainty, as when we buy insurance or accept a wager, or under certainty as when you choose between two pairs of shoes, trading off the better quality of one against the lower price of the other. Most psychological work has focused on decisions that have an interesting degree of complexity, either because outcomes are uncertain and need to be assigned probabilities, or because choices have multiple attributes that need to be weighed against each other. The first of these – risky choice – is discussed in this section, and the second kind of study in the next.

Some authors distinguish between *risk* – in which objective probabilities are known to be associated with outcomes – and *uncertainty* – in which the decision maker must assign subjective probabilities to outcomes (Wu, Zhang, & Gonzales, 2005). The full-blown model is known as SEU (for subjective expected utility) and allows people to combine subjective probabilities and subjective values (utilities) in order to maximize their expectations of achieving happiness though their decisions – an idea also known as *instrumental rationality*. Risk is more tractable to modelling than is uncertainty, and so much attention has been focused on risky prospects of known probability in which only values need to be subjectively defined as utilities, and in which (objective) expected utility provides the criterion for rational choice.

The theory of risky choice was revolutionized by the publication of *prospect theory* by Kahneman and Tversky (1979), which, together with its later revision and extension (Tversky & Kahneman, 1992), helped lay the foundations for the award of the Nobel Prize for Economics to Danny Kahneman (under the rules, this sadly could not be shared posthumously with the legendary Amos Tversky). In this brilliant paper, Kahneman and Tversky both demonstrated numerous violations of expected utility in a series of elegant psychological experiments and also provided a descriptive theory of risky choice, which dealt with all of them. I will do no more here than give a brief flavour of the paper and its conclusions.

Kahneman and Tversky defined a *prospect* as a choice that has a given probability for achieving an outcome of some positive or negative value to the decision maker. The experimental section of the paper provided some ingenious demonstrations of violations of expected utility. For example, if you compare two prospects in which Outcome A is twice as likely as Outcome B, the expected utility will be the same whatever the actual probabilities are. Suppose you compare the following prospects:

A $1000; .45   B $500; .90.

The notation means that Prospect A offers you a .45 chance of winning $1,000 and B a .90 chance of winning $500. Kahneman and Tversky showed that with choices like this most people prefer B. Now consider the following choice:

C $1,000; .001   D $500; .002.

Most people here choose C although decision theory says that if your prefer B to A, you must prefer D to C based on the expected utility. Let the utility (subjective value) of the prizes be U(1000) and U(500). It follows from the first choice that since people prefer B:

$$U(500) \times .90 > U(1,000) \times .45$$
or
$$U(500) > U(1,000)/2.$$

If we now examine the choice between C and D, since the probabilities are still in the ratio 1 to 2, and $500 has more than half the utility of $1,000, then people must also prefer D to C. However, the experiments show the opposite – most people choose C. An intuitive way of putting this is that if winning is probable you go for the better chance of winning, but if it is a long shot then you go for the bigger prize. When people are selling lottery tickets, prospective customers often ask about the value of the prize, but how many ask how many other people are in the draw? This was one of many clever experiments in the paper showing deviations of actual choices from those predicted by expected utility.

What prospect theory really does is to modify the probability and utility functions of standard decision theory in such a way as to better fit people's actual choices. For example, the theory proposes that people overweight small probabilities. The conclusions can be summed very simply as follows:

Gains	Small probabilities	Risk seeking
	Medium to high probabilities	Risk aversion
Losses	Small probabilities	Risk aversion
	Medium to high probabilities	Risk seeking.

In other words, the shape of people's utility functions is such that they are in general risk aversive on prospects of gains and risk seeing on prospects of losses. However, these choice patterns reverse when probabilities are very small indicating that people *overweight* such low probabilities. This explains why people gamble on lotteries (risk seeking on gains) and buy insurance (risk avoiding on losses) as small probabilities are involved in both cases.

Prospect theory is descriptive of what people actually choose, which is very important for economics. In itself, it gives no insight into the cognitive processes involved in choice, although there are some interesting pointers. For example, the original paper identified *framing effects*, showing that the same prospects framed in different ways would lead to different decisions. One finding in the paper was a *certainty effect*, in which people prefer a certain gain to a risky prospect of a greater gain (with reasonably balanced pay-offs). For example, people prefer a sure win of $30 (A) to a .80 chance of winning $45 (B) even though the latter has an expected value of $36. They maintain this preference when this choice is described as a second stage of a process that is reached only with a 25 per cent probability (and a 75 per cent chance of nothing). This is illustrated as Prospect 1 in Figure 5.1. If instead the simple choice is offered between the prospects, C $30; .25 and D $45; .20 (Prospect 2, Figure 5.1) people prefer D to C. It is evident from examination of Figure 5.1 that the two prospects are mathematically equivalent. What seems to be happening here is that the two-stage prospect involves people in

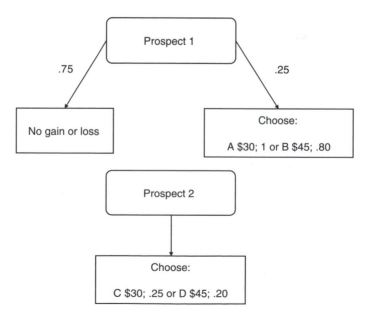

Figure 5.1   One- or two-stage prospects based on Kahneman and Tversky (1979).

a mental simulation in which the certainty effect is manifest under the supposition of successful transition to Stage 2. Analytic processing becomes focused for both prospects on the choice problems identified in the boxes shown in Figure 5.1, only one of which involves the certainty effect (second stage for Prospect 1).

A different kind of framing effect has been shown in research on *support theory* (Tversky & Koehler, 1994) in which participants are shown to attach lower probability (or less weight in decision making) to extensionally equivalent events that are described using implicit disjunctions than when the components are explicitly unpacked. For example, people are willing to pay higher health insurance premiums for hospital treatment for accident or illness than for hospital treatment for any reason! In the same way, the probability of dying in the next five years from any cause will seem to be lower than the probability of dying from heart disease, cancer or some other cause. The more disjuncts are explicitly unpacked, the higher the subjective probability becomes. It seems likely that unpacking is cueing enriched mental models of the prospects (for example, with additional branches) that affect judgements of probability. It also indicates that people do not spontaneously enrich their models by elaboration of alternative possibilities – perhaps a manifestation of the singularity principle.

In the absence of process-oriented research, one can only speculate about the cognitive foundations of research findings on risky choice. For example, the reliable finding that small probabilities are over-weighted in decision making could well be caused by people conducting mental simulations of the prospects they are asked to consider. The very act of entertaining a supposition – introducing a temporary addition to one's set of beliefs – may increase belief in the proposition supposed (Evans, Stevenson, Over, Handley, & Sloman, 2004; Hirt & Sherman, 1985). It seems to me that this effect is likely to be much stronger when the event simulated is of very low probability. It seems that when we add a supposition to our existing beliefs and simulate its consequences, we can't quite put Humpty Dumpty back together again when we finish. Thus our mental fantasy about winning the jackpot in the national lottery provides the event with a reality (and subjective weight) disproportionate to its minute objective probability. In the same way, the skilled insurance salesman increases the subjective weight of a potentially disastrous event, merely by persuading us to imagine its occurrence.

MULTI-ATTRIBUTED DECISION MAKING

Apart from risky choices, decisions involving multiple attributes are psychologically interesting. Suppose you are considering buying a new car and have got your choices down to a list of five. You compare these five on a number of independent attributes (also known as "cues"). For the sake of simplicity, let us assume that you consider only the five attributes listed in Table 5.1 – cost, performance, space, economy and reliability. How do you choose the car that is the best one for you? There is a normative model for this problem that is known as multi-attribute utility theory or MAUT for short (see Shafir & LeBeouf, 2005, for discussion of the origin of this theory). In order to apply the normative analysis you must first assign a weight w_i to each attribute or cue such that where i ranges over the n attributes and

$$\sum_{i=1}^{n} w_i = 1$$

Such weightings are subjective and should reflect the priorities of the individual decision maker. Table 5.1 shows cue weights for an individual who is most concerned about purchase price but least interested in fuel economy (perhaps she expects a rise in income); intermediate in order of importance are reliability, space and performance. Now the next step is to assign a utility for each choice on each attribute: here we allow numbers between 0 (awful) and 100 (perfect) and again assume that for a particular decision maker the utilities are as shown in Table 5.1. The final step is to compute the aggregate utility for each option by multiplying the cue weight by the utility for that cue and summing over the set of cues. For example, for Car A the calculation is

$$(.30 \times 40) + (.15 \times 65) + (.20 \times 40) + (.10 \times 15) + (.25 \times 55) = 45.$$

Note that aggregate utilities must also fall in the range 0–100. According to the computations, D is the best choice, with E close behind and B further back again. A and C are poor choices (you can fill in the makers' names for yourself). Note that according to the principle of *dominance*, we could have eliminated A without the need to do any calculations. A choice is said to be dominated if it is worse than another in some respects and not better in any other. By this definition A is dominated by B and must be inferior no matter what the cue weights. C, though also a poor choice, is not dominated as it scores better than some others on cost.

MAUT is a normative, not a descriptive theory. On grounds of bounded rationality, it seems unlikely that ordinary people would do this full consideration of possibilities, especially as real-world decisions often involve more cues and more options. In fact, numerous deviations from MAUT are observed in the literature, but of particular interest here is the tendency for people to think about one attribute at a time (Shafir & LeBeouf, 2005), just as originally demonstrated by Tversky (1972) in his elimination-by-aspects or EBA model. To understand the EBA strategy, look again at Table 5.1. For this purpose, we

Table 5.1
Utility values and cue weights for a multi-attributed choice problem

	Cost	Performance	Space	Economy	Reliability	Aggregate
Rank	1	4	3	5	2	
Weight	.30	.15	.20	.10	.25	
Car A	40	65	40	15	55	45
Car B	80	70	40	25	60	60
Car C	80	20	50	50	20	47
Car D	50	60	70	75	90	68
Car E	80	60	40	90	60	65

can ignore the cue weights and simply look at their rank order of preference. According to EBA, people look first at the most important cue and eliminate any options that are inferior. Then they move to the next cue and repeat this process and so on, until only one choice remains. Let us apply this strategy to the numbers shown in Table 5.1.

For our imaginary decision maker, the most important attribute is cost, so she looks at this first. Three choices, B, C and E are equally good, so she eliminates A and D. She then looks at reliability considering only the three remaining options and is able to eliminate C, which is clearly inferior, leaving B and E. The third most important cue is space, but the options are equally good, so she moves on to performance. E is inferior to B on this cue, and so is eliminated leaving B as the winner. So a person choosing by EBA would end with choice B even though it is the third-best option according to the MAUT analysis. How can this happen?

From a normative point of view, EBA can go wrong because an option can be eliminated too early before its merits are exposed. In our analysis, this happens with Car D (the best choice in the MAUT analysis), which is eliminated in the first round because of its greater cost, but which scores heavily on all other cues. Car E falls at the last hurdle as it is slightly inferior on performance to B and never gets a chance to show its marked superiority on economy. EBA is psychologically plausible, however, because it conforms with the singularity and satisficing principles of hypothetical thinking – people only have to consider one attribute at a time and maintain options that are good enough at each stage. EBA hence conforms with bounded rationality but also with the fundamental analytic bias.

The operation of the relevance principle can also be shown in multi-attributed choice, as neatly demonstrated in a study by Shafir (1993). In one scenario you have to imagine you are a judge awarding custody of children in a divorce court. Each parent has multiple attributes. Parent A is moderate on all things, but Parent B is highly variable. For example, B may have a better income than A but also has to spend more time away from home. The intriguing finding was that if participants are asked to decide to which parent they would *award* custody they tend to choose B; if asked (in a separate group) to which parent they would *deny* custody, they also tend to choose B! The framing of the choice clearly affects the perceived relevance of the cues. When making a decision to award custody, participants look for reasons to do this – that is, positive attributes that are to be found in B's list. When asked to deny custody, they look for negative attributes, which are also to be found in B's list. This looks to me like preconscious pragmatic processes operating through the heuristic system to bias the attention of the analytic system – an effect comparable to a number discussed in the psychology of reasoning in previous chapters.

On a dual-process view, decisions could be made quickly and intuitively, relying on the heuristic system, or more slowly and reflectively, by application of analytic thinking. However, there is no guarantee that analytic thinking will produce better decisions, especially when problems are complex, as its engagement will tend to focus attention on selected parts of the information available. There are several papers in the social psychological literature that are directly relevant to this (Dijksterhuis, 2004; Dijksterhuis & Smith, 2005; Dijksterhuis et al., 2006; Wilson, Lisle, Schooler, Hodges, Klaaren, & Lafleur, 1993; Wilson & Schooler, 1991). In these experiments, participants are presented with multi-attribute choice problems of varying complexity and are asked to make a decision either immediately, or after conscious reflection, or after a period of time in which conscious attention is distracted by another task. One finding that comes clearly through these studies is that when people make their choices with conscious reflection they are later less satisfied with their decisions than when they make them without reflection. This could simply be because the heuristic processes deliver intuitions of preference for choices that are pretty much the same processes as those responsible for the feelings of satisfaction with these choices.

More interesting is the claim that decisions made unconsciously may be *better* decisions as measured by correspondence with those of expert judgements (Wilson & Schooler, 1991) or by normative analysis (Dijksterhuis et al., 2006). The latter study suggested that this finding interacts with the complexity of the decision and that simple choices may be better made consciously. The authors of these papers agree that conscious decision making causes selective attention due to its limited processing capacity. Intuitive decision making could be superior, due to much greater processing capacity of the heuristic system, but only, of course, if people have had the opportunity to engage in the relevant experiential learning for the context, thus developing veridical implicit models. It is well known that mastery of complex judgemental tasks through experience results in largely implicit learning (Berry & Dienes, 1993) and that efforts to learn complex rules explicitly may be counter-productive (see Reber, 1993). The positive benefits of intuitive thinking are also emphasized in the dual-process account of decision making under risk proposed by Reyna (2004) in what she calls fuzzy-trace theory. On her view, novices rely on fallible explicit reasoning whereas experts develop gist representations and intuitive processes that permit computationally more powerful and accurate decisions. Reyna does, however, concede that intuitive thinking is also the cause of many biases observed in the judgement literature, presumably due to the novel nature of most laboratory tasks.

It seems reasonable to suppose that reliance on rapid heuristic processes or intuitive judgement may be beneficial where appropriate experiential learning has taken place (see also the discussion of Klein's, 1999, work on naturalistic decision making later in this chapter). Much more contentious is the claim of Dijksterhuis et al. (2006) that decision making benefits from unconscious thinking of a *deliberative* nature. The notion of deliberation without awareness has connotations of an entity-like unconscious mind within, acting as a homunculus. There seems to be nothing in the experimental studies that justifies this idea of unconscious deliberation. The unconscious choices are simply ones that are *not* conscious, either because people are given no time to think or because they are distracted by other tasks requiring conscious attention. (This kind of problem may be the reason that many social psychologists prefer the term nonconscious to unconscious processing.) There is no reason why they should not be seen as fast recognition processes in the heuristic system of the kind that I will discuss later in this chapter.

MULTICUE JUDGEMENT

Multicue judgement may sound very similar to multi-attributed decision making but actually relates to the tradition of work called *social judgement theory* (SJT). As mentioned in Chapter 1, this has a quite different origin from the mainstream study of decision making, which came to psychology from economics via Ward Edwards. This field originates in the work of Brunswick, who advocated an ecological approach in which judgement was regarded as analogous to perception and in which the task of psychology was seen as that of relating organisms to their environment (see Doherty, 1996; Goldstein, 2005). A critical concept is that of the *lens model*, which was adapted for the study of judgement by Hammond (1955, 1966), who laid the foundations of SJT. The lens model is so called because it maps the same set of environmental cues on to the world on one side of the lens and on to the judge on the other side (see Figure 5.2).

An example of multicue judgement would be that of a personnel manager selecting candidates on the grounds of multiple criteria such as: (a) education and qualifications; (b) work experience; (c) psychometric tests; (d) interview

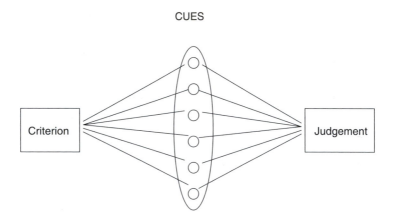

CUES

Achievement = knowledge × task predictability × cognitive control

Figure 5.2   The lens model together with a verbal form of the lens model equation.

performance; and so on. Of course many cues are available in the environment for this judge that she might or might not think (consciously) to be relevant to this judgement, such as gender, age, appearance, accent and so on. The total set of cues predict the criterion on the left side of the lens – performance in the job – and also the judgements made on the right-hand side of the lens. If a set of cues are defined with cue values measured for each case about which a judgement is made, it may be possible to compute two separate multiple regressions: one from the cues to the criterion values and one from the same cues to the judgements made.

Now think about what would measure performance in a judge. Imagine that judgements are made about a large number of cases (in this example candidates for employment) and that in each case the judgement can be compared with some objective criterion of the thing being judged (quality of performance in the job). Then the correlation between the two – known as r_a in the notation of SJT – is the measured *performance* of the judge. If the correlation is high, then she is accurately selecting good candidates. The clever aspect of lens model analysis is that this performance correlation can be broken down into components using the following simplified form of the lens model equation:

$$r_a = G \cdot R_e \cdot R_s$$ 5.1

where R_e is the multiple correlation of the cues with the criterion and R_s is the multiple correlation of the cues with the judgement made (see Cooksey, 1996, for a full exposition of the mathematics of the lens model). G measures the degree of correspondence between the environmental model and the judge's model. If the two multiple regressions are carried out, then G reflects the extent to which the regression coefficients correspond in the two analyses. A verbal statement of the lens model equation (see Figure 5.2) equates G with task knowledge (also known as matching), R_e with task predictability and R_s with cognitive control (consistency of judgements). To understand this better consider that the model differentiates three possible causes of poor performance:

1. The criterion may have poor predictability from the available cues (low R_e).
2. The judge may make unreliable or noisy judgements (low R_s).
3. The judge's model of the task may map poorly on to the environment's model.

The most interesting case is (3) as it may happen that although a task is predictable and the judge is consistent, performance is poor. This is because the judge's model is inaccurate. Suppose the two regressions show strong linear fit but reveal beta weights that diverge sharply. Perhaps the criterion is predicted mostly by qualification and work experience but the judge relies mostly on interview performance, gender and appearance. In this case, however consistent she is, her performance is bound to be poor. We could also describe the performance as *biased*, in that it is based upon personal prejudice rather than an objective understanding of the requirements of the job.

In real-world applications, a performance criterion is not always available, but one can still gain understanding of judges' *tacit* policies by regressing available cues on to their judgements. When only one side of the model is used in this way, the technique is referred to as *judgement analysis* or JA (Stewart, 1988). Many experiments have been reported in the literature studying judgement by both judgement analysis and the full-blown lens model method, particularly in the context of medical decision making (see Wigton, 1996). Typical findings include the following: (a) experts have tacit policies, captured by the regression weights, which are highly variable across individuals, implying large-scale disagreement between experts even in highly qualified groups such as medical consultants; (b) people can utilize quite a small number of cues in their judgements (experts use no more information than novices, although they use it better: e.g., Shanteau, 1992); and (c) judges have poor self-insight, as measured by the correspondence between their tacit policies and the explicit policies that they state.

A study of patient management decisions in general practitioners con-ducted by myself and my colleagues in the early 1990s (Evans, Harries, & Dean, 1995b; Harries, Evans, Dennis, & Dean, 1996) replicated all three of these typical findings. However, using a slightly unorthodox method, we also discovered that while doctors can typically use 2–4 cues they state in interview that they utilize a great many more, around 6–8 (we presented an unusually large number of cues, in the order of 12–13 per case). We also found that doctors could correctly state that they were not using certain cues, but of the ones explicitly identified they had no idea which were and which were not affecting their judgements.

Our tasks were all computer-presented, and in a later experiment we presented only a list of the cue names on the screens shown to the doctors, who had to click the mouse on any cue whose value they required. They were able to self-terminate at any time and give a judgement. What happened was that doctors again chose to inspect more cues than actually influenced their judgements. Moreover, the cues inspected but not used were similar to those that featured only in the explicit policy reports in the earlier study. A reasonable interpretation of these findings is that the doctors attend to the cues that they know from their explicit training to be relevant, but are unaware of the fact that only a subset is actually used. There seems to be clear dissociation between implicit and explicit knowledge on this task.

A problem in studying expert judgement is that the judges have already done their learning. In order to understand the cognitive processes better, we later studied the acquisition of multicue judgement by experiential learning (Evans, Clibbens, Cattani, Harris, & Dennis, 2003a; Evans, Clibbens, & Harris, 2005a). We used a method known as multicue probability learning or MCPL. With this technique, cases are presented one at a time on a computer screen with people asked to predict a given criterion. They are then given outcome feedback that they can compare with their prediction. Cues are, however, *probabilistically* related to the criterion by adding random noise. The idea is to simulate real-world experiential learning as might be experienced by expert judges, whose feedback will inevitably be noisy due to various uncontrolled variables in a real-world scenario. In our case, participants played the role of personnel managers trying to discover which psychometric test results predicted performance in different occupations. We used 80–100 training trials with outcome feedback, followed by 40 transfer trials with no feedback. Multiple regression analyses on the feedback trials were used to discover which cues had been learnt.

In this study, some cues were relevant and some irrelevant, but participants had no information on how many cues were predictive. In a simpler version, the cues were ability tests that were either positively or zero-related to performance. In more complex tasks, the predictors were psychometric tests that could have a positive or negative relation to the criterion (or again be irrelevant). For example, extroversion might improve performance in some jobs but hinder it in others. The latter task is really quite complex as neither the relevance of the cue nor the direction of its effect is known in advance.

Table 5.2

Example set of scores for a particular participant on a given task in the study of Evans et al. (2003a)

	Criterion values	Judgement weights	Explicit cue ratings
Test A	+1	.67	+3
Test B	0	.48	+1
Test C	0	.32	−1
Test D	−1	−.25	−2
Test E	0	−.18	−1
Test F	+1	.49	+2

For each cue we ended up with regression weights, reflecting the tacit policy, and explicit ratings of cue usage taken after the task was finished. An illustrative data set is shown in Table 5.2. A participant who had learnt to predict the criterion would tend to have high positive, high negative or low judgement weights corresponding to positive, negative and zero predictors. Correlating the criterion values with the judgement weights thus gives us a measure of *performance* (see Figure 5.3). Figure 5.3 also shows how two other relationships can be extracted. A correlation between explicit ratings and criterion values, for example, is a measure of *explicit knowledge* acquired. If people have learnt the task explicitly, then they should be able to rate the cues accurately. Finally, the correlation between judgement weights and explicit ratings can be taken as a measure of *self-insight*. That is, it indicates the extent to which people are explicitly aware of what they have learnt.

Note that these three abstracted measures are all independent of one another. What Evans and colleagues (Evans et al., 2003a) found was

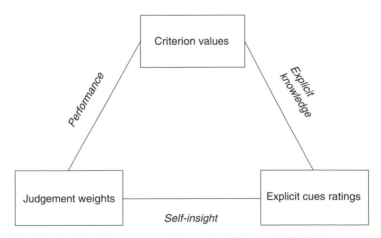

Figure 5.3   Relationship of key measures in the study of Evans et al. (2003a).

that on simpler tasks (fewer cues, only positive predictors) not only was performance well above chance but so was explicit knowledge. On more complex tasks (more cues, negative predictors), however, explicit knowledge of the criterion was not obtained, although performance remained above chance. The strong implication is that simple tasks benefit from explicit learning but more complex ones result only in implicit learning, a conclusion generally consistent with findings in the implicit-learning literature (Berry & Dienes, 1993).

The most novel and important finding in this study was that "self-insight" scores were well above chance on all tasks, even when there was *no* evidence of explicit learning. The interpretation we made of these findings was that there are indeed dual processes controlling such complex judgements and that both implicit and explicit processes contribute to the judgements made. On simpler tasks, performance was higher than on complex tasks, and explicit knowledge was acquired. Hence, we assumed that both implicit and explicit processes contribute to judgements, both in a helpful manner since both implicit and explicit knowledge have been acquired in the training. On complex tasks, although both processes continue to contribute (hence the retained "self-insight" correlation between explicit ratings and judgements made) performance drops because the explicit component is no longer based on any useful learning. In other words, there is always an analytic component to judgements but where the task is too complex to allow explicit learning, only the heuristic-level processes contribute usefully. Explicit reasoning here is mere unfounded opinion. However, with real expert judgement, it may also be that there is both an experiential and explicit component, but the latter is based on book learning and therefore likely to be helpful.

Before moving on, I give a word of caution concerning the dual-process interpretation. As stated in Chapter 1, "System 1" is a rather vague concept, as there may be a number of different forms of implicit cognition residing in distinct subsystems (see also Stanovich, 2004). Heuristic–analytic theory has mostly been focused on linguistic and pragmatic processes that retrieve relevant knowledge from our stores of belief and shape the direction of analytic processing, as discussed in Chapters 3 and 4. It is far from clear that the unconscious element of implicit learning and intuitive judgement involves the same implicit subsystem as the heuristic processes that influence reasoning tasks. Beliefs are forms of *explicit* knowledge (of which we may become aware) but the processes that retrieve and apply them are implicit in nature – and hence described as "heuristic". It seems likely that experiential learning involves a different subsystem in which the knowledge acquired is implicit rather than explicit in nature (weightings in neural networks rather than propositions) and may affect behaviour without ever becoming conscious.

HYPOTHETICAL THINKING IN DECISION MAKING

Despite the cautious comments that ended the previous section, there are various forms of evidence in the decision-making literature that support the three principles of hypothetical thinking theory. As briefly described in Chapter 1, these principles suggest that actual decision making should diverge markedly from the rational model of choice favoured by decision theory. Rather than compare alternative options and try to optimize by choosing the best one, I suggest that people will frequently follow the one-at-a-time model shown in Figure 5.4. That is to say, people will consider the first option that comes to mind (unconsciously cued by context and the current goal in line with relevance principle) and evaluate this option on its own (singularity principle) if necessary by conducting a mental simulation to compute its consequence. This evaluation involves some explicit analytic process even if the cognitively costly use of a mental simulation is not considered necessary. If the option is satisfactory it is "chosen" and acted out; otherwise, it is eliminated, and the next most relevant option is generated for consideration and so on.

One finding that fits this model quite well is the so-called focusing effect in decision making demonstrated by Legrenzi et al. (1993). When people are

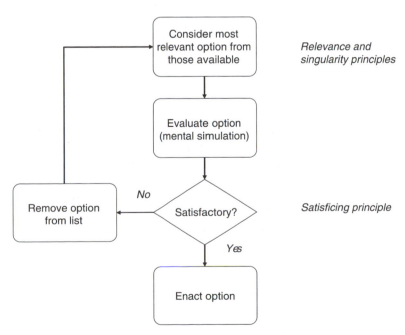

Figure 5.4 One-option-at-a-time decision making, consistent with three principles of hypothetical thinking.

offered an imaginary decision about one explicitly named alternative, they tend to seek information only about that option and not alternatives to it. For example, if people are asked to imagine they are on holiday in a foreign city with a chance to go the opera, they will ask about the cost of tickets, the composer and the artists but not about the other activities that they might do instead. This phenomenon seems related to the disregard of implicit disjunctions demonstrated in research on support theory (Tversky & Koehler, 1994) mentioned earlier. However, a recent study by Cherubini, Mazzocco, and Rumiati (2003) suggests that focusing involves the relevance principle and is not simply to do with explication of alternatives. For example, people ask few questions about the status quo (staying at home) when this is explicitly stated as an alternative and will gather information about implicit alternatives that negate the status quo (not staying at home).

Evidence for the singularity principle in decision making is also supported by research on the *disjunction effect* (LeBeouf & Shafir, 2005; Tversky & Shafir, 1992). In one example people are asked to decide whether they would buy a vacation package (a) knowing that they had just passed an important examination, (b) knowing that they had not passed the examination or (c) not yet knowing whether they had passed or failed. In Group (a) most people decide to take the vacation, as do Group (b). According to Savage's sure-thing principle, it follows that they must prefer to take the vacation in condition (c) as well. If you prefer X to Y when Z is true and your prefer X to Y when Z is false, then you must prefer X to Y when you don't know whether Z is true or not. Surprisingly, participants in Group (c) were unhappy to make the decision and many were willing to pay a premium to defer the decision until after the examination result was known.

Tversky and Shafir suggest that people have a different *reason* for their choice in groups (a) and (b) – to celebrate passing the examination, or to console themselves after failure. In (c) they don't have a reason until the result is known. It seems plausible to suggest that we don't like making decisions that require consideration of alternative mental simulations. That is not to say that people given sufficient time and motivation cannot consider alternatives in decision making, because they clearly can and do. What the singularity principle actually states is that we can consider only one hypothetical alternative *at a time*. In other words, to consider alternatives we have to simulate them separately and store the results in memory for comparison. Such comparisons do not, however, engender the same sense of confidence in decision making that a single mental simulation of the world will allow. We are much more comfortable when we can simulate a single model of the future world resulting from some action and then deciding whether or not to proceed.

The relevance principle of hypothetical thinking theory relates to heuristic processes that rapidly focus attention on some feature of a given problem or enhance our mental representations with prior belief retrieved from memory. In the processing model (extended heuristic–analytic theory) such heuristics can prompt default responses that will cue behaviour if analytic reasoning does not intervene. An important example of this in decision making and problem solving involves *recognition processes*. While some tasks and decisions seem novel, others appear familiar: we recognize them in some way as prototypical of situations encountered before. For example, when a research student comes to me with a research design problem that is novel and baffling her, I usually recognize it as typical of a category of problems I have encountered many times before. As a result, I can give her a solution with little effort of thought. Only occasionally is such a problem novel enough for me to have to give it some hard thought from "first principles".

In their research programme on fast and frugal heuristics, Gigerenzer and colleagues have stressed the importance of the *recognition heuristic* in some kinds of decision making (Gigerenzer, 2004; Goldstein & Gigerenzer, 2002). Their research has shown, for example, that non-natives of a country may do as well as or better than its inhabitants in judging such matters as the relative size of cities or the success of their sporting teams, based on nothing more than the fact that one recognizes one city name rather than another, or that one seems more familiar. The operation of the heuristic is defined as follows: "If one of two objects is recognized and the other is not, then that recognized object has the higher value with respect to the criterion." Although these authors do not employ a dual-process framework, it seems necessary to invoke one in order to fully understand the way in which this heuristic works.

First, it is clear that the recognition heuristic cannot apply to any criterion: you would not use it, for example, as a basis for judging people's height. Goldstein and Gigerenzer state that the heuristic is domain-specific and only used in domains where it is ecologically valid – that is, highly correlated with the criterion being judged. This may be programmed either by evolution or by individual learning experiences. However, this leaves a puzzle: how does the individual know when to use or not use the heuristic, and does this happen at the System 1 or System 2 level? It is in the nature of fast and frugal heuristics that they are both rapid and low in cognitive demands. Coupled with their proposed origin in experiential learning and/or innate modules this points clearly towards a System 1 process. Goldstein and Gigerenzer (2002) seem to reinforce this by the claim that people use this single heuristic without recourse to additional knowledge. However, this argument would seem to predict that reliance on the heuristic would lead us into serious error when applied to exceptional cases. A good example would be cities that we know well (recognize) but also know to be small – for example, those in a locality with which we are familiar. Should not a fast and frugal heuristic lead us to judge these cities to be large? In fact, when people have relevant knowledge of city size they use this knowledge, rather than the recognition heuristic, which will probably come as no surprise (Oppenheimer, 2003).

In line with their default-interventionist dual-process theory, Kahneman and Frederick (2002) suggest that the recognition heuristic must have both an implicit and an explicit component. As in the heuristic–analytic theory, heuristic processes propose default responses that require at least minimal approval by analytic processes before behaviour can occur. In the case of the recognition heuristic, it seems evident that a feeling of recognition cannot directly become a judgement, say, that a city is large without some analytic process of approving this as the basis for responding to the experimental instructions. In addition to inducing feelings of familiarity, presentation of a city name will also (by equally rapid and effortless processes) evoke explicit knowledge of the city, retrieved from semantic memory. When this knowledge conflicts with the recognition heuristic (the city is familiar but small) the heuristic will be inhibited and overridden by analytic processes. This will be a lot easier and more effective, say, than the inhibition of belief biases in reasoning, discussed in Chapter 4. The reason is that no effort of difficult reasoning is required for the analytic system to be aware of the conflict.

Evidence for the importance of recognition processes is also provided by studies of naturalistic decision making. Gary Klein has conducted a large number of studies in which expert decision makers are studied in their natural working environment (see Klein, 1999, for informal review and discussion of many of these). Such decision makers include fire service commanders who in the US system are involved in paramedical decision making as well as in operations to rescue people and property from damage and disaster. Such officers have to make rapid choices in dangerous and critical situations. As Klein points out, such studies differ in many ways from laboratory studies of decision making: decision makers tend to be experts with much relevant prior experience who are making decisions under time pressure, often on the basis of inadequate information. Sometimes goals are unclear, and developing and prioritizing goals may be one of the important requirements in a given situation. Most of the time, these commanders have no feeling of making decisions in the traditional sense at all: that is, there is no conscious deliberation between alternatives. Like me with my students, they mostly recognize a situation and apply a prototypical solution to it: a process that Klein calls *recognition-primed decision making*. Clearly, what makes an expert an expert is to a large extent the development of such knowledge of prototypes and the ability to retrieve those that are relevant and apply them appropriately. There is a clear link here with the claims of Reyna (2004) that experts rely on gist memory and intuitions to a much larger extent than do novices in making their decisions. Note that although recognition-primed and rapid, what is retrieved from long-term memory is a great deal more complex and sophisticated than a feeling of familiarity. It may involve a whole set of learnt procedures with schemas that have to be applied to the specifics of the given situation. It is fast but by no means frugal.

Klein's experts often follow the one-option-at-a-time model shown in Figure 5.4. In discussing one example of a fire commander's thinking he comments, "He thought of several options yet never compared any two of them. He thought of options one a time, evaluated each in turn, rejected it, and turned to the next most typical rescue technique" (Klein, 1999, pp. 19–20). As Klein also shows, such evaluations can be straightforward or can be more complicated involving mental simulations. Such simulations can be purely physical, as when a fire chief works out a novel use of equipment to deal with an unusual hazard and tries to determine whether it will work before putting it into effect. Real-world decision making often involves what is known as higher order intentionality, however, as one person tries to simulate the *mind* of another. Klein discusses some high-profile cases such as the shooting down in 1988 by a US warship of an Iranian commercial airliner whose behaviour was interpreted wrongly as that of an enemy fighter about to attack the ship. Readers may relate to dangerous traffic situations they may have encountered when driving, say of a car overtaking towards you with too little road. Simulating the minds of other drivers around you, in order to predict their behaviour, may be the only way to avoid disaster. Mental simulation is, of course, a fundamental tool of hypothetical thinking that has been discussed in several contexts in this book.

Klein contrasts recognition-primed decision making or RPD with what he calls the "rational choice" model in which alternative actions are considered and compared. RPD is more likely to occur when decision makers are experienced, time pressure is high and the situation is changing and ill-defined. The impression given is that rational choice is largely for bureaucrats who sit in offices with plenty of time to think and with reports to write that will justify their decisions to others. Of course, documentation is one of the ways in which we can try to overcome the natural limits of our hypothetical thinking abilities and to extend our bounded rationality. The rational decision model is embodied in many of the systems that we set up for organizational, economic and political decision making. The extent to which such reports reflect the actual process by which a decision is made, as opposed to an after-the-fact rationalization of it, is another matter entirely.

CONCLUSIONS

Psychological research on decision making has largely been framed by one of two major traditions of distinct origins: economic decision theory and social judgement theory. Neither of these is a traditionally cognitive approach, as the former is concerned largely with demonstrating violations of normative decision theory and the latter with ecological mapping of judgements with the environment. Research findings can, however, be viewed within the framework of dual-process theory and decision researchers are clearly becoming interested in this approach. The research discussed in this chapter provides much evidence consistent with dual-process theory and in particular with heuristically cued relevance and recognition processes together with singularity and satisficing effects in the consideration of options. People rarely engage, it seems, in "rational" decision making in which they deliberate between alternatives, and they frequently rely on choices that are either retrieved from memory or tested one at a time by mental simulations (see Figure 5.4). People are also reluctant to make decisions that require two alternative mental simulations of the future state of the world, even when they point to the same choice of action. Research on decision making also shows that rapid heuristic processes may often form the basis for expert judgement, while novices dealing with unfamiliar problems are more likely to rely on explicit analytic reasoning. This contrasts with claims in reasoning literature that good performance requires analytic reasoning (see Chapters 3 and 4), probably because the latter literature relies on the presentation of novel problems to naïve participants.

What has been omitted from this chapter is consideration of the large body of work within JDM on judgement under uncertainty and the heuristics that people use to make probabilistic inferences. This work, together with more general studies of how people think about chance and probability, is the focus of the following chapter.

CHAPTER SIX

Thinking about chance and probability

We live in an uncertain world, and hence – in the view of many scientists – we were *designed* (by natural selection) to make judgements and decisions under uncertainty. Since all our ancestors had to deal with uncertainty and variability in their environments, it seems inevitable that the mechanisms underlying our cognitive processes have developed means of dealing with this. Of course, animals live an uncertain world also, and it is greatly to their advantage to be responsive to both the absolute and the relative frequencies of events that they experience. For example, if a bear likes to eat berries from a certain kind of bush, it is in its interest to be able to learn that these bushes grow more often in one kind of landscape than another or that they are often found in proximity to another (perhaps inedible) plant. A bear that learns to use such cues in order to find food is acting *as if* it were calculating and responding to conditional probabilities.

Animals do in fact respond to probabilistic cues in their natural environments and can be trained to do so in the laboratory as endless studies of operant conditioning have demonstrated. Hence, there is a strong a priori argument that we have some kind of built-in mechanism (or cognitive module) that enables us to process frequency information in our environment. This leads us into the paradox of rationality (Evans & Over, 1996a), however, since numerous experiments, especially those in the "heuristics and biases" tradition (Gilovich et al., 2002; Kahneman et al., 1982), have demonstrated many errors and biases associated with probability judgement, as we shall see later. Those advocating an innate frequency-processing module (Cosmides &

Tooby, 1996; Gigerenzer & Hoffrage, 1995) have argued that reasoning about probability (as opposed to frequency) has no such innate basis and hence that frequency formats will generally make problems a lot easier to solve. I will examine this argument closely later in this chapter, and we will see that it has run into considerable difficulties when tested experimentally. In my view this is entirely due to the failure of its advocates to recognize the dual-processing nature of human cognition and to understand its implications.

In the dual-process approach it is assumed that we – and other animals – can learn to process frequency information in the environment at the System 1 (heuristic) level without having any explicit concept of probability. To reason explicitly about probabilities on the other hand requires understanding at the System 2 (analytic level), which is another matter entirely. All the evidence suggests that such explicit statistical reasoning is something that people do poorly – maybe even worse than logical reasoning (see Chapters 3 and 4). The concept of probability was not invented by mathematicians until the seventeenth century. However, it is clear that at least some us *can* reason about probabilities, or else there would be no probability calculus and no methodology of inferential statistics for us to apply. To make sense of the literature on judgement under uncertainty, however, we must be very clear that the "as if" processing of probabilities at the heuristic level is an entirely different matter from explicit probabilistic reasoning at the analytic level.

The distinction between the two forms of probabilistic processing was clearly illustrated in some studies carried out by Nisbett and colleagues in the 1980s. In one study (Nisbett, Krantz, Jepson, & Kunda, 1983) the ability of people untrained in statistics to give statistical explanations of real-world phenomena was examined. Most people have rather poor understanding, for example, of the law of large numbers (LLN), which dictates that only large samples provide reliable information about the populations from which they are drawn. For example, if asked why the highest baseball batting averages recorded in early season always drop, many people will give nonstatistical explanations (e.g., the guys get overconfident and lose concentration) rather than recognizing the problem of small samples. However, people with much real-world experience of the domain (such as sports coaches) will be much more likely to recognize the LLN. The key point here, though, is that when such domain experts are tested in another domain – in which they lack experience – they perform no better than anyone else. What this strongly suggests is that their correct statistical understanding reflects an experiential and implicit learning process that is typically domain-specific (Berry & Dienes, 1993).

This study contrasts strongly with the findings of another (Fong, Krantz, & Nisbett, 1986) that showed that formal training in statistical principles – based on statistics courses, or even a 25-minute laboratory session – improved statistics reasoning in a whole range of everyday settings – a domain-*general* effect. Such training apparently enables people to apply analytic reasoning at the System 2 level as they have access to explicit rules. Converging evidence for this dual-process account comes from more recent studies by Klaczynski and colleagues (Klaczynski, 2000; Klaczynski & Robinson, 2000). They employed a task in which a brief scenario was given with an argument based on generalization from small samples, thus violating the LLN. The arguments gave a conclusion that was either compatible or incompatible with the participants' own beliefs. Participants were then asked (a) to rate the strength of the argument and (b) to give a verbal justification of their ratings. The latter were assessed qualitatively for the degree to which they recognized statistical concepts (sample size, random variation and so on).

As mentioned several times in this book, one of the forms of evidence for dual-process theory is that heuristic processes appear to be independent of cognitive ability and working-memory capacity whereas problems requiring analytic reasoning are much better solved by those of higher ability (Stanovich, 1999; Stanovich & West, 2000). The primary measure of bias in the Klaczynski studies was the rating of argument strength on problems where the conclusions were consistent or inconsistent with prior belief – an effect similar to belief bias in deductive reasoning (see Chapter 4) or what is called "myside bias" in studies of argumentation and informal reasoning (Baron, 1995; Stanovich & West, in press). Klaczynski's studies revealed a strong belief bias on these LLN problems, which was unrelated to developmental variables and cognitive ability. However, the quality of reasoning found in the justifications *was* related to cognitive ability, with young adults being superior to both adolescents and older adults. These findings strongly suggest that the ability to reason analytically about probabilistic issues is related to cognitive ability but does not mean that more able reasoners are any less prejudiced by their beliefs – presumably because their judgements are pre-empted by heuristic processes. This work also supports the view that one function of analytic processes is to rationalize the outcome of unconsciously caused behaviour (see Chapter 7).

Bearing in mind this dual-process distinction, I will now examine some of the phenomena associated with thinking about probabilities and making judgements under uncertainty.

SUBJECTIVE PERCEPTION OF PROBABILITY AND RANDOMNESS

There are two major academic schools of thought on probability. The classical or objectivist position is that probability is a relative frequency and can only be considered when there is a frequency distribution of some kind. This is the theory that psychologists teach to their students even though it involves such convolutions as sampling distributions (imagine you ran the experiment many times when the null hypothesis was true) to make it work. The Bayesian or subjectivist view is that a probability is no more nor less than a degree of belief in something. While both schools define a probability as ranging between 0 and 1, and both endorse the probability calculus, the philosophical difference is considerable. In an uncertain world, we cannot simply believe that things are true and false in the manner of propositional logic but we must believe things to an extent. One drawback of the frequentist position is that it does not allow us to quantify our uncertainty about one-off events, which are the kind often involved in real-world decision making.

The Bayesian approach is also associated with Bayes' theorem or Bayesian revision, which I will discuss later in the chapter. In essence, it means that your degree of belief in some proposition or hypothesis is revised in a gradual manner as you encounter evidence for or against it. Translated into a philosophy of science this provides a stark contrast with Popperian philosophy (Popper, 1959, 1962) in which current theories are no more than conjectures to be given up whole when falsifying evidence is encountered. The Bayesian approach to science (Evans, 2005; see Howson & Urbach, 1993) was discussed briefly in Chapter 2. It is difficult to see how one can understand hypothetical thinking without a subjective notion of probability – a key feature, for example, of the epistemic mental models that feature in hypothetical thinking theory.

To what extent do ordinary people have a subjective understanding of chance and probability? Western languages at least have many words designed to express concepts of likelihood and uncertainty: terms such as "often", "frequently", "rarely", "occasionally", "likely", "improbable" and so on. Such terms are in the ordinary language and are not derived from formal study of probability theory and indicate that at least a rudimentary concept of probability is endemic in our culture. Although the word "random" is rather technical and perhaps infrequently used by ordinary people, the terms "chance" and "luck" are common. Thus although we may be predisposed to think about the world in causal terms (Sloman, 2005) we certainly have the concept that some of the events around us occur by chance. For example, if one side dominates a soccer match without scoring and the other scores from their only chance in the game, most people would describe this as a lucky win, implying in some way that the "odds" favoured the team who actually lost.

Luck of course is a dubious concept from the viewpoint of probability theory. It is reasonable to say that someone *was* lucky or unlucky after the event, when chance was affecting their outcomes (as in the case of our soccer team). However, the concept is often applied as though luck was a state that one could achieve, as in the case of the gambler who believes from early successes that he is lucky tonight, as if this gave him the basis for further successful gambling. A great psychological puzzle is why people persist in gambling, particularly on casino games, when the odds are always against them. Gamblers have many false beliefs about the nature of chance games (Wagenaar, 1988) and employ systems that assume (fallaciously) that the outcome of a previous event affects the probability of a later one even in games like roulette that are based on statistically independent sequences. This suggests that the "folk" theory of probability is pretty weak. The simple heuristics that people apply in this domain definitely do not make them smart.

Randomness is a really difficult concept for most people. Most commonly the term is used to refer to Bernoulli sequences such as successive tosses of a coin, or successive numbers spun on a roulette wheel where each event is predictable only as a random variable with some distribution and where successive events are completely independent of prior outcomes. It has been known for many years (Wagenaar, 1972) that people have a poor subjective understanding of randomness (for a more recent review, see Falk & Konold, 1997). Essentially, people believe that random (Bernoulli) sequences alternate their outcomes more often than actually happens in a chance sequence. They will both generate sequences that alternate too often and similarly misperceive presented sequences.

It is important to understand that a sequence of, say, coin tosses can violate independence while maintaining an overall probability of .5 for heads or tails. To generate such sequences all you have to do is to specify a probability of alternation that is:

$$P(\text{heads}|\text{current spin is tails}) = P(\text{tails}|\text{current spin is heads}) = r.$$

If r is set to .5 then the sequence is Bernoulli. If $r < .5$ then it will produce sequences in which the runs of heads and tails are longer than they should be. If $r > .5$ then sequences will be shorter than they should be (relative alternation or outcomes). Examine the two sequences printed in Table 6.1. Which of these simulates the random tossing of a coin? The answer is A, but most people think that this does not look random, as the runs of heads and tails are longer than expected. Sequence B was generated with an alternation probability (r) of .6, which corresponds more closely to what most people perceive as a random sequence. Most people given these sequences would choose B as the random sequence.

This striking feature of subjective randomness leads to two biases, known as positive and negative recency. Negative recency bias – also known as the gambler's fallacy – means that when people are viewing a sequence of events believed to be random, they tend to predict the next event as being the opposite of the previous one. The myth embodied in our language as "the law of averages" is that if a sequence of one outcome is observed with a random process then it is likely to switch to another in order to compensate and even things out. This bias underlies the useless betting strategies that people employ to try to beat the roulette wheel. In fact, casinos are happy to provide

Table 6.1

Computer simulation of a sequence of coin tosses: which one is the random sequence?

Sequence A

T	T	T	H	T	H	T	T	T	T
H	H	T	T	T	T	T	T	T	T
H	T	H	T	H	H	H	H	H	H
T	T	T	H	T	H	H	T	H	H
H	H	T	H	T	H	T	T	T	H
T	H	T	T	T	T	H	H		

Sequence B

H	T	H	H	T	T	T	H	H	T
H	T	H	T	T	H	T	T	H	T
T	T	H	H	T	H	H	H	T	H
T	H	T	H	H	H	H	H	T	H
T	H	H	H	T	H	T	H	H	H
T	H	H	T	H	T	H	H		

customers with printed sequences of the outcomes on their wheels, so that they can apply their systems and lose all the quicker! Presumably people bet more money with the false confidence that their systems inspire.

Positive recency bias occurs when a person who is actually viewing a random sequence of events believes that it is patterned (like Sequence A in Table 6.1) and that a given outcome is on a "streak". Then they are likely to predict that the current streak will continue. The best documented example of positive recency bias is the "hot hand effect" in basketball, originally published in a famous and much cited paper by Gilovich, Vallone, and Tversky (1985). Gilovich et al. showed that basket ball fans perceive shooters as having hot streaks where they can shoot successive baskets, whereas statistical analysis shows that the sequences are consistent with statistical independence. Of course, better players do have longer streaks, but only because their probability of completing a basket on any one attempt is higher. If this effect is interesting, so too have been some of the reactions to it in the academic literature reviewed recently by Alter and Oppenheimer (2006). Despite frequent replications (mostly in sporting contexts) many authors have tried to dispute the findings, convinced that there really are streaks in sports. (The whole concept of sporting "form", so beloved by the media, may be called into question.) Of course, the effect is really part of a domain-general misperception of randomness.

The biases of subjective randomness are very interesting and almost certainly underlie the apparently irrational tendency for many people to gamble on chance events like roulette, even though they incur a totally predictable financial loss by doing so (Evans & Coventry, 2006). Subjective randomness would seem to be a System 1-level effect, although the false beliefs about chance and probability that people use to justify their gambling behaviour (Wagenaar, 1988) require analytic reasoning in System 2. While it is commonly assumed that these false beliefs are the cause of gambling, from a dual-process point of view it is more likely that they are confabulated in order to rationalize unconsciously caused behaviour. Such rationalizations may then help to maintain the behaviour in future. Why, however, do we have such biases? If there is an innate frequency-processing module, for example, it certainly is not adaptive in this context. However, as Stanovich (2004) has argued, biases can arise where a mechanism that evolved in one environment gets applied in a different and modern context. Noisy but natural environments are most unlikely to produce random sequences of events with statistically independent outcomes of the kind generated in the casinos.

THE HEURISTICS AND BIASES
RESEARCH PROGRAMME

One of the most influential research programmes in the study of human reasoning and decision making has been that known as "heuristics and biases". This work was initiated by a series of brilliant papers published by Amos Tversky and Daniel Kahneman in the early 1970s (for two important collections of papers on this topic, see Gilovich et al., 2002; Kahneman et al., 1982). The term "heuristic" represents here a hypothetical construct used to explain "biases", which were observable systematic errors in people's judgements about probability. It was not clear in the early work whether these heuristics were intended to be specified at the unconscious or conscious level, or perhaps a mixture of both. Curiously enough, both (a) this programme, in which the role of heuristics in causing biases is emphasized, and (b) the "rival" programme of Gigerenzer and colleagues (Gigerenzer & Todd, 1999), in which the adaptive nature of heuristics is stressed, have their origins in Herb Simon's work on heuristic reasoning and bounded rationality.

The term "heuristic" used as a noun does not necessarily map on to the notion of heuristic processes as applied in the heuristic–analytic theory of reasoning. The basic idea is that a heuristic is a short-cut technique for solving problems that would otherwise be intractable given our cognitive processing capacity. In their famous early studies of problem solving, Newell and Simon (1972) demonstrated that people can solve problems that have very large search spaces. What this means is that if you could generate all possible solutions and then search through them one at a time to check whether each was a valid solution, this would be an impossibly slow strategy, even for a high-speed computer. What heuristics do is to cut down the search to a manageable number of possibilities, making it possible – but not certain – that a solution can be found. For example, experienced crossword puzzlers may solve anagrams with as many as 15 letters although they clearly could not possibly generate and examine 26^{15} possible solutions! Heuristics must be employed, based on the meaning of the solution provided in the cue and the presence of possible familiar letter groups within the anagram and so on, to reduce the search.

Kahneman and Tversky applied the concept of a heuristic to judgement rather than problem solving. A good example is the *availability* heuristic (Schwarz & Vaughn, 2002; Tversky & Kahneman, 1973), which comes into play when people try to estimate the likelihood of some event. Essentially, it was proposed, people will rely on their memories and assume that the more instances that come to mind, the more frequent must be the event. Suppose, as an experienced experimental psychologist, a student asks you how often your predicted effects were observed in the many experiments you have run (published and unpublished) in your career. How could you go about answering a question like this? What most people appear to do is to try to generate examples of event category by retrieving them from memory. For example, if I were asked about my experimental predictions, I might retrieve significantly more examples of successful than unsuccessful ones and on this basis answer around 75 per cent. It is not difficult to see, however, that this reliance on the availability heuristic might produce systematic biases. For example, I might well recall disproportionately more successful cases as these led to published papers and forget older unpublished studies altogether. If I had had a particularly good or bad run of experimental results in the past year, this could influence my recall and my judgement. If I was feeling depressed when asked the question, I might generate more failed examples. And so on and so on.

Whether heuristics make you smart or biased is really a question of emphasis. Heuristics do both because they can enable you to solve otherwise intractable problems but they can also lead you into errors and systematic biases. The heuristics and biases programme consists of studies largely designed to show when heuristics will lead to biases but this does not necessarily mean that these are "bad" heuristics. For example, you can imagine that an experienced doctor faced with a patient with unusual symptoms might well recall several similar cases from his long career that turned out to have a common diagnosis and on this basis infer the probable disease from which the patient is suffering. Use of the availability heuristic here is likely to support expert decision making in a similar way to the mechanism described by Klein (1999) as recognition-primed decision making (see Chapter 5), which seems to serve expert decision makers so well in many real-life situations.

The heuristic that has been most productive in terms of experimental studies of intuitive probability judgement is that of *representativeness* (Kahneman & Tversky, 1972). The representativeness heuristic comes into play when people are judging conditional probabilities: for example, the like-lihood of a sample having been drawn from a population, or of an event given a hypothesis. In such cases, perceived similarity is the key concept. A sample will appear representative of a population, for example, if it is similar to it in essential properties. This led Kahneman and Tversky (1972) originally to predict that people would ignore sample size when inferring properties of populations from samples, as sample size is a property only of the sample. Hence, the similarity of the sample mean or proportion to that of the popu-lation would determine its perceived likelihood regardless of the size of the sample. However, early research on this issue quickly led to the view that people do have some intuitive understanding that larger samples are more reliable. They nevertheless underweight (rather than neglect) the influence of sample size in their intuitive judgements (Evans, 1989; Kahneman & Tver-sky, 1982a). As reviewed earlier, we now also know that the ability to under-stand and apply the law of large numbers is related both to cognitive ability and to the receipt of formal training in statistical theory. Hence, the tendency to rely on similarity of sample and population to the relative neglect of sample size does look like a heuristic *process* that may be overridden by analytic reasoning.

It does seem that ordinary people lack reliable intuitions about statistical samples. For example, I once saw a letter published in a British newspaper during a general election campaign claiming that all opinion-polling evidence was useless. This was based on adding together the size of samples used in all the published polls and showing that they constituted a tiny proportion of the population. Of course, the accuracy of samples actually depends only on their absolute size, unless the population size is so small that sampling without replacement would cause measurable error. However, undergraduate students who have had some statistical training also act as though sample to population size ratio was important (Bar-Hillel, 1979; Evans & Bradshaw, 1986) in making intuitive judgements. If we do have an innate cognitive mod-ule for frequency processing, it does not deliver accurate intuitions about sample size at the System 1 level. It is not clear that we should expect it to, however, since the properties of the sample you have is always the *best* esti-mate of those of the population even if it is not a good one. However, it has been argued that the problem of sampling error is a significant one for those who favour the theory of natural sampling (Over, 2003).

The conjunction fallacy

The representativeness heuristic was the prime motivator for the important experimental demonstrations by Kahneman and Tversky of two phenom-ena known as the *conjunction fallacy* and *base-rate neglect*. Tversky and Kahneman (1983) demonstrated the conjunction fallacy first with regard to people's stereotypes and social judgements as in the case of the famous Linda problem. Participants were given the following brief vignette:

> Linda is 31 years old, single, outspoken, and very bright. At University, she studied philosophy. As a student, she was deeply concerned with issues of discrimination and social justice, and also participated in anti-nuclear demonstrations.

Using different methods (both between and within participants), Tversky and Kahneman obtained ratings of the relative likelihood of the three following statements:

> Linda is a bank teller (A).
> Linda is a feminist (B).
> Linda is a feminist and a bank teller (BA).

Regardless of the method, people's perceived likelihood for these three statements was B ≥ BA > A. Thus people rate the likelihood of A&B to be greater than that of A, which is a mathematical impossibility: the conjunction of two events cannot be more likely than either on its own, as A&B logically implies A. This paper created enormous interest as evidenced by an astonishing 493 citations of it in the academic literature (*Web of Science*, April 2006). There has been much argument about the interpretation of the finding and dozens of experimental studies of the effect reported in subsequent literature. However, the phenomenon itself was thoroughly established in Tversky and Kahneman's original paper. For example, they showed that the effect was not restricted to situations involving stereotypes. In one scenario, they showed that people thought Bjorn Borg, the then dominant tennis player, was more likely to lose the first set and win a match at Wimbledon, than he was to lose the first set! They even anticipated the finding that has been of much concern in the later literature – that fewer errors are made when the task is presented in terms of relative frequencies rather than probabilities (see next section). Few people will state that there are more cases of A and B than of A as it becomes apparent that the former are a subset of the latter.

While representativeness seems to give a plausible account of the Linda problem (her description fits the stereotype of a feminist much better than that of a bank teller), it is not clear that it provides the correct account of the conjunction fallacy. As Kahneman and Frederick (2002) note, there have been numerous claims in the subsequent literature about pragmatic effects and the interpretation of words like "probability". However, their interpretation that the bias reflects a lack of extensional reasoning in System 2 in which A&B is correctly perceived to be a subset of A appears to be correct. As will become clear, the reason that frequency formats often facilitate correct solutions on the Linda problem and other problems involving probability judgement is that they help to explicate the set relationships involved.

An explanation of the conjunction fallacy in terms of the principles of hypothetical thinking is as follows. In accordance with the singularity principle, people conduct a single mental simulation of the proposition that they are asked to judge. When that proposition is "bank teller", they imagine a person based on their stereotype of bank tellers. This model fits poorly to the description of Linda so they evaluate the hypothesis as improbable. When the proposition is "feminist bank teller", however, the addition of *feminist* signals that they are thinking about an atypical bank teller and hence cancels much of the stereotype. Their simulation of "feminist bank teller" thus incorporates *compatible* elements of their stereotypes of both feminists and bank tellers, resulting in a simulation that fits much better to the description of Linda and is thus evaluated as more probable. People consider only the most likely possibilities in their mental simulations and so "Linda is a bank teller" effectively becomes "Linda is a bank teller who is not a feminist", which they are quite entitled to think is more likely than "Linda is a bank teller who is a feminist". This account is compatible with those based on pragmatic principles (e.g., Maachi, 1995) while incorporating the general thrust of the representativeness concept.

Base-rate neglect

The other main phenomenon inspired by representativeness is the base-rate fallacy, which has engendered an even bigger literature, with Kahneman and Tversky's (1973) original paper logging 1,315 citations (*Web of Science*, April 2006). There is a stereotype version similar to the Linda problem in which participants are given a thumbnail description of an individual who sounds more like an engineer than a lawyer. In such a case, participants are relatively insensitive to being told that he was among a group who were 80 per cent lawyers and 20 per cent engineers, or 20 per cent lawyers and 80 per cent engineers when asked to judge how likely he was to be one or the other. From a statistical viewpoint, even if this description is strongly (but imperfectly) diagnostic of an engineer, the base rate makes a lot of difference.

As with the conjunction fallacy, base-rate neglect is not dependent upon the use of stereotypes, and I will explain it with reference to the medical diagnosis problem administered to medical students and junior doctors by Casscells, Schoenberger, and Graboys (1978). The original problem was worded by Casscells et al. as follows:

If a test to detect a disease whose prevalence is 1/1,000 has a false positive rate of 5 per cent, what is the chance that a person found to have a positive result actually has the disease, assuming that you know nothing about the person's symptoms or signs? ____%.

Participants found this problem very hard with the most common response being 95 per cent whereas the correct answer is close to 2 per cent! This is a strong case of base-rate neglect since people are apparently reasoning that the test is 95 per cent accurate on the basis of the false-positive rate of 5 per cent and are therefore ignoring the fact that the disease being tested for is rare, having a prior probability of only .001. What is the correct answer here? Recall that Bayes' theorem gives the following relationship:

$$\frac{P(H_1/D)}{P(H_2/D)} = \frac{P(H_1)}{P(H_2)} \times \frac{P(D/H_1)}{P(D/H_2)} \tag{2.6}$$

which can be read as posterior odds = prior odds times the likelihood ratio. In this case we take D, the datum, to be the observation that the person has a positive test result, H_1 the hypothesis that the person has the disease and H_2 the hypothesis that they do not. We have been told that the false-positive rate is 5 per cent, which is the chance of a positive test given H_2. We assume that the hit rate is 100 per cent (often specified in better-worded versions of the problem) so that a person with the disease always tests positive. The prior odds are 999 to 1 in favour of H_2 (not having the disease). Substituting these values we get:

$$\frac{P(H_1/D)}{P(H_2/D)} = \frac{1}{999} \cdot \frac{1}{.05}.$$

This gives us odds of .02002, which convert into a posterior probability (which was asked for) of .0204, or approximately 2 per cent. How could we expect any naïve participant to do such a calculation! Actually, it is quite easy if you think about it in the following way. Consider that (on average) of 1,000 people tested just 1 will have the disease and test positive. Of the remaining 999 healthy people, 5 per cent – about 50 – will also test positive. Hence, the probability of a positive tester having the disease is about 1 in 50, or 2 per cent. We shall see later that versions of the problem that facilitate correct responding are ones that explicate these nested-set relationships.

The base-rate fallacy is often described as a tendency to ignore base rates – or relevant prior probabilities – in making posterior probability judgements. If Fred sounds like an engineer then we think he probably is one and are not very interested in whether he was taken from a group who were predominantly engineers or lawyers. While this problem is amenable to an explanation in terms of representativeness, the medical diagnosis problem is not. However, people are still apparently ignoring the base rate. Actually, this is a simplification. First of all, a survey of a large number of studies of the base-rate fallacy by Koehler (1996) revealed that the data are mostly compatible with the view that people *underweight* rather than ignore the base rate. Second, there is evidence that people do understand the relevance of base rates under a variety of circumstances. If people are given wholly nondiagnostic information (Fred is married with two children) then they will tend to give the base-rate probability as their answer, as was shown in the original study of Kahneman and Tversky (1973). In the medical diagnosis problem, both Cosmides and Tooby (1996) and Evans *et al.* (Evans, Handley, Perham, Over, & Thompson, 2000) found that a sizeable minority of participants who got the problem wrong gave the answer $\frac{1}{1,000}$ rather than 95 per cent, which is the base-rate probability specified in the question. This suggests that in standard versions of the tasks, people are having great difficulty in *integrating* the base rate and diagnostic information. Instead they base their mental simulations *either* on the base rate or (more frequently) on the diagnostic data in line with the singularity principle.

There is evidence that when base rates are provided by experiential learning rather than by presented statistics, they are more likely to influence probability judgements (Koehler, 1996). In fact, the almost universal use of base-rate statistics to create prior probabilities is probably the main cause of the difficulties that people have in taking them into account. In my view, it brings strongly into question the ecological validity of these experiments as a test of Bayesian reasoning. Remember that Bayesian probabilities are subjective, representing beliefs. So real-world Bayesian inference involves weighting the immediate evidence for hypotheses by one's prior belief in them. It would be surprising if people were to ignore these prior beliefs, given the strong evidence of confirmation and belief bias effects discussed in Chapters 2 and 4. Recall, for example, that scientists usually question their methodology and repeat their experiments before deciding to revise or abandon their hypotheses (Fugelsang et al., 2004). The deductive reasoning literature also shows that it very hard to stop people taking into account their prior beliefs about statements, even when the instructions clearly make them logically irrelevant to the task.

How often would statistical information form the basis for beliefs in everyday life? The answer, surely, is very rarely. How many people consult actuarial statistics on road accidents before purchasing a motor cycle or on divorce rates before entering into marriage? Even when such statistics are available and known to the individual, they are not much help. People are not deluding themselves when they believe that such statistics do not apply to individuals. Take the case of actuarial calculation of insurance premiums. These tend to be high for male drivers under the age of 25 because this group have a high rate of accidents. From the viewpoint of the insurance company this makes sense because they are calculating their risk for their entire group of under-25 male clients. However, this does not mean that a particular individual driver in this group necessarily has a raised risk. He might be (or believe himself to be) an unusually skilled and careful driver and would hence reject such statistics in computing his own subjective risk of an accident. In fact, base-rate statistics never apply accurately to any particular individual case and are at most one element that a person might take into account in determining their subjective probability. The same applies in expert judgement. A doctor might have statistics to help her assess a patient's risk of heart disease, for example, but these will be based on placing the patient in broad categories according to age, gender, smoking etc. and will not take into account the much more detailed knowledge that she may have about the patient and his medical history.

In the study of medical decision making described in Chapter 5 (Evans et al., 1995b) we found that doctors' willingness to treat raised blood cholesterol was relatively unaffected by factors related only statistically and not causally to heart disease, such as presence of the disease in primary relatives. A parallel finding in the base-rate neglect literature is that people are much more likely to take account of base rates if a scenario is provided that links them *causally* to the hypothesis under investigation (Ajzen, 1977; Bar-Hillel, 1980). The findings might reflect the fact that some people switch to mental simulations founded on the base rate when a causal mental model is suggested and does not necessarily indicate that individuals can integrate the two pieces of information.

Given our concern about the almost universal use of base-rate statistics to provide Bayesian prior probabilities, my colleagues and I decided to investigate the use of prior probabilities supplied by real beliefs that people bring with them to the laboratory (Evans, Handley, Over, & Perham, 2002). To do this, we first measured our student participants' stereotypical beliefs about the interests of students studying different subjects. Specifically, we measured their beliefs that students would join different student societies as a function of the faculty in which they were placed and vice versa. In one experiment, we presented prior probabilities as base-rate statistics and left diagnostic information implicit in people's beliefs, in line with earlier research. For example, participants were given questions like the following:

40 per cent (10 per cent) of students are in the Engineering faculty
What is the probability that a member of the Drama (Computer) society is also in the Engineering faculty? ____%

The pre-test showed that participants believed on average that 31 per cent of Engineering students would join the Drama society compared with 77 per cent who would join the Computer society. These background beliefs provide the diagnostic evidence P(D|H), whereas the stated base rate provided the prior probability P(H). The question required them to provide the posterior probability P(H|D). From a Bayesian point of view both the explicit base rate and the implicit belief should influence the judgement equally. Both factors were significant in an analysis of variance – that is, people gave significantly higher estimates for higher base rates and for more believable faculty–society connections. However, Bayesian analysis of individual participants showed that the weighting given to diagnostic information was very much higher. Hence, this experiment conforms with the general finding in the literature that base rates are underweighted but not ignored.

The key experiments in this study were ones where the problems were turned around so that prior probabilities were supplied by belief and diagnostic information by statistics. We devised problems in which exactly the same beliefs were used to supply base-rate information as had been used previously to give the diagnostic information. An example of the problem used is the following:

> A survey was conducted to discover the recreational activities of Engineering students. It was discovered that those Engineering students who belonged to the Computer society owned a PC. However, it was also the case that there were Engineering students who did not belong to the Computer society but who also owned a PC. Specifically, 5 per cent of Engineering students who did not belong to the Computer society owned PCs. Suppose that a group of Engineering students were randomly selected and asked (a) if they owned a PC and (b) what societies they belonged to. Giving your best estimate, what percentage of those Engineering students who own PCs would you expect to belong to the Computer society? ____%

In this problem, the diagnostic information (D) is ownership of a PC, and the hypothesis (H) is society membership. Since the domain of inference is now limited to Engineering students only, the Bayesian prior, P(H), is provided by the stereotypical beliefs that people have about society preferences for Engineers – the same beliefs as were used to provide diagnostic evidence in the earlier experiments. For example, P(H) will be high for the Computer society but low for the Drama society. The diagnosticity of the evidence is supplied statistically in the scenario: 100 per cent ownership for Computer society members and 5 per cent for non-members. The actual false positive rate was varied among 5 per cent, 15 per cent, 30 per cent and 50 per cent across different scenarios.

Evans et al. (2002, Exp. 4) initially found that false-positive rates influenced probability judgements in the expected manner but that implicit base rates did not. However, when participants' personal base rates (as opposed to group norms) were examined these did predict judgements. In a subsequent experiment, participants were asked to give the relevant personal base rates ("What percentage of Engineers belong to the Computer society?") immediately before reading each scenario. Presented in this way, personal base rates exerted a much *larger* influence than false positive rates. These findings suggest, however, that people do not spontaneously introduce their beliefs as prior probabilities in the same way that they do to provide diagnostic evidence. There is still a bias towards focusing on the individual evidence of the case in hand. However, the data also show that if base rates are made salient enough – both personal and judged immediately before the inferential task – then they may dominate judgements. Once again, however, it seems that people use one cue or the other.

The frequency/probability debate

The evidence examined to date suggests that most people asked to judge posterior probabilities conduct mental simulations that are based on either diagnostic or base-rate information, with a strong bias towards the former. People have been shown to switch to base rates when diagnosticity of the specific evidence is weak, when base rates are causally linked to the hypo- thesis or when base rates are derived from personal beliefs and made salient to the task. However, there are circumstances in which people can engage in analytic reasoning in Bayesian inference in which they succeed in correctly integrating base-rate and diagnostic information. This requires that people construct mental models that correctly represent the nested-set relationships. For example, the solution of the medical diagnosis problem requires imagina- tion of a model such as that shown in Figure 6.1. Here, we can see that of

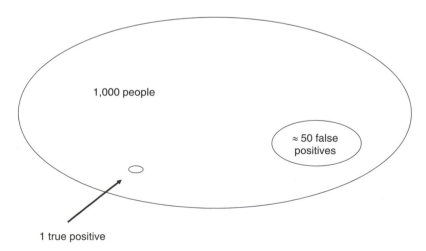

Figure 6.1   Nested-set relationships for the medical diagnosis problem.

1,000 people, 1 has the disease and will test positive and about 50 (5 per cent of 999) will give false positive tests, making the solution of around 2 per cent (1 in 50) transparent. However, it seems that few people spontaneously construct such a model unless the presentation of the problem is designed specifically to help them do so.

Cosmides and Tooby (1996, p. 24) presented the following version of the medical diagnosis problem to their participants:

> 1 out of every 1,000 Americans has disease X. A test has been developed to detect when a person has disease X. Every time the test is given to a person who has the disease, the test comes out positive (i.e. the "true positive rate" is 100 per cent). But sometimes the test also comes out positive when it is given to a person who is completely healthy. Specifically, out of every 1,000 people who are perfectly healthy, 50 of them test positive for the disease (the "false positive" rate is 5 per cent).

Participants are then told that a sample of 1,000 Americans were selected by lottery and given the test. They were asked to judge how many people who test positive for the disease would actually have the disease, expressed as a fraction _____ out of _____. Cosmides and Tooby found that 56 per cent of participants gave the correct 2 per cent answer on this version compared with only 12 per cent on the original version used by Casscells et al. (1978). It is evident that the two versions vary in a number of ways, so the question is: what is it about the Cosmides and Tooby version that produces the facilitation?

This literature has been marked by a rather heated debate about frequency formats. This goes back to the early 1990s when Gigerenzer (e.g., 1991, 2002; see also Gigerenzer & Hoffrage, 1995) argued that cognitive illusions including the conjunction fallacy and base-rate neglect could be made to "disappear" by use of frequency formats. The argument was originally based on the idea that we have evolved some mechanism to deal with frequencies in our environment but not with one-case probabilities, which are a relatively recent invention of mathematicians. Cosmides and Tooby (1996) developed this idea within their evolutionary psychology framework to include the idea of an innate frequency-processing module. They applied a similar logic to that associated with their work on social contract theory and the Wason selection task discussed in Chapter 4. Hence, they argued that the above version of the medical diagnosis problem was much easier than the probability version of Casscells et al. because the frequency format allowed the innate module to be applied.

Cosmides and Tooby's interpretation of their experiments was met with scepticism by a number of reasoning researchers who believed instead that the frequency version was simply cueing a mental model of the kind shown in Figure 6.1. This led to several experimental papers (e.g., Evans et al., 2000;

Girotto & Gonzalez, 2001; Sloman, Over, & Slovack, 2003) designed to distinguish between the frequency module and the nested-set hypotheses. These experiments include demonstrations that frequency versions can be difficult and probability versions can be easy. Manipulations that explicate the nested-set relationships facilitate performance while those that obscure it (even if frequencies are used) have the opposite effect. In response, Hoffrage, Gigerenzer, Krauss, and Martigon (2002) have argued that the nested-set hypothesis is intrinsic to what they call *natural sampling*, which must apparently be done in such a way as to make the set relationships transparent. It is now unclear whether anyone wishes to defend the view that frequencies *per se* are sufficient to facilitate statistical reasoning. For further comment on the natural sampling hypothesis and the credibility of the evolutionary argument, the reader is referred to Over (2003).

My purpose here is to comment on these findings from the viewpoint of dual-process theory. It seems reasonable to suppose that we – and other animals – may have evolved some specialized cognitive mechanism for processing frequency information in our environments. In fact, I have suggested that this could be an underlying cause for problem gambling, when such a mechanism is misapplied in a casino environment (Evans & Coventry, 2006). However, such a module – if it exists – would be an implicit form of cognition resident in System 1 and hence affect our learning and interaction with environments in which frequency information was a reliable cue. What such a mechanism would *not* do, according to the dual-process account, is to facilitate reasoning about quantitative word problems, presented with explicit verbal instructions. It is noticeable that advocates of natural sampling do not actually run experiments in which people encounter events with natural frequency relationships at all, but rather present people with word problems in which frequency statistics have already been collated. I feel that if the natural sampling theory is to be properly investigated it needs to involve situations where people learn frequency information experientially. This could be done using computer simulations, as in the manner of our own work on multicue probability learning (Evans et al., 2003a) discussed in Chapter 5.

It seems to me that quantitative word problems of the kinds used in the heuristics and biases literature have little to do with natural sampling mechanisms but instead provide difficult problems for analytic reasoning in the same way as do many of the tasks used in the deductive reasoning literature (see Chapters 3 and 4). As with logic problems, these probability tasks are given to people who generally lack training in the relevant normative systems of reasoning (logic, probability theory). In such cases, people will attempt to solve them using explicit mental models and simulations in accordance with the general principles of hypothetical thinking. Just as people make many fallacies in deductive reasoning by satisficing on single models, so they similarly may construct simplified mental models of probability problems that fail to reflect their formal properties (see also Kahneman & Frederick, 2002, for their discussion of attribute substitution in naïve probabilistic reasoning). Frequency formats have been successful in debiasing phenomena such as the conjunction fallacy and base-rate neglect because they directly cue mental models that encode the relevant nested-set relationships and thus facilitate analytic system solution of the problems. However, such study of quantitative word problems provides no evidence one way or the other as to whether we have any kind of natural frequency processing module that shapes our learning and behavioural interaction with the environment. Addressing that question requires an entirely different kind of research methodology.

PSEUDODIAGNOSTICITY

While most of the literature on Bayesian reasoning has focused on use of base rates or prior probabilities, there is a different and much smaller literature on how people reason about diagnostic information. Specifically, there is a claim in the literature that people reason "pseudodiagnostically" by focusing on evidence for a hypothesis without considering the extent to which that evidence discriminates it from its alternatives. Recall the formula for Bayes' theorem:

$$\frac{P(H_1/D)}{P(H_2/D)} = \frac{P(H_1)}{P(H_2)} \times \frac{P(D/H_1)}{P(D/H_2)}.$$

The likelihood ratio – the last part of the equation – compares the probability of a piece of evidence given each of the alternative hypotheses under consideration. The larger the ratio, the more diagnostic of H_1 is the evidence. Now consider the situation described in Table 6.2 in which two symptoms are probabilistically related to two diseases. Which provides better evidence of Disease A, Symptom 1 or 2? The answer is Symptom 2, because it yields a likelihood ratio of 4:1 in favour of A, as compared with 8:7 for Symptom 1. However, a person reasoning *pseudodiagnostically* would be more impressed

Table 6.2

Diagnosticity of cues: percentage of patients showing symptoms as a function of their disease

	Symptom 1	Symptom 2
Disease A	80	40
Disease B	70	10

with Symptom 1 because 80 per cent of Disease A patients have this compared with only 40 per cent for Symptom 2.

The pseudodiagnosticity (henceforth PD) effect was first demonstrated by Doherty et al. (1979), who saw it as a form of confirmation bias (see Chapter 2). Their participants were given a scenario in which they had to imagine that they were undersea explorers who had discovered a pot and wished to return it to its homeland—one of two islands. They were provided with a description of six characteristics of the pot, for example, whether the clay was smooth or rough and whether or not it had handles. Subjects were then permitted to seek 6 pieces of information from a possible 12 pieces. The information concerned the probability of each characteristic being present in pots from both islands.

In order to gain diagnostic evidence relevant to the decision, participants should choose to discover three pairs of probabilities, so that they know for three of the features their relative likelihood of being found on either of the islands. The analysis showed, however, that a large number of them formed a favoured hypothesis about a particular island at the outset and then sampled mostly or exclusively evidence about that island, ignoring the other. The basic finding has been replicated in a number of subsequent studies using a number of variants on the task (e.g., Beyth-Marom & Fischhoff, 1983; Doherty, Chadwick, Garavan, Barr, & Mynatt, 1996; Evans, Feeney, & Venn, 2001a; Mynatt et al., 1993; Ofir, 1988; Skov & Sherman, 1986). These studies also include manipulations that induce people to reason diagnostically, for example by getting them to focus on a particular cue rather than a particular hypothesis. However, it seems that in unstructured tasks lacking such cues people will generally consider only one hypothesis, a striking example of the singularity principle. In fact, the principle has never been more clearly stated than by Mynatt et al. (1993), who comment on the basis of this work that "We propose that the number of objects that can be maintained and operated upon in working memory is one. ... A corollary of this ... assumption is that subjects will continue to test the hypothesis in working memory, unless prompted to change it". In general, work on this form of statistical reasoning provides strong evidence for the kind of hypothesis-testing behaviour observed when reasoning deterministically about hypotheses that I reviewed in Chapter 2.

Mynatt et al. developed a rather more elegant version of the PD tasks in the following form:

Your sister has a car she bought a couple of years ago. It's either a car X or a car Y but you can't remember which. You do remember that her car does over 25 miles per gallon and has not had any major mechanical problems in the two years she's owned it.

You have the following information:
  A. 65 per cent of car Xs do over 25 miles per gallon.
Three additional pieces of information are also available:
  B. The percentage of car Ys that do over 25 miles per gallon.
  C. The percentage of car Xs that have had no major mechanical
       problems for the first two years of ownership.
  D. The percentage of car Ys that have had no major mechanical
       problems for the first two years of ownership.
Assuming you could find out only one of these three pieces of information
(B, C or D), which would you want in order to help you to decide which
car your sister owns? Please circle your answer.

With problems of this kind (in a number of different scenarios) Mynatt et al.
observed 28 per cent choices of B (correct), 59 per cent C (the PD response)
and 13 per cent D.

On the PD task, X is referred to as the *focal* hypothesis because this is the
one that people are induced to think about by the information given. We can
think of this as the supposition on which their singular mental simulation is
based. However, the effect depends upon people being given initial evidence
to support the focal hypothesis so that it satisfies. When belief in the focal
hypothesis is undermined by weak evidence, there is a noticeable shift
towards more diagnostic choices (see Mynatt et al., 1993, Exp. 2, and Evans
et al., 2002, Exp. 1) or to D responses, which can be interpreted as PD choices
for the alternative hypothesis. A plausible interpretation of these findings is
that when the focal hypothesis is unbelievable it fails to satisfy and people
simulate the alternative hypothesis instead.

Studies by Aidan Feeney and colleagues have shown that people are
sensitive to the rarity of features, which is implicitly relevant to their diagnosticity. For example, suppose you are told that your sister's car had
power-assisted steering and a top speed of 140 mph. Many modern cars
have power steering but few can do such high speeds, so we have a common
and rare feature. Feeney, Evans, and Clibbens (1997) found that if told in A
that most car Xs have the rare feature (top speed of over 140 mph) many
people will switch to the diagnostic choice C, in order to find out whether Y
also had this feature. Rare information is implicitly diagnostic because
background beliefs tell you that other makes of car (in general) are not
likely to have it. However, Feeney, Evans, and Venn (2000) argued that there
was a rarity heuristic operating at an unconscious level, as a bias towards
rarity persisted regardless of relevant explicit and statistical information.
For example, if a context is given in which all cars are high-performance
sports cars, the preference for the "rare" cue continues, even though its diagnostic value is much less in this context. Hence, it is unlikely that people's
interest in rare features reflects any process of explicit analytic reasoning

and more likely that it operates through the relevance principle at the System 1 level.

There is also evidence that analytic reasoning is involved in the PD task, as responses can be shifted quite significantly by variants in instructional framing, as several studies have shown (e.g., Beyth-Marom & Fischhoff, 1983; Evans et al., 2001a; Mynatt et al., 1993). For example, participants are more likely to make the diagnostic choice when asked to choose information that would help them decide "whether the car was X or Y" as opposed to "whether or not the car was X" (Feeney, Evans, & Venn, 2001). However, research on this topic most strikingly supports hypothetical thinking theory by showing that people tend to become focused on a single hypothesis by unconscious cues to its relevance and thereafter to think only about this focal hypothesis.

CONCLUSIONS

In this chapter, I have reviewed a number of studies that concern the way in which people reason about statistical information and probabilities. It is clear that probability problems are very difficult for most ordinary people who have not received special training in mathematics and statistics. For example, heuristic processes seem generally to focus people on selective aspects of the problem information. Hence, in Bayesian reasoning, for example, people will usually think about either the base rate or (more often) the diagnostic evidence and fail to combine the two unless problem formats are used that make the nested-set relationships transparent. In effect, people often answer a different question from the one they were asked (Kahneman & Frederick, 2002). However, if they are cued to construct the right kinds of mental model, then their analytic reasoning will deliver the correct answers. In general, normative solutions are more likely to be found by high-ability participants on such tasks, just as they are on deductive-reasoning problems (Stanovich, 1999). Combining information about base rates and diagnostic evidence is hard to do and only appears possible when the analytic system is involved.

It is possible that we do have some innate cognitive module in System 1 cognition that enables us to process frequency information. There are good a priori arguments that this should be so, as both we and other animals would gain benefit from veridical processing of frequency information in the natural world. It is clear from the psychological research that we have very poor intuitions about random events, but it could be argued that true randomness is rarely manifest in the natural world and that we were designed by evolution to detect patterns in noisy environments. That we see such patterns where there is only randomness, in an artificial casino environment, might account for the apparently nonadaptive tendency for people to bet in the face of expected losses. Having said this, I do feel that most research conducted by those interested in evolutionary and ecological adaptation has been misdirected on to the study of quantitative word problems that strongly load on to general-purpose reasoning process in System 2. For example, the undoubted debiasing that can be achieved by use of frequency formats can be accounted for in terms of the assistance that it provides in constructing the kinds of mental models needed for successful analytic reasoning.

There is much evidence in these literatures consistent with hypothetical thinking theory. The singularity principle is strongly indicated by the pseudo-diagnosticity effect, for example, which shows clearly how people tend to focus on one hypothesis or the other, rather than thinking about both together. Other phenomena, such as the conjunction effect, are also amenable to explanation with these principles. We seem to construct singular mental simulations whose nature is strongly constrained by preconscious heuristic processes in line with relevance principle. As Kahneman and Tversky have demonstrated in several studies, social stereotypes can strongly influence our thinking about individual cases but these default processes can also be altered. Hence, our default stereotypical thinking about a bank teller is sharply altered when we think about a *feminist* bank teller, leading to the paradoxical conclusions known as the conjunction fallacy.

I have deliberately left some issues hanging in this chapter concerning the implications that research in the heuristics and biases tradition has for human rationality. Are Kahneman and his colleagues right to emphasize the biases that result from heuristic thinking or do Gigerenzer's research group have the better idea in showing the adaptive nature of such thinking? The implications of research on biases for human rationality is one of several broader issues that are dealt with in the following and final chapter of this book.

CHAPTER SEVEN

Broader issues

In this book, I have developed and applied a theory of hypothetical thinking built around three key principles: singularity, relevance and satisficing. The processing model for this theory is a substantially revised version of the heuristic–analytic theory of reasoning that falls within the more general class of dual-process theories that have been widely applied in cognitive and social psychology. Processes described as heuristic (fast, parallel, implicit, high capacity) and analytic (slow, sequential, explicit, low capacity) in this theory map on to the distinction between System 1 and System 2 processing in the general family of dual-process theories (Evans, 2003; Stanovich, 1999). In the preceding chapters, the three principles and the role of dual-processes have been discussed in a wide range of cognitive tasks, including hypothesis testing, inductive reasoning, deductive reasoning, decision making and statistical inference.

Accounting for cognitive tasks in this way actually opens up several broader issues with which this final chapter is concerned. A problem that has been alluded to several times is that many of the phenomena take the form of cognitive *biases*, a term that seems to imply irrationality. The debate about rationality and its relation to dual-process theories is the first of the issues to be addressed. The second broad issue that has so far been mentioned only in passing is that of self-knowledge. If much of our behaviour is caused unconsciously at the heuristic or System 1 level, then to what extent are we consciously in control of our actions and aware of the mental events that underlie them? In the third and final section of this chapter, I will address the relation of the heuristic–analytic theory to other dual-process theories of cognition, including those developed in areas such as social psychology that lie outside of the main research topics reviewed in this book.

BIAS AND RATIONALITY

There is no single and agreed definition of what it means to be rational. The term is used in several different (not necessarily exclusive) ways in the philosophical and psychological literature, including the following:

- Personal rationality (also known as individual or instrumental rationality): the extent to which an individual succeeds in achieving their personal goals
- Normative rationality: the extent to which a person's behaviour conforms with the rules of a formal normative system used to define correct reasoning or decision making
- Bounded rationality: the idea that people have instrumental rationality (achieve their goals) within the constraints of their cognitive apparatus with its limited processing capacity
- Ecological rationality: the extent to which people's behaviour is adapted to the environment in which they find themselves
- Evolutionary rationality: the extent to which an organism's behaviour serves the goals of their genes.

A concern – obsession even – with normative rationality has marked all of the research fields reviewed in this book. We have seen in all the previous chapters that phenomena described as biases are explicitly or implicitly linked to some normative system of correct reasoning. Table 7.1 lists a number of the major biases that have been reviewed in this book. In each case, the term "bias" is explicitly linked in the relevant literature to violation of some normative theory. Confirmation bias violates Popperian falsificationism; belief bias is illogical because validity concerns only the relation of premises to conclusions; the disjunction effect violates Savage's sure-thing principle; base-rate neglect violates Bayes' theorem and so on. These biases constitute the main phenomena in these research fields and hence appear to demonstrate that people are normatively irrational, a conclusion that many authors have found disturbing or inappropriate (see, for example, Cohen, 1981; Funder, 1987; Gigerenzer, 1991; O'Brien, 1993; Oaksford & Chater, 1993).

The problem is that it seems paradoxical to accuse people of being irrational on the basis of their susceptibility to cognitive biases in the laboratory. This is because the human species is evidently very smart and accomplished, and indeed all animals appear to have high ecological rationality: that

Table 7.1
Some of the main cognitive biases reviewed in this book

Bias	Description	Research paradigm	Normative system
Confirmation bias	Acting so as to discover confirming and avoid falsifying evidence	Hypothesis testing; concept learning	Popperian philosophy of science
Positive testing bias	Considering only positive predictions of a focal hypothesis	Hypothesis testing	Various philosophies of science
Matching bias	Focusing on cases that match lexical content of propositional rules	Deductive reasoning	Logic
Belief bias	Judging the validity of arguments on the believability of their conclusions	Deductive reasoning	Logic
Double negation effect	Failing to recognize that not-(not-p) implies p	Deductive reasoning	Logic
Positive/negative recency biases	Systematic misperception of random sequences	Probability judgement; gambling	Probability theory
Overweighting of small probabilities		Decision making under risk	Expected utility
Disjunction effect	Failure to prefer A to B when an irrelevant event C is unknown	Decision making	Savage's sure-thing principle
Conjunction fallacy	Judging P(A&B) to be more likely than P(A)	Probability judgement	Probability theory
Base-rate neglect	Insufficient consideration of prior probabilities in posterior probability judgements	Probability judgement	Bayes' theorem
Pseudodiagnosticity	Judging a hypothesis on the basis of $P(D|H)$ without considering $P(D|\neg H)$	Probabilistic hypothesis testing	Bayes' theorem

is, to be adapted by some combination of evolution and learning to successful life in their normal environments. So a lot of authors have felt that something must be wrong in these endless demonstrations of normative irrationality: the question is what? My own analysis (Evans, 1993; Evans & Over, 1996a) suggests that answers to this question fall into three broad categories:

1. *The normative system problem.* This is the argument that psychologists

apply the wrong normative system to the problems administered to their participants. If the correct system were applied, behaviour would appear rational. Advocates of this approach include Mike Oaksford and Nick Chater, who, for example, have argued that choices on the Wason selection task are rational if viewed in terms of expected information gain (Oaksford & Chater, 1996) and that, more generally, deductive-reasoning performance is rational if assessed from the viewpoint of probability theory rather than standard logic (Oaksford & Chater, 2001).

2. *The interpretation problem.* This argument attributes deviations from normative theory not to faulty reasoning processes but to participants adopting alternative mental representations of the problem information from those intended by the experimenters (for examples, see Henle, 1962; Revlin, Leirer, Yopp, & Yopp, 1980; Smedslund, 1970, 1990). For example, if a participant takes "if p then q" to be a biconditional "if and only if p then q" then they will, by a process of logical reasoning, deduce conclusions that appear to be fallacious.

3. *The external validity problem.* A number of authors (e.g., Cohen, 1981; Funder, 1987) have argued that problems chosen to demonstrate cognitive "illusions" in the laboratory are not representative of reasoning accuracy in the real world. They are rather analogous to visual illusions, such as the Muller-Lyer, which demonstrate the fallibility – by special tricks – of a generally veridical and adaptive process.

Arguments (2) and (3) do not really stand up to close scrutiny. The interpretation argument fails because there are biases that cannot be accounted for a process of logical reasoning from any consistent interpretation of the tasks given. For example, all theories of conditionals (see Evans & Over, 2004, and Chapter 3 of this book) agree that Modus Tollens is a valid inference and that the not-q card should be selected on the Wason selection task. The same applies if the conditional is read as a biconditional. In spite of this, people often fail to make MT arguments and very frequently fail to pick the not-q card. The external validity argument is not credible either: laboratory demonstrations of biases and normative violations are so many and varied that it beggars belief that each could be the result of a carefully engineered illusion. Also, many of these biases have been demonstrated with expert judges or in everyday contexts (see Gilovich et al., 2002, for many examples).

This leaves us with the problem of normative rationality, which is much more tricky. Before considering this further, it is worth noting Stanovich's (1999, 2004) analysis of the alternative positions that authors take on the rationality debate. He characterizes three positions, as follows:

1. *Panglossian* (named for Voltaire's fictional philosopher). Roughly speaking, this is the view that people are rational no matter what they do.

Panglossian authors (such as Cohen, 1981) are happy to explain all apparent deviations from rational behaviour on the basis of one of the three arguments listed above. People are being assessed by the wrong normative system, or they are misunderstanding the question, or the experiment creates by trickery an unrepresentative cognitive illusion, and so on. Such arguments are apparently motivated by *a priori* beliefs that people must be rational.

2. *Meliorist.* On this view, people can be and often are irrational, but not inherently so. They often get it wrong due to lack of education, lack of mental effort and so on, but can be improved. Meliorists are keen to find ways of helping people to improve their reasoning and judgements, which requires them to concede that they are often less than optimal to start with. Meliorist authors include Stanovich himself (e.g., 2004) and Jonathan Baron (e.g., Baron, 1985, 1994).

3. *Apologist.* This is the bounded rationality approach. Apologists, like Meliorists, concede that behaviour can often be suboptimal but attribute this to failures in cognitive capacity. Such authors tend to assume that people have been shaped by evolution and/or learning to be as rational as they can be. The research programme of Gigerenzer and colleagues that demonstrates fast and frugal heuristics that can apparently make us smart, with minimal demands on our cognitive resources, falls into this category (Gigerenzer, 2004; Gigerenzer & Todd, 1999).

Of these three groups, Meliorists – who want to improve reasoning and judgement – are the most willing to concede the reality of errors and biases and the most favourably inclined to normative theories or at least *prescriptive* theories (Baron, 1985) that people can realistically be taught to aid their everyday reasoning and decision making.

For many years, I conducted experimental research on biases in reasoning without thinking that I was doing anything more than cognitive psychology – documenting and understanding phenomena that revealed the nature of human thinking. However, when Panglossian authors began to attack all work on cognitive biases, a response was required. My own was to argue that the word "rational" was being used in two distinct ways termed rationality$_1$ and rationality$_2$ (Evans, 1993). These correspond to personal and normative rationality, respectively. The argument was that demonstrating people to be irrational$_2$ (non-normative) by no means necessarily meant that they were irrational$_1$ (failing to achieve their personal goals). For example, standard logic, which deals in propositions that can only be true or false, maps poorly on to a real world full of uncertainty in which people must actually reason. Hence, logic may be a poor normative model against which to assess human reasoning (Evans, 2002a; Oaksford & Chater, 1991).

In my subsequent collaboration with the philosopher David Over (Evans

& Over, 1996a), the concept of the two kinds of rationality was developed so that the definition of rationality$_2$ now included the phrase "acting when one has a reason for what one does sanctioned by a normative theory". David insisted that to be termed rational in this sense, one had to be following rules explicitly, not simply complying with rules in the manner of a bumblebee apparently maximizing expected utility in its observed behaviour (Real, 1991). However, this subtly shifted the terminology to represent two different concepts of rationality, rather than two different ways of using the word. This was also the starting point for the revised dual-process theory of reasoning with which this collaborative book ended. It was not our intention simply to equate rationality$_1$ with System 1 and rationality$_2$ with System 2 as some readers apparently inferred. However, it is true that thinking deeply about these two concepts of rationality forced us to make the dual-process distinction.

Here is the reason. If you think about instrumental rationality (rationality$_1$) then it is fairly evident that many organisms (even plants) must be deemed "rational" in this sense due to either evolutionary programming or operant conditioning or a combination of both. A cat achieves the goal of eating by following a complex but stereotyped pattern of hunting behaviours that are evidently genetically programmed. A domestic cat can also learn to find food by reminding its owner to put food in its bowl. Whether such processes are genetically hard-wired or experientially acquired they appear to be automatic and implicit. It seemed to us that much human behaviour is like this also, achieving rationality$_1$ without requiring any effort of conscious or deliberative thinking. However, humans can also solve problems and make decisions in quite a different way, by conscious reflection and hypothetical thought about imaginary possibilities.

A potential confusion arose in this analysis which I hope I have avoided in the present volume. If rationality$_2$ were to be equated with System 2 or analytic thinking, then it would imply that the analytic system was a kind of mental logic, following normative rules. This is most definitely *not* what I believe to the case. In fact, the discussion in this book of cognitive biases has relied on the idea of *two* fundamental biases – one heuristic and the other analytic. It has been argued that considering a single hypothesis and maintaining it in line with the satisficing principle – the *fundamental analytic bias* – is a major factor underlying many of the phenomena discussed. This combines with the *fundamental heuristic bias* to contextualize problems with regard to prior knowledge and belief in line with the relevance principle (see also Stanovich, 1999). However, it would be correct to say that rationality$_2$ (as defined by Evans & Over, 1996a) cannot be achieved *without* the use of reflective, analytic thinking. It now seems preferable to emphasize the nature of analytic thinking and to avoid any reference to rationality in its definition. What matters is that it is a different kind of cognitive resource (from heuristic processing) that is available to human beings. Use of this resource can also serve rationality₁ by helping us to achieve our goals.

In favour of the value of normative rationality is the empirical observation that participants of high cognitive ability often provide normatively correct answers to problems in reasoning and judgement that are known to generate biases in their less able colleagues. Stanovich (1999) has used this as an argument against Panglossian claims that these biases are but disguised forms of rationality. However, even Stanovich reported exceptions to this finding, and further research is suggesting a more complex picture of individual differences in reasoning. For example, Newstead et al. (2004) found evidence that participants of medium cognitive ability may be better at pragmatic forms of reasoning than are those of lower ability, but worse at abstract reasoning than are those of higher ability. This corresponds with findings that retrieval of knowledge from memory relevant to contextualized reasoning develops with age (e.g., Klaczynski, 2000; Markovits & Quinn, 2002) and is better developed in adults with higher working-memory capacity (De Neys et al., 2005b). This works in contrast with traditional Piagetian theory (e.g., Inhelder & Piaget, 1958) in which it was assumed that children develop concrete thinking that is replaced by abstract logical thought in adults. The contemporary developmental researchers cited above assume that both kinds of thought develop in parallel, and the evidence suggests that most adults are more competent with concrete than abstract thinking problems.

Normative rationality is essentially a philosophical and not a psychological concept. Analytic reasoning may (or may not) involve following explicit rules as some theorists argue (e.g., Sloman, 1996), but the relation of those rules to formal normative theories cannot form part of our psychological definition of System 2 thinking. Higher ability participants do appear to think more analytically (or to do so more effectively) but not necessarily more in accordance with standard normative theories. For example, we have recent evidence that high-ability participants show very strongly defective truth tables (see Chapter 3) in line with the suppositional theory of conditionals, but in conflict with standard textbook treatments of material conditionals (Evans et al., in press). This does not mean that there is anything "wrong" with propositional logic and its material conditional – it is very useful in developing computer logic, for example. However, it does illustrate that we cannot build our theory of analytic thinking around standard normative systems.

The notions of evolutionary and ecological rationality can seem to get confused (Over, 2000a, 2000b; Todd, Fiddick, & Krauss, 2000). The distinction is that ecological rationality is manifested when an organism is well adapted to its environment, and evolutionary rationality is that programmed by genes. Because the dominant evolutionary theory is that of adaptationism based on Darwinian principles, one might expect these to be the same.

However, this is not necessarily so. First, there is the problem of how specific or general our genetic programming might be. When our behaviour is well adapted, is this due to application of an innate cognitive module with encapsulated software (see Chapter 4) or the application of some domain-general learning mechanism? Of course, our ability to learn is provided by the genes, but there is a big distinction between custom-programmed modules and general-purpose cognition on a "long-leash" from the genes (Stanovich, 2004; Stanovich & West, 2003).

A second issue is that we evolved in an environment that was in many ways strikingly different from the one in which we now operate. Hence, evolutionary rationality may conflict with ecological rationality, something that has not generally been recognized in the influential tradition of evolutionary psychology led by Tooby and Cosmides (e.g., 1992). These authors have been criticized for always emphasizing the adaptive nature of human behaviour in the modern environment as though this was an inevitable consequence of evolutionary processes (Stanovich, 2004, chap. 5; Stanovich & West, 2003). We could turn this on its head and argue that evolutionary psychologists ought to be looking for *biases* resulting from mechanisms adapted to ancient environments that are no longer relevant. The problem with looking for adaptations, such as the cheater detection algorithm proposed by Cosmides (1989; see Chapter 4), is that any behaviour adapted to the modern environment may have come about through some general process of learning.

Evolutionary considerations are relevant to broader forms of dual-process theory, if System 1 is viewed as including innate cognitive modules as well as implicit knowledge acquired through experiential learning. For this reason, some dual-process theorists have looked closely and critically at the arguments of evolutionary psychologists and especially the claim that the mind is massively modular, thus apparently precluding any powerful role of general-purpose reasoning in System 2 (Over, 2003; Stanovich, 1999, 2004). However, such considerations are well beyond the scope of the present book with its focus on the heuristic–analytic theory of reasoning and judgement. The implicit heuristic processes on which this book is focused are principally those that deliver prior knowledge and belief to consciousness for analytic processing in line with the relevance principle. Whether this fundamental heuristic bias has an ancient evolutionary origin is obviously highly questionable. However, it is sufficient for our present purposes to focus on the nature of the heuristic processes that carry this out and the interaction with the analytic processes that is reflected in our response to cognitive tasks.

SELF-KNOWLEDGE

Common sense (folk psychology) tells us that we are consciously in control of our actions. However, experimental psychology tells us that much of our behaviour is controlled by processes that are partially or wholly unconscious. Common sense tells us that since our behaviour is consciously controlled we can introspect to derive the reasons for our actions and report them to others. For example, we can tell opinion pollsters not only how we intended to vote, but the reasons we have for doing so. Once again, experimental psychology tells us otherwise: as Nisbett and Wilson (1977) famously put it, we cannot tell what we do not know. While lack of insight into our own thought processes is attributed to motivation and repression in Freudian theory, a much more convincing reason is that many of our cognitive processes are simply unconscious and automatic and therefore inaccessible to introspection (Wilson, 2002; Wilson & Dunn, 2004).

It is important to understand that this book has not been focused on the many kinds of implicit cognitive processes that may affect us in *wholly* unconscious ways. Such processes include those associated with attention, perceptual and motor skills, language processing and the acquisition and application of implicit knowledge through low-level associative learning processes. There are many kinds of implicit cognitive processes in the mind beyond the type of heuristic processes discussed in this book. Since we have focused on explicit reasoning and judgement tasks that involve hypothetical thinking, some element at least of analytic thinking is generally involved, in order to generate a response that complies with the verbal instructions. Such processing may be superficial and minimal, however, effectively delivering default heuristically cued responses. For example, this happens when a conclusion to an argument that appears congenial is accepted as valid (belief bias) or when an example that comes readily to mind is interpreted as being probable (availability bias). We have also seen how more active intervention by the analytic system can lead to such default responses being discarded and replaced by ones based on more deliberative and appropriate reasoning.

It is hardly surprising that people will lack insight into mental processes that are wholly implicit. For example, no one would seriously expect that people could, by introspection, explain the processes underlying their recognition of a familiar face, or their construction of the meaning of a spoken sentence. However, psychologists have seriously addressed the question of whether people have insight into reasoning, judgement and decision making – all tasks that appear to involve conscious thinking. Let us reprise a couple of examples that have arisen in the main review chapters of this book. In the study of multicue judgement there has been some debate about the degree to which people are aware of the "policies" that are implicit in their judgements and which can be extracted by the methods of social judgement theory using multiple regression analysis. Our own research on this, described in Chapter 5, accords with the traditional view in this literature that such self-insight is limited at best. For example, we found that doctors knew which cues they were *not* using to make a judgement, but reported use of all cues to which they consciously attended (Harries et al., 1996), whereas only a subset actually affected their judgements. Subsequent research indicated that such judgements are influenced by a combination of implicit and explicit knowledge (Evans et al., 2003a).

The multicue judgement work actually takes us beyond the bounds of the heuristic–analytic theory and into more general forms of dual-process theory. This is because implicit learning falls into the category of processes that can influence our behaviour directly, even though they appear to combine with explicit processes in producing the judgements observed in this paradigm. More relevant for our current purposes are phenomena such as matching bias and belief bias that fall centrally within the remit of the heuristic–analytic account. The difference in these cases is that heuristic processes are forming default mental models for analytic processing either by focusing attention on selected aspects of the problem or by retrieving relevant prior knowledge from memory. What level of self-insight can we expect in such cases?

It would be surprising indeed if people were to report that their responses were based on matching or belief bias. Verbal reports – including "introspections" – require the analytic system for their generation, a system that has been motivated by the experimental instructions to engage in logical reasoning. If people were aware that they were choosing cards because they match, or conclusions because they were believable, they presumably would refrain from doing so! The fallacy, as so well exposed by Nisbett and Wilson (1977), is to assume that a request for someone to explain their choices would somehow cause them to retrieve the memory of a conscious thought process responsible for the behaviour. In fact, such requests constitute a new cognitive task that necessarily involves heavy use of the analytic system. In effect, people think – given my response and given the task I was set, what is the reason for this choice? As Wason and Evans (1975; see also Lucas & Ball, 2005) showed, people actually *rationalize* their choices in such reports. For example, choice of a matching card may be justified on the basis of verification or falsification depending on how it maps on to the logic of the problem. In the same way, Nisbett and Wilson (1977) showed how unconsciously controlled social judgements were often explained by use of a priori causal theories that are culturally available.

As argued by Ericsson and Simon (1980, 1984), concurrent verbal protocols (think aloud) are much more useful than retrospective reports as they provide evidence about the current locus of participants' attention. These are not introspections but process-tracing methods, like eye-movement tracking or neural imaging. Only by this method, for example, could we discover the presence of "secondary matching bias" (Lucas & Ball, 2005; Wason & Evans, 1975) in which people think about matching values on the *hidden* sides of cards. Such protocols have also shown us that participants who attend to the premises (rather than just the conclusion) of a syllogistic argument are less prone to belief bias (Evans et al., 1983). In essence, people can report the contents of their verbal working memories, but this is best done concurrently to avoid forgetting. Moreover, these reports do not reveal *reasons*: it is the task of the experimenter and not the participant to infer the underlying cognitive processes.

The literature on judgement includes study of several meta-cognitive biases that have not so far been discussed in this book. One such is hindsight bias or the "knew it all along effect" (Fischhoff, 1982; Hawkins & Hastie, 1990; Roese, 2004). There are two paradigms, which Roese (2004) calls the *hypothetical paradigm* and the *memory paradigm*. The memory paradigm has been popular in recent research and involves showing that when people answer questions and later are asked to recall either their answers or confidence ratings with the correct answers known, their memories shift in a self-serving manner. That is, they are inclined to believe that they gave more correct answers or had more confidence in answers that turned out to be correct than they actually did. Of more interest here is the hypothetical paradigm as employed in Fischhoff's original studies. In this method people judge the a priori probability of outcomes with and without outcome knowledge. When outcomes are known, people overestimate the probability that they could have predicted them. For example, Fischhoff (1975) asked participants to estimate the probability of various outcomes of an historical battle (A won, B won, truce, stand-off etc.). Each group were given the same scenario but told that different outcomes occurred. Not only did participants allocate higher probabilities to the "known" outcomes, but they also attributed causes in the scenario according to the outcome. For example, if a guerrilla force was said to have beaten an organized army, then the presence of a hilly terrain with good cover might be cited as a key causal factor.

Hindsight bias (in the hypothetical paradigm) is highly consistent with hypothetical thinking theory. It seems that people construct a single mental simulation of the causal factors leading to the outcome that is biased by the knowledge of what that outcome was. This process can lead to selective rewriting of the past and failure to learn from history (Fischhoff, 1982). It is also very interesting to compare hindsight judgements to counterfactual thinking (Roese, 2004; Teigen, 1998). Logically, they should have an inverse relationship. If there are two possible outcomes, A and B, and you know that A occurred, hindsight bias should lead you to overestimate the probability of A and underestimate the probability of B. However, the relevant research shows that this is not necessarily so. What determines the counterfactual judgements is their perceived closeness (Evans & Over, 2004, chap. 7) or what Teigen (1998) calls the *proximity* heuristic. To understand what may be going on here, consider a real-world example.

In April 2006, Arsenal and Villareal met in the second leg of a European Champions' League semifinal. Arsenal had a 1–0 lead from the first leg and were favourites to go through. In the game, the score remained 0–0 until three minutes from the end at which point Villareal were awarded a disputed penalty kick. The Arsenal goalkeeper, Jens Lehman, saved the penalty, and Arsenal progressed to the final. I have no actual data on this case, but the research literature suggests that the following would occur if people were asked after the game to judge the probability of different results. If they were asked the probability of the actual outcome (drawn second leg) they would do this by considering a priori causal factors, such as the quality of the two teams, their prior record in European competition and the tactical advantage (to Arsenal) of holding a 1–0 lead. They might well overestimate the probability of the draw as they could focus on causal factors relevant to it (for example, Arsenal could play defensively as they only needed a draw). This is hindsight bias. Now suppose instead that they were asked to give the probability of a counterfactual outcome – Villareal won 1–0. In this case, the late penalty save would influence their thinking, making this counterfactual possibility a close one that they would therefore judge probable. This information would not influence the factual judgement, however, explaining the dissociation between factual and counterfactual probability judgements. In this case, it is quite possible that a group asked to judge the likelihood of a draw and another group asked to judge that of a Villareal win might give probabilities adding to well in excess of one.

The findings here are similar to those of the work on reasons pro and con discussed in Chapter 5 (Shafir, 1993). In that case people might choose the same option when asked to select one of two actions as when asked to reject one. In all of these cases, people are constructing single mental simulations. The biasing factor is the relevance principle by which unconscious cues to relevance flesh out the content of the simulation. What is relevant to accepting an option appears different from what is relevant to rejecting one. Similarly, what is relevant for judging a factual probability is different from what is relevant for judging a counterfactual probability. Although people consciously evaluate their mental simulations, much of their content is determined by unconscious heuristic processes. Note, however, that when people simply compare the probability of factual and counterfactual conditional statements (see Over et al., in press; see also Chapter 4) they seem to use a similar process, presumably because both appear to concern the causal connection between p and q. However, psychological research on closeness in counterfactual conditional sentences to date has been minimal (see Evans & Over, 2004, chap. 7).

People – including expert judges – are chronically overconfident of their judgements, giving confidence ratings that actually overestimate their probability of correctly answering questions or making predictions (Fischhoff & McGreggor, 1982; Koriat, Lichtenstein, & Fischhoff, 1980). This is one of a number of biases that can be seen as "self-serving" along with hindsight bias and *myside bias* (Baron, 1995; Stanovich & West, in press) – the tendency to see arguments as stronger when they support your own beliefs. Clearly there could be motivational factors in self-serving biases, but I prefer a cognitive account. For example, forecasting a future event requires conducting a mental simulation. In accordance with the relevance and singularity principles, people will tend to focus on the most plausible scenario (most relevant by default). This process is almost bound to bias any subsequent question about confidence in an upward direction as the mere act of simulation will make the chosen alternative more available. In fact, there is evidence that just asking someone to imagine a possible scenario will increase their degree of belief that it will come about (Hirt & Sherman, 1985).

All in all, our insight into our own cognitive processes seems to be very limited. This appears problematic for dual-process theories that place a lot of emphasis on the automatic-controlled distinction (see Evans, 2006a), since such views suggest that at least some of our decision making is conscious and controlled in the manner expected by folk psychology. However, my argument is not that such intentional level decision making does not occur, but rather that it does not result in self-insight. First, no action is ever entirely controlled by conscious analytic thinking as much of its content and directional focus is determined by preconscious processes. Moreover, any question that we ask to try to determine self-insight introduces a reactive measurement whether it be an introspective report or a confidence rating. Giving your reasons for choosing cards on the selection task, for example, is a different cognitive task from that of actually choosing them. If asked retrospectively for reasons, a process very similar to that of hindsight bias operates. If you know you have chosen the 3 card and that you were asked to make the rule true or false, then you solve this (new) task by coming up with a reason that links the two together, just as in the hindsight bias paradigm you seek and find causal factors relevant to the outcome you know to have occurred.

LINKS WITH OTHER RESEARCH ON DUAL PROCESSES

In the discussion of the cognitive literatures on reasoning, judgement and decision making in this book, a specific dual-process account has largely been applied: the revised heuristic–analytic theory (Evans, 2006b). There are actually a large number of dual-process theories in psychology applied both in these fields and in others, most notably in the psychology of learning and in social psychology. Some of the major ones are listed in Table 7.2. On a superficial examination, it may seem that they are all drawing a broadly similar distinction, that between fast, automatic processes on the one hand (System 1) and slow, deliberative and conscious ones on the other (System 2). However, more detailed consideration reveals that any attempt either (a) to

Table 7.2
Some of the major dual-process theories of cognition

	System 1	System 2
Fodor (1983, 2001)	Input modules	Higher cognition
Epstein (1994); Epstein and Pacini (1999)	Experiential	Rational
Chaiken (1980); Chen and Chaiken (1999)	Heuristic	Systematic
Reber (1993); Evans and Over (1996a); Sun (2001)	Implicit/tacit	Explicit
Evans (1989; 2006b)	Heuristic	Analytic
Schneider and Schiffrin (1977)	Automatic	Controlled
Hammond (1996)	Intuitive	Analytic
Stanovich (1999, 2004); Kahneman and Frederick (2002)	System 1 (TASS)	System 2 (analytic)
Nisbett et al. (2001)	Holistic	Analytic
Wilson (2002)	Adaptive unconscious	Conscious
Toates (2006)	Stimulus-bound	Higher order

map these theories on to each other or (b) to map each on to two underlying cognitive systems is fraught with difficulties (see Evans, 2006a).

Dual-process theories of learning have been around for many years, and the account of Reber (1993) was an inspiration in the development of more broadly based two-system theories of reasoning (Evans & Over, 1996a; Stanovich, 1999). Dual-process learning theories propose that there are two distinct forms of learning: implicit and explicit, which lead correspondingly to distinct implicit and explicit forms of knowledge (see also Berry & Dienes, 1993; Dienes & Perner, 1999; French & Cleeremans, 2002; Osman, 2005; Sun, 2001; Sun, Slusarz, & Terry, 2005). At a computational level, these two forms of learning can be modelled using neural networks for the implicit processes and some form of rule induction for the explicit learning (Sun et al., 2005), with the added psychological assumption that the latter process is explicit and limited by working memory capacity. On this basis, dual-process theories of learning seem to map well on to Sloman's (1996) distinction between associative and rule-based processes in reasoning.

Evidence for implicit learning has been accumulated from several distinct paradigms such as artificial-grammar learning (Reber, 1976) and tasks involving control of complex systems (Berry & Broadbent, 1987, 1988). For example, in the latter case, participants might be asked to set variables in order to control output of a factory within a computer simulation. The system to be controlled has rules that are unknown to the participants. Instead, they make adjustments and then receive outcome feedback on a trial-by-trial basis. Eventually, they learn to control the system to the specified criteria but without ever being able to state explicitly the rules that govern its behaviour. In the artificial-grammar paradigm, participants are asked to judge the grammaticality of letter strings that are generated (or not) by a phrase structure grammar. Again, with outcome feedback over a number of trials, people learn to tell grammatical and ungrammatical strings apart, but are not able to state the explicit rules that underlie their definition.

In other kinds of learning tasks, people can explicitly describe the basis of their learning, and the difference between this and implicit learning has led some theorists to postulate two distinct forms of cognitive processes and two distinct forms of knowledge representation as noted above. However, this position has become quite controversial (e.g., Cleeremans & Jiminez, 2002; Shanks & St John, 1994), with some recent theorists favouring a single-process approach in which knowledge structures lie on a continuum of strength. Conscious attention may be more or less required – or involved initially but later replaced by well-learnt processes that become "automatic". By analogy with this, some authors have argued against dual-process accounts of reasoning (Osman, 2005; Stevenson, 1997) as though these also might be on a continuum. Newstead (2000) has also argued (on different grounds) for the continuum approach, something also incorporated into the distinction between intuitive and analytic thinking in the cognitive continuum theory of Hammond (1996).

I am less inclined now than previously (Evans & Over, 1996a) to think that dual processes in learning can easily be related to the kinds of dual-process distinctions in reasoning and judgement discussed in this book. There is a clear distinction between implicit and explicit *knowledge*, which is that the former affects our behaviour without becoming conscious, and the latter has the potential to be retrieved and posted in consciousness. The complication is that the kind of heuristic processes discussed in this book are mostly concerned with the retrieval and application of *explicit* knowledge from long-term and semantic memory, albeit by *implicit* processes. Explicit knowledge is not what we are aware of at a given time (which is very little), but what has the potential to become conscious. The heuristic–analytic theory is concerned with the kind of implicit cognitive processes that deliver content for conscious analytic processing and shape its direction in line with the relevance principle. Although fast and automatic in themselves, these heuristic processes clearly fall into the category of implicit processes that post their results into consciousness.

In essence, while System 2 still stands up as a unitary concept, System 1 does not. It is in reality a collection of quite different kinds of implicit cognitive systems (see also Stanovich, 2004; Wilson, 2002). Heuristic processes shape our conscious thinking both by retrieving relevant prior knowledge and by directing attention to different parts of the presented information. More than one mechanism probably underlies these but they are at least coherently linked by the relevance principle. These are different from the processes involved in the acquisition of and application of implicit knowledge to our behaviour, which is the focus of dual-process research in learning. There are also forms of implicit knowledge that appear to be acquired initially through a process of explicit learning and later become automated and hence rapid and effortless (Monsell & Driver, 2000; Schneider & Shiffrin, 1977). There are also undoubtedly cognitive modules in the mind with encapsulated and domain-specific processes such as those involved in language processing and vision (Fodor, 1983) even though attempts to explain higher level reasoning and decision processes with reference to such modules has proved highly controversial (see Chapters 4 and 6).

Failures to distinguish between different kinds of implicit processes is a source of potential confusion in broader dual-system accounts. Thus, while Sloman's (1996) distinction between associative and rule-based processing is highly appropriate to the literature on inductive and categorical learning, it may be an oversimplification to try to generalize this, as he does, to decision-making and deductive-reasoning tasks. Most dual-process theorists in reasoning are focused on the distinction between belief-based and analytic reasoning but if you accept the account of such tasks given in this book, it should be apparent that these heuristic processes are not associative. They might better be termed *pragmatic*, as they are highly sensitive to context and deliver relevant content. On a somewhat different track, Evans and Over (1996a) and Stanovich (1999) may have confused matters by applying the idea from learning theory that the two processes might be old (implicit) and new (explicit) in evolutionary terms to dual-process accounts of reasoning. As Goel (2005) has shown in his neural-imaging studies of reasoning, belief biases are located in frontal regions of the brain that are recently evolved and distinctively human. There is clearly something wrong with the concurrent proposals of reasoning theorists (Evans, 2003) that System 1 is ancient and shared with other animals and that belief bias is part of System 1. What is wrong is that there is no singular implicit system with a particular evolutionary history that competes with analytic reasoning in System 2. Nor can it be the case that the most cognitive biases observed in reasoning research are primarily due to cognitive modules that evolved for different purposes in an ancient environment as Stanovich (2004) appears to suggest.

Dual-process theories have also been strongly applied in cognitive social psychology for many years (for recent reviews and collections of papers, see Chaiken & Trope, 1999; Hassin et al., 2005; Wilson, 2002) but with little or no cross-reference to the literatures in reasoning, judgement and decision making. Again, the distinctions made seem superficially to correspond well with the generic Systems 1 and 2 of reasoning theory. Social psychologists distinguish between processes that are fast and automatic on the one hand and slow, deliberative and conscious on the other. The rational–experiential theory of Epstein (1994; Epstein & Pacini, 1999) proposed two systems that are also distinguished by being evolutionarily old (experiential) and recent (rational) with the latter being distinctively human. The heuristic–systematic model of Chaiken (1980; Chen & Chaiken, 1999) is based on distinctions that seem very similar to those between heuristic and analytic reasoning processes. Automatic versus controlled processing has been a major construct in accounting for studies of social cognition (e.g., Bargh & Ferguson, 2000) but social psychologists also seem to draw upon the distinction between implicit and explicit *knowledge* as when they assert dissociation between implicit and explicit levels of attitudes (Wilson, Lindsey, & Schooler, 2000) and stereotypes (Bargh, 1999).

Research in social psychology provides evidence for dual processing primarily by demonstrating dissociations between implicit and explicit levels of processing or knowledge. For example, some individuals express explicit stereotypical attitudes about gender, race and so on, and some do not. (Those who do not can still state explicitly what the stereotypes in their culture are.) Many experimental studies have shown, however, that almost everyone can be shown to possess these stereotypes at the implicit level (Bargh, 1999). A typical method used is that of semantic priming borrowed from the cognitive literature on implicit memory (see Lucas, 2000). For example, McRae and colleagues (Macrae, Bodenhausen, Milne, Thorn, & Castelli, 1997) showed people pictures followed by a lexical decision task (judging whether a letter string is a word or nonword). Some of the pictures were of women, and, provided that a semantic judgement was required (animate–inanimate), a marked priming effect was observed on the lexical decision tasks. Stereotype-consistent words (e.g., caring, emotional) were recognized much faster than counter-stereotypical words (e.g., confident, assertive). However, the effect did not occur if people simply examined the pictures for visual features. Hence, although stereotype activation is automatic, its operation is influenced by the consciously controlled locus of attention.

There is a debate in the social cognition literature as to whether people have any control over activation and application of stereotypes in their social thinking. A relatively optimistic view is that while activation is automatic, stereotypical thoughts can be consciously suppressed and inhibited (e.g., Devine, 1989). The argument here would seem to parallel those of reasoning researchers who suggest that belief biases in reasoning can be inhibited provided that the participants are properly motivated by instructions and of sufficient cognitive ability (Chapter 4). However, a more pessimistic view is taken by Bargh (1999), who reviews evidence showing that people cannot effectively inhibit stereotypical thinking even when made consciously aware that it might influence their judgements. Bargh implies that social psychologists have suffered from wishful thinking on this topic and also argues that both psychologists and their participants suffer from the illusion that "controlled" cognitive processes are somehow freely willed and lacking in deterministic mechanism (Bargh, 2005; Bargh & Ferguson, 2000). His views clearly support those of other social psychologists such as Wilson (2002) that people lack self-insight (see previous section).

The literature on dual processes in social psychology is huge, and effective review of it is well beyond the scope of this book. Social psychologists appear to have been less concerned than their cognitive colleagues with issues of cognitive architecture and evolution but are engaged in detailed argument about what forms of social knowledge are implicit and explicit and the extent to which social processes are automatic or under voluntary control. They have also had rather more to say about the issues of self-knowledge and free will. Social psychologists, dealing rather more directly with the real world, have also addressed concerns about the extent to which individuals can be held morally and legally responsible for their social attitudes and behaviour, in the light of the massive accumulation of evidence of automatic processing of social information.

In summary, dual-processing accounts of reasoning and judgement that have been the focus of this book are clearly linked in some way with those developed in other fields of psychology, especially in the study of learning and of social cognition. Integrating these literatures is, however, a formidable task. There do appear to be distinct implicit and explicit forms of knowledge representation that are acquired by different mechanisms of learning, and it is likely that the implicit form evolved much earlier. However, these implicit processes largely differ from the kinds of heuristic processes discussed in this book, which concern the locus and content of conscious attention in the analytic thinking system and often also the implicit processes that retrieve and apply explicit knowledge. Social psychologists have concerned themselves with the distinction between implicit and explicit knowledge, but in a manner that relates more closely to the literature on implicit memory than on implicit learning, with the use of semantic priming being a very popular methodology. Social psychologists are also interested in the ways in which automatic and controlled processes appear to compete for control of social judgements that provide potential links with dual-processing accounts of reasoning and judgement.

FINAL THOUGHTS

This book has been focused on hypothetical thinking. This is the kind of thought that occurs when we attempt explicitly to make an inference, judgement or decision that requires imagination of hypothetical possibilities. The theory of hypothetical thinking offered incorporates a particular dual-processing account in order to deal with the cognitive processes underlying such thinking. While there are many kinds of implicit and automatic processes in the brain that control much of our behaviour, including associative learning, and encapsulated modules that control perceptual and language processing, these are not the main concern of the heuristic–analytic theory of thinking. The focus here has been, rather, on the kinds of implicit processes – which I term "heuristic" – that bias and shape our analytic reasoning.

The original heuristic–analytic theory of reasoning (Evans, 1989) was designed to explain cognitive biases that arise in reasoning, judgement and decision making. This was based upon the idea that we can only think about limited representations of problem information and that the attentional and pragmatic processes that determine these representations are of necessity preconscious. In this book, I have also been interested in explaining biases and have used this idea – the fundamental heuristic bias – extensively in this exercise. It does indeed seem that we automatically and rapidly contextualize problems in the light of prior knowledge and that this process can bias our conscious reasoning (see also Stanovich, 1999). Where this book departs from these previous analyses is in attributing biases of reasoning not only to this fundamental bias of the heuristic system, but also to an equally fundamental bias in the analytic system. We tend to think about only one possibility at a time and accept this as the basis for inference, decisions or action if it seems good enough. Taken together, this account of hypothetical thinking involves the three principles of relevance, singularity and satisficing that have been illustrated with respect to a wide range of psychological literatures.

In discussing hypothetical thought, I have also made extensive use of the concepts of epistemic mental models and of mental simulations. The popular and successful mental model theory of reasoning (Johnson-Laird, 1983; Johnson-Laird & Byrne, 1991) has, I believe, had limited success in trying to account for the accumulation of evidence that human reasoning is primarily pragmatic and not deductive in nature. In common with mental logic theories, mental modellers have tried to account for reasoning on the grounds that it is a logical process subject to influence by pragmatic factors relating to prior knowledge and belief. To this end, Johnson-Laird and colleagues have promoted the idea of *semantic* mental models that represent situations in the world. Such models are truth-verifiable and well suited to an account of human reasoning in terms of extensional logic.

The view of human reasoning taken here is radically different. People do indeed make use of mental models in their reasoning and decision making, but these models are *epistemic* in nature. This means that they do not simply represent the states of the world (as in semantic models) but rather the beliefs that people hold about these states. Such models are not truth-verifiable, because if I believe that, say, the Republicans will win the next US election with subjective probability .6, this belief can never be confirmed. The Republicans will win or they will not but they cannot win .6. Nor is there any relevant frequency distribution to be considered for such a one-off event. But epistemic mental models can do much more than represent subjective probabilities. They can represent any kind of belief or propositional attitude that we hold with regard to their content. For example, they can represent beliefs about causal relations in line with accumulated evidence that causal mental models are prevalent in human thought (Sloman, 2005). They can represent counterfactual thoughts about past possibilities that never occurred and which can now never be verified. Crucially, they can represent the fact that the models themselves are hypothetical or suppositional, so that we can distinguish our thought experiments from our beliefs about reality.

Epistemic mental models should not be thought of as static structures that are retrieved unaltered from memory, although we probably do store such models that are commonly used in our thinking. Normally, we engage in hypothetical thinking in order to deal with a novel problem. We are invited to dinner by someone for the first time and need to work out the route of travel and estimate its duration. We decide to take a holiday and need to choose a destination and form of accommodation that will fit our requirements and suit our budget. We are offered tickets to a sporting event and try to work out whether we will enjoy it enough to be worth the time and expense of attending. Real-world decision making is like this. We usually consider one possibility at a time but often lack any preformed belief or knowledge to determine our action. In such cases, we conduct thought experiments or mental simulations in order to develop epistemic mental models that are well enough defined to be useful.

Mental simulation is an idea that links together many of the diverse literatures discussed in this book. It is the primary tool that the analytic system uses to evaluate possibilities. We use mental simulations to think and reason about conditional statements, to evaluate hypotheses, to make forecasts, to evaluate options that we can choose and so on. Mental simulation always engages the analytic system with its conscious but slow and capacity-limited processes. Any form of hypothetical thinking requires explicit representation of its suppositional nature. However, mental simulations are also constrained by the three principles of hypothetical thinking, including the relevance principle that reflects heuristic processing. We tend to think about one possibility at a time (singularity principle), which is the one that appears most appropriate in the context (relevance principle). Our imagination of possibilities is limited and predictable (see Byrne, 2005, for many examples), and we are unable to keep track of possible but less likely branches when we build the simulation forward in time (Kahneman & Tversky, 1982b). We may revise or abandon the mental representations that are generated, but have a strong tendency to accept them unless there is clear reason to do otherwise (satisficing).

This process of hypothetical thinking has bounded rationality because it allows us to function in a world of great complexity and uncertainty, while taking actions that achieve our goals much of the time. However, it is hardly surprising that those experimental psychologists who are interested in finding error and bias have little difficulty in doing so. We have seen, for example, that

different research programmes can treat heuristics more or less sympatheti-
cally: some finding situations where short-cut rules of thumb lead to effective
solutions to otherwise intractable problems and some devising tasks where
systematic biases result. For example, people may appear to be biased by
prior beliefs and to be stereotypical and prejudiced in their social perception
and judgements. The ability to inhibit such beliefs and to reason in abstract
manner appears to be related both to cognitive ability and to cognitive style.
Some people are more able to think analytically than others; some are also
more inclined to do so than others.

I sometimes think that we should call a halt to all psychological experimentation for ten years or so and instead spend our time just reading what
has already been done and thinking about it. The literatures are so large that
no one person can know more than a fraction of the work in any detail. If we
were not all so busy running and analysing our experiments, perhaps we
would make more sense of what has already been reported. It is no wonder
that parallel literatures have developed on dual processes in several distinct
fields of psychology that make little or no cross-reference to each other.
In this book, I have at least tried to connect several literatures that are normally studied separately – hypothesis testing, deductive reasoning, statistical
reasoning, judgement and decision making. While the tasks that are given
to participants in these fields are many and varied, they engage the same
cognitive systems. I hope that I have been able to show how a dual-process
framework with a common set of principles can usefully be applied in all of
these.

References

Adams, E. (1975). *The logic of conditionals: An application of probability to deductive logic*. Dordrecht: Reidel.

Ajzen, I. (1977). Intuitive theories of events and the effects of base rate information on prediction. *Journal of Personality and Social Psychology, 35*, 303–314.

Almor, A. (2003). Specialised behaviour without specialised modules. In D. E. Over (Ed.), *Evolution and the psychology of thinking* (pp. 101–120). Hove, UK: Psychology Press.

Alter, A. L., & Oppenheimer, D. M. (2006). From a fixation on sports to an exploration of mechanism: The past, present and future of hot hand research. *Thinking & Reasoning, 12*, 431–444.

Anderson, J. R. (1990). *The adaptive character of thought*. Hillsdale, NJ: Erlbaum.

Ball, L. J., Lucas, E. J., Miles, J. N. V., & Gale, A. G. (2003). Inspection times and the selection task: What do eye-movements reveal about relevance effects? *Quarterly Journal of Experimental Psychology, 56A*, 1053–1077.

Ball, L. J., Wade, C. N., & Quayle, J. D. (2006). Effects of belief and logic on syllogistic reasoning: Eye-movement evidence for selective processing models. *Experimental Psychology, 53*, 77–86.

Bargh, J. A. (1999). The cognitive monster: The case against the controllability of automatic stereotype effects. In S. Chaiken & Y. Trope (Eds.), *Dual-process theories in social psychology* (pp. 361–382). New York: Guilford Press.

Bargh, J. A. (2005). Bypassing the will: Demystifying the nonconscious control of social behavior. In R. R. Hassin, J. S. Uleman, & J. A. Bargh (Eds.), *The new unconscious* (pp. 37–58). Oxford, UK: Oxford University Press.

Bargh, J. A., & Ferguson, M. J. (2000). Beyond behaviorism: On the automaticity of higher mental processes. *Psychological Bulletin, 126*, 925–945.

Bar-Hillel, M. (1979). The role of sample size in sample evaluation. *Organizational Behavior and Human Performance, 24*, 245–257.

Bar-Hillel, M. (1980). The base-rate fallacy in probability judgements. *Acta Psychologica, 44*, 211–233.

Barkow, J. H., Cosmides, L., & Tooby, J. (Eds.) (1992). *The adapted mind: Evolutionary psychology and the generation of culture.* Oxford, UK: Oxford University Press.

Baron, J. (1985). *Rationality and intelligence.* Cambridge, UK: Cambridge University Press.

Baron, J. (1994). Nonconsequentialist decisions. *Behavioral and Brain Sciences, 17*, 1–42.

Baron, J. (1995). Myside bias in thinking about abortion. *Thinking & Reasoning, 1*, 221–235.

Barrett, L., Dunbar, R. I. M., & Lycett, J. (2002). *Human evolutionary psychology.* Basingstoke, UK: Macmillan.

Barston, J. L. (1986). *An investigation into belief biases in reasoning.* Plymouth, UK: University of Plymouth.

Bennett, J. (2003). *A philosophical guide to conditionals.* Oxford, UK: Oxford University Press.

Berry, D. C., & Broadbent, D. E. (1987). Explanation and verbalization in a computer assisted search task. *Quarterly Journal of Experimental Psychology, 39A*, 585–609.

Berry, D. C., & Broadbent, D. E. (1988). Interactive tasks and the implicit-explicit distinction. *British Journal of Psychology, 79*, 251–273.

Berry, D. C., & Dienes, Z. (1993). *Implicit learning.* Hove, UK: Erlbaum.

Beyth-Marom, R., & Fischhoff, B. (1983). Diagnosticity and pseudodiagnosticity. *Journal of Personality and Social Psychology, 45*, 1185–1197.

Braine, M. D. S., & O'Brien, D. P. (1991). A theory of If: A lexical entry, reasoning program, and pragmatic principles. *Psychological Review, 98*, 182–203.

Braine, M. D. S., & O'Brien, D. P. (Eds.) (1998a). *Mental logic.* Mahwah, NJ: Erlbaum.

Braine, M. D. S., & O'Brien, D. P. (1998b). The theory of mental-propositional logic: Description and illustration. In M. D. S. Braine & D. P. O'Brien (Eds.), *Mental logic* (pp. 79–89). Mahwah, NJ: Erlbaum.

Bruner, J. S., Goodnow, J. J., & Austin, G. A. (1956). *A study of thinking.* New York: Wiley.

Bueler, R., Griffin, D., & Ross, M. (2002). Inside the planning fallacy: The causes and consequences of optimistic time predictions. In T. Gilovich, D. Griffin, & D. Kahneman (Eds.), *Heuristics and biases: The psychology of intuitive judgement* (pp. 250–270). Cambridge, UK: Cambridge University Press.

Buller, D. J. (2005). Evolutionary psychology: The emperor's new paradigm. *Trends in Cognitive Sciences, 9*, 227–283.

Byrne, R. M. J. (2005). *The rational imagination.* Cambridge, MA: MIT Press.

Byrne, R. M. J., & Handley, S. J. (1996). Reasoning strategies for suppositional deductions. *Cognition, 62*, 49.

Byrne, R. M. J., & Tasso, A. (1999). Deductive reasoning with factual, possible and counterfactual conditionals. *Memory and Cognition, 27*, 726–740.

Canter, D., & Alison, L. (Eds.) (2000). *The social psychology of crime: Groups, teams and networks.* Aldershot, UK: Ashgate.

Caporael, L. R. (2001). Evolutionary psychology: Toward a unifying theory and a hybrid science. *Annual Review of Psychology, 52,* 607–628.

Casscells, W., Schoenberger, A., & Graboys, T. B. (1978). Interpretation by physicians of clinical laboratory results. *New England Journal of Medicine, 299,* 999–1001.

Chaiken, S. (1980). Heuristic versus systematic information processing and the use of source versus message cues in persuasion. *Journal of Personality and Social Psychology, 39,* 752–766.

Chaiken, S., & Trope, Y. (Eds.). (1999). *Dual-process theories in social psychology.* New York: Guilford Press.

Chater, N., & Oaksford, M. (1999). The probability heuristics model of syllogistic reasoning. *Cognitive Psychology, 38,* 191–258.

Chen, S., & Chaiken, S. (1999). The heuristic-systematic model in its broader context. In S. Chaiken & Y. Trope (Eds.), *Dual-process theories in social psychology* (pp. 73–96). New York: Guilford Press.

Cheng, P. W., & Holyoak, K. J. (1985). Pragmatic reasoning schemas. *Cognitive Psychology, 17,* 391–416.

Cheng, P. W., & Holyoak, K. J. (1989). On the natural selection of reasoning theories. *Cognition, 33,* 285–314.

Cheng, P. W., Holyoak, K. J., Nisbett, R. E., & Oliver, L. M. (1986). Pragmatic versus syntactic approaches to training deductive reasoning. *Cognitive Psychology, 18,* 293–328.

Cherubini, P., Mazzocco, A., & Rumiati, R. (2003). Rethinking the focusing effect in decision making. *Acta Psychologica, 113,* 67–81.

Cleeremans, A., & Jiminez, L. (2002). Implicit learning and consciousness: A graded, dynamic perspective. In R. M. French & A. Cleeremans (Eds.), *Implicit learning and consciousness.* Hove, UK: Psychology Press.

Cohen, L. J. (1981). Can human irrationality be experimentally demonstrated? *Behavioral and Brain Sciences, 4,* 317–370.

Colom, R., Rebollo, I., Palacios, A., Juan-Espinosa, M., & Kyllonen, P. C. (2004). Working memory is (almost) perfectly predicted by g. *Intelligence, 32,* 277–296.

Cooksey, R. W. (1996). The methodology of social judgement theory. *Thinking & Reasoning, 2,* 141–173.

Cosmides, L. (1989). The logic of social exchange: Has natural selection shaped how humans reason? *Cognition, 31,* 187–276.

Cosmides, L., & Tooby, J. (1992). Cognitive adapations for social exchange. In J. H. Barkow, L. Cosmides, & J. Tooby (Eds.), *The adapted mind: Evolutionary psychology and the generation of culture* (pp. 163–228). Oxford, UK: Oxford University Press.

Cosmides, L., & Tooby, J. (1996). Are humans good intuitive statisticians after all? Rethinking some conclusions from the literature on judgment under uncertainty. *Cognition, 58,* 1–73.

Cosmides, L., & Tooby, J. (2000). Consider the source: The evolution of adaptations for decoupling and metarepresentation. In D. Sperber (Ed.), *Metarepresentations* (pp. 53–115). Oxford, UK: Oxford University Press.

Cummins, D. D., Lubart, T., Alksnis, O., & Rist, R. (1991). Conditional reasoning and causation. *Memory and Cognition, 19,* 274–282.

De Neys, W. (2006a). Automatic-heuristic and executive-analytic processing during reasoning: Chronometric and dual-task considerations. *Quarterly Journal of Experimental Psychology*, *59*, 1070–1100.

De Neys, W. (2006b). Dual processing in reasoning: Two systems but one reasoner. *Psychological Science*, *17*, 428–433.

De Neys, W., Schaeken, W., & d'Ydewalle, G. (2005a). Working memory and counterexample retrieval for causal conditionals. *Thinking & Reasoning*, *11*, 123–150.

De Neys, W., Schaeken, W., & d'Ydewalle, G. (2005b). Working memory and everyday conditional reasoning: Retrieval and inhibition of stored counterexamples. *Thinking & Reasoning*, *11*, 349–381.

Devine, P. G. (1989). Stereotypes and prejudice: Their automatic and controlled components. *Journal of Personality and Social Psychology*, *56*, 680–690.

Dienes, Z., & Perner, J. (1999). A theory of implicit and explicit knowledge. *Behavioral and Brain Sciences*, *22*, 735–808.

Dieussaert, K., Schaeken, W., & d'Ydewalle, G. (2002). The relative contribution of content and context factors on the interpretation of conditionals. *Experimental Psychology*, *49*, 181–195.

Dijksterhuis, A. (2004). Think different: The merits of unconscious thought in preference development and decision making. *Journal of Personality and Social Psychology*, *87*, 586–598.

Dijksterhuis, A., Bos, M. W., Nordgren, L. F., & von Baaren, R. B. (2006). On making the right choice: The deliberation-without-attention effect. *Science*, *311*, 1005–1007.

Dijksterhuis, A., & Smith P. K. (2005). What do we do unconsciously? And how? *Journal of Consumer Psychology*, *15*, 225–229.

Doherty, M. E. (Ed.) (1996). Social judgement theory. *Thinking & Reasoning*, *2 (2/3)*.

Doherty, M. E., Chadwick, R., Garavan, H., Barr, D., & Mynatt, C. R. (1996). On people's understanding of the diagnostic implications of probabilistic data. *Memory and Cognition*, *24*, 644–654.

Doherty, M. E., Mynatt, C. R., Tweney, R. D., & Schiavo, M. D. (1979). Pseudodiagnosticity. *Acta Psychologica*, *43*, 11–21.

Edgington, D. (1995). On conditionals. *Mind*, *104*, 235–329.

Edgington, D. (2003). What if? Questions about conditionals. *Mind & Language*, *18*, 380–401.

Edwards, W. (1954). The theory of decision making. *Psychological Bulletin*, *41*, 380–417.

Edwards, W. (1961). Behavioral decision theory. *Annual Review of Psychology*, *67*, 441–452.

Elqayam, S. (2006). The collapse illusion: A semantic-pragmatic illusion of truth and paradox. *Thinking & Reasoning*, *12*, 144–180.

Epstein, S. (1994). Integration of the cognitive and psychodynamic unconscious. *American Psychologist*, *49*, 709–724.

Epstein, S., & Pacini, R. (1999). Some basic issues regarding dual-process theories from the perspective of cognitive-experiential theory. In S. Chaiken & Y. Trope (Eds.), *Dual-process theories in social psychology* (pp. 462–482). New York: Guilford Press.

Epstein, S., Pacini, R., Denes-Raj, V., & Heier, H. (1996). Individual differences in intuitive-experiential and analytic-rational thinking styles. *Journal of Personality and Social Psychology*, *71*, 390–405.

Ericsson, K. A., & Simon, H. A. (1980). Verbal reports as data. *Psychological Review*, *87*, 215–251.

Ericsson, K. A., & Simon, H. A. (1984). *Protocol analysis: Verbal reports as data.* Cambridge, MA: MIT Press.

Evans, J. St. B. T. (1982). *The psychology of deductive reasoning.* London: Routledge.

Evans, J. St. B. T. (1984). Heuristic and analytic processes in reasoning. *British Journal of Psychology*, *75*, 451–468.

Evans, J. St. B. T. (1989). *Bias in human reasoning: Causes and consequences.* Hove, UK: Erlbaum.

Evans, J. St. B. T. (1993). Bias and rationality. In K. I. Manktelow & D. E. Over (Eds.), *Rationality: Psychological and philosophical perspectives* (pp. 6–30). London: Routledge.

Evans, J. St. B. T. (1995). Relevance and reasoning. In S. E. Newstead & J. St. B. T. Evans (Eds.), *Perspectives on thinking and reasoning* (pp. 147–172). Hove, UK: Erlbaum.

Evans, J. St. B. T. (1996). Deciding before you think: Relevance and reasoning in the selection task. *British Journal of Psychology*, *87*, 223–240.

Evans, J. St. B. T. (1998). Matching bias in conditional reasoning: Do we understand it after 25 years? *Thinking & Reasoning*, *4*, 45–82.

Evans, J. St. B. T. (2000). Thinking and believing. In J. A. Garcia-Madruga, N. Carriedo, & M. J. Gonzales-Labra (Eds.), *Mental models in reasoning* (pp. 41–56). Madrid, Spain: UNED.

Evans, J. St. B. T. (2002a). Logic and human reasoning: An assessment of the deduction paradigm. *Psychological Bulletin*, *128*, 978–996.

Evans, J. St. B. T. (2002b). Matching bias and set sizes: A discussion of Yama (2001). *Thinking & Reasoning*, *8*, 153–163.

Evans, J. St. B. T. (2002c). The influence of prior belief on scientific thinking. In P. Carruthers, S. Stich, & M. Siegal (Eds.), *The cognitive basis of science* (pp. 193–210). Cambridge, UK: Cambridge University Press.

Evans, J. St. B. T. (2003). In two minds: Dual process accounts of reasoning. *Trends in Cognitive Sciences*, *7*, 454–459.

Evans, J. St. B. T. (2004). History of the dual process theory of reasoning. In K. I. Manktelow & M. C. Chung (Eds.), *Psychology of reasoning: Theoretical and historical perspectives* (pp. 241–266). Hove, UK: Psychology Press.

Evans, J. St. B. T. (2005). *How to do research: A psychologist's guide.* Hove, UK: Psychology Press.

Evans, J. St. B. T. (2006a). Dual system theories of cognition: Some issues. *Proceedings of the 28th Annual Meeting of the Cognitive Science Society, Vancouver.* [Available from http://www.cogsci.rpi.edu/CSJarchive/proceedings/2006/docs/p202.pdf]

Evans, J. St. B. T. (2006b). The heuristic–analytic theory of reasoning: Extension and evaluation. *Psychonomic Bulletin and Review*, *13*, 378–395.

Evans, J. St. B. T. (in press). On the resolution of conflict in dual-process theories of reasoning. *Thinking & Reasoning.*

Evans, J. St. B. T., Barston, J. L., & Pollard, P. (1983). On the conflict between logic and belief in syllogistic reasoning. *Memory and Cognition*, *11*, 295–306.

Evans, J. St. B. T., & Bradshaw, H. (1986). Estimating sample size requirements in research design: A study of intuitive statistical judgement. *Current Psychological Research and Reviews*, *5*, 10–19.

Evans, J. St. B. T., Clibbens, J., Cattani, A., Harris, A., & Dennis, I. (2003a). Explicit and implicit processes in multicue judgement. *Memory and Cognition*, *31*, 608–618.

Evans, J. St. B. T., Clibbens, J., & Harris, A. (2005a). Prior belief and polarity in multicue learning. *Quarterly Journal of Experimental Psychology*, *58A*, 651–666.

Evans, J. St. B. T., Clibbens, J., & Rood, B. (1995a). Bias in conditional inference: implications for mental models and mental logic. *Quarterly Journal of Experimental Psychology*, *48A*, 644–670.

Evans, J. St. B. T., Clibbens, J., & Rood, B. (1996a). The role of implicit and explicit negation in conditional reasoning bias. *Journal of Memory and Language*, *35*, 392–409.

Evans, J. St. B. T., & Coventry, K. (2006). A dual-process approach to behavioral addiction. The case of gambling. In W. W. Reinout & A. W. Stacy (Eds.), *Handbook of implicit cognition and addiction*. Thousand Oaks, CA: Sage.

Evans, J. St. B. T., & Curtis-Holmes, J. (2005). Rapid responding increases belief bias: Evidence for the dual-process theory of reasoning. *Thinking & Reasoning*, *11*, 382–389.

Evans, J. St. B. T., Ellis, C. E., & Newstead, S. E. (1996b). On the mental representation of conditional sentences. *Quarterly Journal of Experimental Psychology*, *49A*, 1086–1114.

Evans, J. St. B. T., Feeney, A., & Venn, S. (2001a). Implicit and explicit processes in an hypothesis evaluation task. *British Journal of Psychology*, *93*, 31–46.

Evans, J. St. B. T., & Handley, S. J. (1999). The role of negation in conditional inference. *Quarterly Journal of Experimental Psychology*, *52A*, 739–769.

Evans, J. St. B. T., Handley, S. J., & Harper, C. (2001b). Necessity, possibility and belief: A study of syllogistic reasoning. *Quarterly Journal of Experimental Psychology*, *54A*, 935–958.

Evans, J. St. B. T., Handley, S. J., Harper, C., & Johnson-Laird, P. N. (1999a). Reasoning about necessity and possibility: A test of the mental model theory of deduction. *Journal of Experimental Psychology: Learning, Memory, and Cognition*, *25*, 1495–1513.

Evans, J. St. B. T., Handley, S. J., Neilens, H., & Over, D. E. (in press). Thinking about conditionals: A study of individual differences. *Memory & Cognition*.

Evans, J. St. B. T., Handley, S. J., & Over, D. E. (2003b). Conditionals and conditional probability. *Journal of Experimental Psychology: Learning, Memory, and Cognition*, *29*, 321–355.

Evans, J. St. B. T., Handley, S. J., Over, D. E., & Perham, N. (2002). Background beliefs in Bayesian inference. *Memory and Cognition*, *30*, 179–190.

Evans, J. St. B. T., Handley, S. J., Perham, N., Over, D. E., & Thompson, V. A. (2000). Frequency versus probability formats in statistical word problems. *Cognition*, *77*, 197–213.

Evans, J. St. B. T., Harries, C. H., & Dean, J. (1995b). Tacit and explicit policies in general practioners' prescription of lipid lowering agents. *British Journal of General Practice*, *45*, 15–18.

Evans, J. St. B. T., Legrenzi, P., & Girotto, V. (1999b). The influence of linguistic form on reasoning: The case of matching bias. *Quarterly Journal of Experimental Psychology*, *52A*, 185–216.

Evans, J. St. B. T., & Lynch, J. S. (1973). Matching bias in the selection task. *British Journal of Psychology*, *64*, 391–397.

Evans, J. St. B. T., & Newstead, S. E. (1980). A study of disjunctive reasoning. *Psychological Research*, *41*, 373–388.

Evans, J. St. B. T., Newstead, S. E., & Byrne, R. M. J. (1993). *Human reasoning: The psychology of deduction*. Hove, UK: Erlbaum.

Evans, J. St. B. T., & Over, D. E. (1996a). *Rationality and reasoning*. Hove, UK: Psychology Press.

Evans, J. St. B. T., & Over, D. E. (1996b). Rationality in the selection task: Epistemic utility versus uncertainty reduction. *Psychological Review*, *103*, 356–363.

Evans, J. St. B. T., & Over, D. E. (1997). Rationality in reasoning: The case of deductive competence. *Current Psychology of Cognition*, *16*, 3–38.

Evans, J. St. B. T., & Over, D. E. (1999). Explicit representations in hypothetical thinking. *Behavioral and Brain Sciences*, *22*, 763–764.

Evans, J. St. B. T., & Over, D. E. (2004). *If*. Oxford, UK: Oxford University Press.

Evans, J. St. B. T., Over, D. E., & Handley, S. J. (2003). A theory of hypothetical thinking. In D. Hardman & L. Maachi (Eds.), *Thinking: Psychological perspectives on reasoning, judgement and decision making* (pp. 3–22). Chichester, UK: Wiley.

Evans, J. St. B. T., Over, D. E., & Handley, S. J. (2005b). Supposition, extensionality and conditionals: A critique of Johnson-Laird & Byrne (2002). *Psychological Review*, *112*, 1040–1052.

Evans, J. St. B. T., Stevenson, R. J., Over, D. E., Handley, S. J., & Sloman, S. A. (2004). *Belief revision and uncertain reasoning*. ESRC End of Award Report, R000239074. Plymouth, UK: University of Plymouth.

Falk, R., & Konold, C. (1997). Making sense of randomness: Implicit encoding as a basis for judgement. *Psychological Review*, *104*, 301–318.

Feeney, A., Evans, J. St. B. T., & Clibbens, J. (1997). Probabilities, utilities and hypothesis testing. In *Proceedings of the 19th Annual Conference of the Cognitive Science Society* (pp. 217–222). Mahwah, NJ: Erlbaum.

Feeney, A., Evans, J. St. B. T., & Venn, S. (2000). A rarity heuristic for hypothesis testing. In *Proceedings of the 22nd Annual Conference of the Cognitive Science Society* Mahwah, NJ: Erlbaum.

Feeney, A., Evans, J. St. B. T., & Venn, S. (2001). *Rarity and hypothesis testing*. Unpublished manuscript, Durham University, UK.

Feeney, A., & Handley, S. J. (2000). The suppression of q card selections: Evidence for deductive inference in Wason's selection task. *Quarterly Journal of Experimental Psychology*, *53A*, 1224–1243.

Feynman, R. P. (1985). *Surely you are joking Mr Feynman!* London: Vintage.

Fiddick, L., Cosmides, L., & Tooby, J. (2000). No interpretation without representation: The role of domain-specific representations and inferences in the Wason selection task. *Cognition*, *77*, 1–79.

Fiddick, L., Spampinato, M. V., & Grafman, J. (2005). Social contracts and precautions activate different neurological systems: An fMRI investigation of deontic reasoning. *NeuroImage*, *28*, 778–786.

Fischhoff, B. (1975). Hindsight /= foresight: The effect of outcome knowledge on judgment under uncertainty. *Journal of Experimental Psychology: Human Perception and Performance*, *1*, 288–299.

Fischhoff, B. (1982). For those condemned to study the past: Heuristics and biases in hindsight. In D. Kahneman, P. Slovic, & A. Tversky (Eds.), *Judgement under uncertainty: Heuristics and biases* (pp. 335–351). Cambridge, UK: Cambridge University Press.

Fischhoff, B., & McGreggor, D. (1982). Subjective confidence in forecasts. *Journal of Forecasting*, *1*, 155–172.

Fodor, J. (1983). *The modularity of mind*. Scranton, PA: Crowell.

Fodor, J. (2000). Why we are so good at catching cheaters? *Cognition*, *75*, 29–32.

Fodor, J. (2001). *The mind doesn't work that way*. Cambridge, MA: MIT Press.

Fong, G. T., Krantz, D. H., & Nisbett, R. E. (1986). The effects of statistical training on thinking about everyday problems. *Cognitive Psychology*, *18*, 253–292.

French, R. M., & Cleeremans, A. (Eds.) (2002). *Implicit learning and consciousness*. Hove, UK: Psychology Press.

Fugelsang, J. A., Stein, C. B., Green, A. E., & Dunbar, K. N. (2004). Theory and data interactions of the scientific mind: Evidence from the molecular and cognitive laboratory. *Canadian Journal of Experimental Psychology*, *58*, 86–95.

Fugelsang, J. A., & Thompson, V. A. (2003). A dual-process model of belief and evidence interactions in causal reasoning. *Memory and Cognition*, *31*, 800–815.

Funder, D. C. (1987). Errors and mistakes: Evaluating the accuracy of social judgements. *Psychological Bulletin*, *101*, 75–90.

George, C. (1995). The endorsement of the premises: Assumption-based or belief-based reasoning. *British Journal of Psychology*, *86*, 93–111.

George, C. (1997). Reasoning from uncertain premises. *Thinking & Reasoning*, *3*, 161–190.

George, C. (1999). Evaluation of the plausibility of a conclusion derivable from several arguments with uncertain premises. *Thinking & Reasoning*, *5*, 245–281.

Gigerenzer, G. (1991). How to make cognitive illusions disappear: Beyond "heuristics and biases". In W. Stroebe & M. Hewstone (Eds.), *European review of social psychology* (pp. 83–115). Chichester, UK: Wiley.

Gigerenzer, G. (1996). Reasoning the fast and frugal way: Models of bounded rationality. *Psychological Review*, *103*, 650–669.

Gigerenzer, G. (2002). *Reckoning with risk*. London: Penguin Books.

Gigerenzer, G. (2004). Fast and frugal heuristics: The tools of bounded rationality. In D. J. Koehler & N. Harvey (Eds.), *Blackwell handbook of judgment and decision making* (pp. 62–88). Oxford, UK: Blackwell.

Gigerenzer, G., & Hoffrage, U. (1995). How to improve Bayesian reasoning without instruction: Frequency formats. *Psychological Review*, *102*, 684–704.

Gigerenzer, G., & Hug, K. (1992). Domain-specific reasoning: Social contracts, cheating and perspective change. *Cognition*, *43*, 127–171.

Gigerenzer, G., & Murray, D. J. (1987). *Cognition as intuitive statistics*. Hillsdale, NJ: Erlbaum.

Gigerenzer, G., & Todd, P. M. (1999). *Simple heuristics that make us smart*. New York: Oxford University Press.

Gilovich, T., Griffin, D., & Kahneman, D. (2002). *Heuristics and biases: The psychology of intuitive judgement*. Cambridge, UK: Cambridge University Press.

Gilovich, T., Vallone, R., & Tversky, A. (1985). The hot hand in basketball: On the misperception of random sequences. *Cognitive Psychology, 17*, 295–314.

Girotto, V., & Gonzalez, M. (2001). Solving probabilistic and statistical problems: A matter of information structure and question form. *Cognition, 78*, 247–276.

Girotto, V., & Johnson-Laird, P. N. (2004). The probability of conditionals. *Psychologia, 47*, 207–225.

Goel, V. (2005). Cognitive neuroscience of deductive reasoning. In K. Holyoak & R. G. Morrison (Eds.), *The Cambridge handbook of thinking and reasoning* (pp. 475–492). Cambridge, UK: Cambridge University Press.

Goel, V., & Dolan, R. J. (2003). Explaining modulation of reasoning by belief. *Cognition, 87*, B11–B22.

Goldstein, D. G., & Gigerenzer, G. (2002). Models of ecological rationality: The recognition heuristic. *Psychological Review, 109*, 75–90.

Goldstein, W. M. (2005). Social judgment theory: Applying and extending Brunswick's probabilistic functionalism. In D. J. Koehler & N. Harvey (Eds.), *Blackwell handbook of judgment and decision making* (pp. 37–61). Oxford, UK: Blackwell.

Goldvarg, Y., & Johnson-Laird, P. N. (2000). Illusions in modal reasoning. *Memory and Cognition, 28*, 282–294.

Gorman, M. E., & Gorman, M. E. (1984). Comparison of disconfirmatory, confirmatory and control strategies on Wason's 2–4–6 task. *Quarterly Journal of Experimental Psychology, 36A*, 629–648.

Gorman, M. E., Stafford, A., & Gorman, M. E. (1987). Disconfirmation and dual hypotheses on a more difficult version of Wason's 2–4–6 task. *Quarterly Journal of Experimental Psychology, 39A*, 1–28.

Griggs, R. A., & Cox, J. R. (1982). The elusive thematic materials effect in the Wason selection task. *British Journal of Psychology, 73*, 407–420.

Hadjichristidis, C., Stevenson, R. J., Over, D. E., Sloman, S. A., Evans, J. St. B. T., & Feeney, A. (2001). On the evaluation of *If p then q* conditionals. In *Proceedings of the 23rd Annual Meeting of the Cognitive Science Society, Edinburgh*. [Available from http://www.cogsci.rpi.edu/CSJarchive/Proceedings/2001/cogsci01.pdf]

Hammond, K. R. (1955). Probalistic functionalism and the clinical method. *Psychological Review, 62*, 255–262.

Hammond, K. R. (1966). *The psychology of Egon Brunswik*. New York: Holt, Reinhart & Winston.

Hammond, K. R. (1996). *Human judgment and social policy*. New York: Oxford University Press.

Handley, S. J., & Evans, J. St. B. T. (2000). Supposition and representation in human reasoning. *Thinking & Reasoning, 6*, 273–312.

Handley, S. J., Evans, J. St. B. T., & Thompson, V. A. (2006). The negated conditional: A litmus test for the suppositional conditional? *Journal of Experimental Psychology. Learning, Memory, and Cognition, 32*, 559–569.

Handley, S. J., Feeney, A., & Harper, C. (2002). Alternative antecedents, probabilities and the suppression of fallacies on Wason's selection task. *Quarterly Journal of Experimental Psychology, 55A*, 799–813.

Harries, C., Evans, J. St. B. T., Dennis, I., & Dean, J. (1996). A clinical judgement analysis of prescribing decisions in general practice. *Le Travail Humain, 59,* 87–111.

Hassin, R. R., Uleman, J. S., & Bargh, J. A. (Eds.) (2005). *The new unconscious.* Oxford, UK: Oxford University Press.

Hastie, R. (2001). Problems for judgement and decision making. *Annual Review of Psychology, 52,* 653–683.

Hawkins, S. A., & Hastie, R. (1990). Hindsight: Biased judgments of past events after the outcomes are known. *Psychological Bulletin, 107,* 311–327.

Henle, M. (1962). On the relation between logic and thinking. *Psychological Review, 69,* 366–378.

Hinton, P. R. (2000). *Sterotypes, cognition and culture.* Hove, UK: Psychology Press.

Hirt, E. R., & Sherman, S. J. (1985). The role of prior knowledge in explaining hypothetical events. *Journal of Experimental Social Psychology, 21,* 519–543.

Hoffrage, U., Gigerenzer, G., Krauss, S., & Martigon, L. (2002). Representation facilitates reasoning: What natural frequencies are and what they are not. *Cognition, 84,* 343–352.

Holyoak, K., & Cheng, P. W. (1995). Pragmatic reasoning with a point of view. *Thinking & Reasoning, 1,* 289–314.

Houdé, O., Zago, L., Mellet, E., Moutier, S., Pineau, A., Mazover, B., Tzourio-Mazover, N. (2000). Shifting from the perceptual brain to the logical brain: The neural impact of cognitive inhibition training. *Journal of Cognitive Neuroscience, 12,* 721–728.

Howson, C., & Urbach, P. (1993). *Scientific reasoning* (2nd ed.). Chicago: Open Court.

Inhelder, B., & Piaget, J. (1958). *The growth of logical thinking.* New York: Basic Books.

Johnson-Laird, P. N. (1983). *Mental models.* Cambridge, UK: Cambridge University Press.

Johnson-Laird, P. N. (2005). If bears eat in the woods . . .? *Trends in Cognitive Sciences, 9,* 43–44.

Johnson-Laird, P. N., & Bara, B. G. (1984). Syllogistic inference. *Cognition, 16,* 1–61.

Johnson-Laird, P. N., & Byrne, R. M. J. (1990). Meta-logical reasoning: Knights, knaves and rips. *Cognition, 36,* 69–84.

Johnson-Laird, P. N., & Byrne, R. M. J. (1991). *Deduction.* Hove, UK: Erlbaum.

Johnson-Laird, P. N., & Byrne, R. M. J. (2002). Conditionals: A theory of meaning, pragmatics and inference. *Psychological Review, 109,* 646–678.

Johnson-Laird, P. N., & Savary, F. (1999). Illusory inferences: A novel class of erroneous deductions. *Cognition, 71,* 191–299.

Johnson-Laird, P. N., & Tagart, J. (1969). How implication is understood. *American Journal of Psychology, 2,* 367–373.

Kahneman, D. & Frederick, S. (2002). Representativeness revisited: Attribute substitution in intuitive judgement. In T. Gilovich, D. Griffin, & D. Kahneman (Eds.), *Heuristics and biases: The psychology of intuitive judgement* (pp. 49–81). Cambridge, UK: Cambridge University Press.

Kahneman, D., & Frederick, S. (2005). A model of heuristic judgment. In K. Holyoak & R. G. Morrison (Eds.), *The Cambridge handbook of thinking and reasoning* (pp. 267–294). Cambridge, UK: Cambridge University Press.

Kahneman, D., Slovic, P., & Tversky, A. (1982). *Judgment under uncertainty: Heuristics and biases.* Cambridge, UK: Cambridge University Press.

Kahneman, D., & Tversky, A. (1972). Subjective probability: A judgment of representativeness. *Cognitive Psychology, 3,* 430–454.

Kahneman, D., & Tversky, A. (1973). On the psychology of prediction. *Psychological Review, 80,* 237–251.

Kahneman, D., & Tversky, A. (1979). Prospect theory: An analysis of decision under risk. *Econometrica, 47,* 263–291.

Kahneman, D., & Tversky, A. (1982a). On the study of statistical intuition. *Cognition, 12,* 325–326.

Kahneman, D., & Tversky, A. (1982b). The simulation heuristic. In D. Kahneman, P. Slovic, & A. Tversky (Eds.), *Judgment under uncertainty: Heuristics and biases* (pp. 201–210). Cambridge, UK: Cambridge University Press.

Kirby, K. N. (1994). Probabilities and utilities of fictional outcomes in Wason's four card selection task. *Cognition, 51,* 1–28.

Klaczynski, P. A. (2000). Motivated scientific reasoning biases, epistemological beliefs, and the theory polarization: A two-process approach to adolescent cognition. *Child Development, 71,* 1347–1366.

Klaczynski, P. A. (2001). Analytic and heuristic processing influences on adolescent reasoning and decision-making. *Child Development, 72,* 844–861.

Klaczynski, P. A., & Cottrell, J. M. (2004). A dual-process approach to cognitive development: The case of children's understanding of sunk cost decisions. *Thinking & Reasoning, 10,* 147–174.

Klaczynski, P. A., & Lavallee, K. L. (2005). Domain-specific identity, epistemic regulation, and intellectual ability as predictors of belief-biased reasoning: A dual-process perspective. *Journal of Experimental Child Psychology, 92,* 1–24.

Klaczynski, P. A., & Robinson, B. (2000). Personal theories, intellectual ability and epistemological beliefs: Adult age differences in everyday reasoning biases. *Psychology and Aging, 15,* 400–416.

Klaczynski, P. A., Schuneman, M. J., & Daniel, D. B. (2004). Theories of conditional reasoning: A developmental examination of competing hypotheses. *Developmental Psychology, 40,* 559–571.

Klauer, K. C., Musch, J., & Naumer, B. (2000). On belief bias in syllogistic reasoning. *Psychological Review, 107,* 852–884.

Klayman, J. (1995). Varieties of confirmation bias. *The Psychology of Learning and Motivation, 32,* 385–417.

Klayman, J., & Ha, Y. W. (1987). Confirmation, disconfirmation and information in hypothesis testing. *Psychological Review, 94,* 211–228.

Klein, G. (1999). *Sources of power.* Cambridge, MA: MIT Press.

Koehler, D. J., & Harvey, N. (Eds.). (2004). *Blackwell handbook of judgment and decision making.* Oxford, UK: Blackwell.

Koehler, J. J. (1996). The base rate fallacy reconsidered: Descriptive, normative and methodological challenges. *Behavioral and Brain Sciences, 19,* 1–53.

Kokis, J. V., MacPherson, R., Toplak, M. E., West, R. F., & Stanovich, K. E. (2002). Heuristic and analytic processing: Age trends and associations with cognitive ability and cognitive styles. *Journal of Experimental Child Psychology, 83,* 26–52.

Koriat, A., Lichtenstein, S., & Fischhoff, B. (1980). Reasons for confidence. *Journal of Experimental Psychology: Human Learning and Memory, 6*, 107–118.

Kyllonen, P., & Christal, R. E. (1990). Reasoning ability is (little more than) working memory capacity!? *Intelligence, 14*, 389–433.

LeBeouf, R. A., & Shafir, E. (2005). Decision making. In K. Holyoak & R. G. Morrison (Eds.), *The Cambridge handbook of thinking and reasoning* (pp. 243–265). Cambridge, UK: Cambridge University Press.

Legrenzi, P., Girotto, V., & Johnson-Laird, P. N. (1993). Focussing in reasoning and decision making. *Cognition, 49*, 37–66.

Levine, M. (1966). Hypothesis behaviour by humans during discrimination learning. *Journal of Experimental Psychology, 71*, 331–338.

Liu, I.-M., Lo, K.-C., & Wu, J.-T. (1996). A probabilistic interpretation of "If-Then". *Quarterly Journal of Experimental Psychology, 49A*, 828–844.

Lord, C., Ross, L., & Lepper, M. R. (1979). Biased assimilation and attitude polarisation: The effect of prior theories on subsequently considered evidence. *Journal of Personality and Social Psychology, 37*, 2098–2109.

Lott, J. (1999). *Developmental trends in conditional reasoning.* Unpublished masters thesis, University of Plymouth, Plymouth, UK.

Lucas, E. J., & Ball, L. J. (2005). Think-aloud protocols and the selection task: Evidence for relevance effects and rationalisation processes. *Thinking & Reasoning, 11*, 35–66.

Lucas, M. (2000). Semantic priming without association: A meta-analytic review. *Psychonomic Bulletin and Review, 7*, 618–630.

Maachi, L. (1995). Pragmatic aspects of the base-rate fallacy. *Quarterly Journal of Experimental Psychology, 48A*, 188–207.

Macrae, C. N., Bodenhausen, G. V., Milne, A. B., Thorn, T. M. J., & Castelli, L. (1997). Out of mind but back in sight: Stereotypes on the rebound. *Journal of Experimental Social Psychology, 33*, 471–489.

Mandel, D. R., Hilton, D. J., & Catellani, P. (Eds.) (2005). *The psychology of counterfactual thinking.* London: Routledge.

Manktelow, K. I. (1999). *Reasoning and thinking.* Hove, UK: Psychology Press.

Manktelow, K. I., & Over, D. E. (1991). Social roles and utilities in reasoning with deontic conditionals. *Cognition, 39*, 85–105.

Markovits, H., & Barrouillet, P. (2002). The development of conditional reasoning: A mental model account. *Developmental Review, 22*, 5–36.

Markovits, H., Fleury, M.-L., Quinn, S., & Venet, M. (1998). The development of conditional reasoning and the structure of semantic memory. *Child Development, 69*, 742–755.

Markovits, H., & Nantel, G. (1989). The belief bias effect in the production and evaluation of logical conclusions. *Memory and Cognition, 17*, 11–17.

Markovits, H., & Quinn, S. (2002). Efficiency of retrieval correlates with "logical" reasoning from causal conditional premises. *Memory and Cognition, 30*, 696–706.

Mithen, S. (1996). *The prehistory of the mind.* London: Thames & Hudson.

Monsell, S., & Driver, J. (2000). *Control of cognitive processes.* Cambridge, MA: MIT Press.

Morley, N. J., Evans, J. St. B. T., & Handley, S. J. (2004). Belief bias and figural bias in syllogistic reasoning. *Quarterly Journal of Experimental Psychology, 57A*, 666–692.

Mynatt, C. R., Doherty, M. E., & Dragan, W. (1993). Information relevance, working memory and the consideration of alternatives. *Quarterly Journal of Experimental Psychology*, *46A*, 759–778.

Mynatt, C. R., Doherty, M. E., & Tweney, R. D. (1977). Confirmation bias in a simulated research environment: An experimental study of scientific inference. *Quarterly Journal of Experimental Psychology*, *24*, 326–329.

Mynatt, C. R., Doherty, M. E., & Tweney, R. D. (1978). Consequences of confirmation and disconfirmation in a simulated research environment. *Quarterly Journal of Experimental Psychology*, *30*, 85–96.

Newell, A., & Simon, H. A. (1972). *Human problem solving*. Englewood Cliffs, NJ: Prentice-Hall.

Newstead, S. E. (2000). Are there two different kinds of thinking? *Behavioral and Brain Sciences*, *23*, 690–691.

Newstead, S. E., Girotto, V., & Legrenzi, P. (1995). The THOG problem and its implications for human reasoning. In S. E. Newstead & J. St. B. T. Evans (Eds.), *Perspectives on thinking and reasoning* (pp. 261–286). Hove, UK: Erlbaum.

Newstead, S. E., Handley, S. J., Harley, C., Wright, H., & Farelly, D. (2004). Individual differences in deductive reasoning. *Quarterly Journal of Experimental Psychology*, *57A*, 33–60.

Newstead, S. E., Pollard, P., Evans, J. St. B. T., & Allen, J. L. (1992). The source of belief bias effects in syllogistic reasoning. *Cognition*, *45*, 257–284.

Newstead, S. E., Thompson, V. A., & Handley, S. J. (2002). Generating alternatives: A key component in human reasoning? *Memory and Cognition*, *30*, 129–137.

Nickerson, R. S. (1996). Hempel's paradox and the Wason selection task: Logical and psychological puzzles of confirmation. *Thinking & Reasoning*, *2*, 1–32.

Nisbett, R. E., Krantz, D. H., Jepson, D. H., & Kunda, Z. (1983). The use of statistical heuristics in everyday inductive reasoning. *Psychological Review*, *90*, 339–363.

Nisbett, R. E., Peng, K., Choi, I., & Norenzayan, A. (2001). Culture and systems of thought: Holistic vs analytic cognition. *Psychological Review*, *108*, 291–310.

Nisbett, R. E., & Wilson, T. D. (1977). Telling more than we can know: Verbal reports on mental processes. *Psychological Review*, *84*, 231–295.

Oakhill, J., & Johnson-Laird, P. N. (1985). The effects of belief on the spontaneous production of syllogistic conclusions. *Quarterly Journal of Experimental Psychology*, *37A*, 553–569.

Oakhill, J., Johnson-Laird, P. N., & Garnham, A. (1989). Believability and syllogistic reasoning. *Cognition*, *31*, 117–140.

Oaksford, M. (2002). Contrast classes and matching bias as explanations of the effects of negation on conditional reasoning. *Thinking & Reasoning*, *8*, 135–151.

Oaksford, M., & Chater, N. (1991). Against logicist cognitive science. *Mind & Language*, *6*, 1–38.

Oaksford, M., & Chater, N. (1993). Reasoning theories and bounded rationality. In K. I. Manktelow & D. E. Over (Eds.), *Rationality* (pp. 31–60). London: Routledge.

Oaksford, M., & Chater, N. (1994). A rational analysis of the selection task as optimal data selection. *Psychological Review*, *101*, 608–631.

Oaksford, M., & Chater, N. (1995). Information gain explains relevance which explains the selection task. *Cognition, 57,* 97–108.

Oaksford, M., & Chater, N. (1996). Rational explanation of the selection task. *Psychological Review, 103,* 381–391.

Oaksford, M., & Chater, N. (1998). *Rationality in an uncertain world.* Hove, UK: Psychology Press.

Oaksford, M., & Chater, N. (2001). The probabilistic approach to human reasoning. *Trends in Cognitive Sciences, 5,* 349–357.

Oaksford, M., Chater, N., & Larkin, J. (2000). Probabilities and polarity biases in conditional inference. *Journal of Experimental Psychology: Learning, Memory, and Cognition, 26,* 883–889.

Oaksford, M., & Stenning, K. (1992). Reasoning with conditionals containing negated constituents. *Journal of Experimental Psychology: Learning, Memory, and Cognition, 18,* 835–854.

Oberauer, K., & Wilhelm, O. (2003). The meaning(s) of conditionals: Conditional probabilities, mental models and personal utilities. *Journal of Experimental Psychology: Learning, Memory, and Cognition, 29,* 680–693.

O'Brien, D. P. (1993). Mental logic and human irrationality: We can put a man on the moon, so why can't we solve those logical reasoning problems? In K. I. Manktelow & D. E. Over (Eds.), *Rationality* (pp. 110–135). London: Routledge.

Ofir, C. (1988). Pseudodiagnosticity in judgement under uncertainty. *Organizational Behavior and Human Decision Processes, 42,* 343–363.

Oppenheimer, D. M. (2003). Not so fast! (and not so frugal!): Rethinking the recognition heuristic. *Cognition, 90,* B1–B9.

Osman, M. (2005). An evaluation of dual-process theories of reasoning. *Psychonomic Bulletin and Review, 11,* 988–1010.

Oswald, M. E., & Grosjean, S. (2004). Confirmation bias. In R. Pohl (Ed.), *Cognitive illusions* (pp. 79–98). Hove, UK: Psychology Press.

Over, D. E. (2000a). Ecological issues: A reply to Todd, Fiddick and Krause. *Thinking & Reasoning, 6,* 385–388.

Over, D. E. (2000b). Ecological rationality and heuristics. Review of G. Giberenzer & P. M. Todd (1999), Simple heuristics that make us smart. *Thinking & Reasoning, 6,* 182–192.

Over, D. E. (2003). From massive modularity to metarepresentation: The evolution of higher cogntion. In D. E. Over (Ed.), *Evolution and the psychology of thinking: The debate* (pp. 121–144). Hove, UK: Psychology Press.

Over, D. E., & Evans, J. St. B. T. (2003). The probability of conditionals: The psychological evidence. *Mind & Language, 18,* 340–358.

Over, D. E., Hadjichristidis, C., Evans, J. St. B. T., Handley, S. J., & Sloman, S. A. (in press). The probability of causal conditionals. *Cognitive Psychology.*

Over, D. E., & Manktelow, K. I. (1993). Rationality, utility and deontic reasoning. In K. I. Manktelow & D. E. Over (Eds.), *Rationality* (pp. 231–259). London: Routledge.

Pearl, J. (2000). *Causality: Models, reasoning and inference.* Cambridge, UK: Cambridge University Press.

Pinker, S. (1997). *How the mind works.* New York: Norton.

Poincaré, H. (1927). *The foundations of science.* New York: Science House.

Poletiek, F. (1996). Paradoxes of falsification. *Quarterly Journal of Experimental Psychology, 49A*, 447–462.

Poletiek, F. (2001). *Hypothesis-testing behaviour*. Hove, UK: Psychology Press.

Politzer, G., & Nguyen-Xuan, A. (1992). Reasoning about conditional promises and warnings: Darwinian algorithms, mental models, relevance judgements or pragmatic schemas? *Quarterly Journal of Experimental Psychology, 44A*, 401–412.

Popper, K. R. (1959). *The logic of scientific discovery*. London: Hutchinson.

Popper, K. R. (1962). *Conjectures and refutations*. London: Hutchinson.

Quelhas, A. C., & Byrne, R. M. J. (2003). Reasoning with deontic and counterfactual conditionals. *Thinking & Reasoning, 9*, 43–65.

Quinn, S., & Markovits, H. (1998). Conditional reasoning, causality and the structure of semantic inference. *Cognition, 68*, B93–B101.

Quinn, S., & Markovits, H. (2002). Conditional reasoning with causal premises: Evidence for a retrieval model. *Thinking & Reasoning, 8*, 179–192.

Ramsey, F. P. (1931). *The foundations of mathematics and other logical essays*. London: Routledge and Kegan Paul.

Real, L. A. (1991). Animal choice behaviour and the evolution of cognitive architecture. *Science, 253*, 980–979.

Reber, A. S. (1976). Implicit learning of synthetic languages: The role of instructional set. *Journal of Experimental Psychology: Human Learning and Memory, 2*, 88–94.

Reber, A. S. (1993). *Implicit learning and tacit knowledge*. Oxford, UK: Oxford University Press.

Reber, R. (2004). Availability. In R. Pohl (Ed.), *Cognitive illusions* (pp. 147–164). Hove, UK: Psychology Press.

Revlin, R., Leirer, V., Yopp, H., & Yopp, R. (1980). The belief bias effect in formal reasoning: The influence of knowledge on logic. *Memory and Cognition, 8*, 584–592.

Reyna, V. F. (2004). How people make decisions that involve risk: A dual-processes approach. *Current Directions in Psychological Science, 13*, 60–66.

Rips, L. J. (1989). The psychology of knights and knaves. *Cognition, 31*, 85–116.

Rips, L. J. (1994). *The psychology of proof*. Cambridge, MA: MIT Press.

Rips, L. J., & Marcus, S. L. (1977). Suppositions and the analysis of conditional sentences. In M. A. Just & P. A. Carpenter (Eds.), *Cognitive processes in comprehension* (pp. 185–219). New York: Wiley.

Roberts, M. J. (1998). Inspection times and the selection task: Are they relevant? *Quarterly Journal of Experimental Psychology, 51A*, 781–810.

Roberts, M. J., & Newton, E. J. (2002). Inspection times, the change task, and the rapid-response selection task. *Quarterly Journal of Experimental Psychology, 54A*, 1031–1048.

Roese, N. J. (2004). Twisted pair: Counterfactual thinking and hindsight bias. In N. Harvey & D. J. Koehler (Eds.), *Blackwell handbook on judgment and decision making* (pp. 258–273). Oxford, UK: Blackwell.

Samuels, R. (1998). Evolutionary psychology and the mass modularity hypothesis. *British Journal for the Philosophy of Science, 49*, 575–602.

Schaeken, W., DeVooght, G., Vandierendonck, A., & d'Ydewalle, G. (2000). *Deductive reasoning and strategies*. Mahwah, NJ: Erlbaum.

Schneider, W., & Shiffrin, R. M. (1977). Controlled and automatic human information processing I: Detection, search and attention. *Psychological Review, 84*, 1–66.

Schroyens, W., & Schaeken, W. (2004). Guilt by association: On Iffy propositions and the proper treatment of mental models theory. *Current Psychology Letters, 12* (http://cpl.revues.ord/document411.html).

Schroyens, W., Schaeken, W., & d'Ydewalle, G. (2001). The processing of negations in conditional reasoning: A meta-analytic study in mental models and/or mental logic theory. *Thinking & Reasoning, 7*, 121–172.

Schroyens, W., Schaeken, W., Fias, W., & d'Ydewalle, G. (2000). Heuristic and analytic processes in propositional reasoning with negative conditionals. *Journal of Experimental Psychology: Learning, Memory, and Cognition, 26*, 1713–1734.

Schroyens, W., Schaeken, W., Verschueren, N., & d'Ydewalle, G. (1999). Conditional reasoning with negations: Matching bias and implicit versus explicit affirmation or denial. *Psychological Belgica, 39*, 235–258.

Schwarz, N., & Vaughn, L. A. (2002). The availability heuristic revisited: Ease of recall and content of recall as distinct sources. In T. Gilovich, D. Griffin, & D. Kahneman (Eds.), *Heuristics and biases: The psychology of intuitive judgment* (pp. 103–119). Cambridge, UK: Cambridge University Press.

Segal, E. (2004). Incubation in insight problem solving. *Creativity Research Journal, 16*, 141–148.

Shafir, E. (1993). Choosing versus rejecting: Why some options are both better and worse than others. *Memory and Cognition, 21*, 546–556.

Shafir, E., & LeBeouf, R. A. (2005). Context and conflict in multiattribute choice. In D. J. Koehler & N. Harvey (Eds.), *Blackwell handbook of judgment and decision making* (pp. 341–359). Oxford, UK: Blackwell.

Shanks, D. R., & St John, M. F. (1994). Characteristics of dissociable human learning systems. *Behavioral and Brain Sciences, 17*, 367–447.

Shanteau, J. (1992). How much information does an expert use? Is it relevant? *Acta Psychologica, 81*, 75–86.

Simon, H. A. (1982). *Models of bounded rationality*. Cambridge, MA: MIT Press.

Skov, R. B., & Sherman, S. J. (1986). Information-gathering processes: Diagnosticity, hypothesis-confirmatory strategies, and perceived hypothesis confirmation. *Journal of Experimental Social Psychology, 22*, 121.

Sloman, S. A. (1996). The empirical case for two systems of reasoning. *Psychological Bulletin, 119*, 3–22.

Sloman, S. A. (2005). *Causal models*. Oxford, UK: Oxford University Press.

Sloman, S. A., Over, D. E., & Slovack, L. (2003). Frequency illusions and other fallacies. *Organizational Behavior and Human Decision Processes, 91*, 296–309.

Smedslund, J. (1970). Circular relation between understanding and logic. *Scandinavian Journal of Psychology, 11*, 217–219.

Smedslund, J. (1990). A critique of Tversky and Kahneman's distinction between fallacy and misunderstanding. *Scandinavian Journal of Psychology, 31*, 110–120.

Smullyan, R. M. (1978). *What is the name of this book? The riddle of Dracula and other logical puzzles*. Englewood Cliffs, NJ: Prentice-Hall.

Spellman, B. A., Lopez, A. L., & Smith, E. E. (1999). Hypothesis testing: Strategy selection for generalising versus limiting hypotheses. *Thinking & Reasoning, 5*, 67–91.

Sperber, D., Cara, F., & Girotto, V. (1995). Relevance theory explains the selection task. *Cognition, 57*, 31–95.

Sperber, D., & Girotto, V. (2002). Use or misuse of the selection task? Rejoinder to Fiddick, Cosmides and Tooby. *Cognition, 85*, 277–290.

Sperber, D., & Wilson, D. (1995). *Relevance* (2nd ed.). Oxford, UK: Basil Blackwell.

Stalnaker, R. (1968). A theory of conditionals. *American Philosophical Quarterly Monograph Series, 2*, 98–112.

Stanovich, K. E. (1999). *Who is rational? Studies of individual differences in reasoning.* Mahwah, NJ: Erlbaum.

Stanovich, K. E. (2004). *The robot's rebellion: Finding meaning in the age of Darwin.* Chicago: Chicago University Press.

Stanovich, K. E. (2006). Is it time for a tri-process theory? Distinguishing the reflective and the algorithmic mind. *In two minds: Dual process theories of reasoning and rationality.* Open University Conference, Cambridge, 5–7 July.

Stanovich, K. E., & West, R. F. (1998). Cognitive ability and variation in selection task performance. *Thinking & Reasoning, 4*, 193–230.

Stanovich, K. E., & West, R. F. (2000). Individual differences in reasoning: Implications for the rationality debate. *Behavioral and Brain Sciences, 23*, 645–726.

Stanovich, K. E., & West, R. F. (2003). Evolutionary versus instrumental goals: How evolutionary psychology misconceives human rationality. In D. E. Over (Ed.), *Evolution and the psychology of thinking* (pp. 171–230). Hove, UK: Psychology Press.

Stanovich, K. E., & West, R. F. (in press). Natural myside bias is independent of cognitive ability. *Thinking & Reasoning.*

Stevenson, R. J. (1997). Deductive reasoning and the distinction between implicit and explicit processes. *Current Psychology of Cognition, 16*, 222–229.

Stevenson, R. J., & Over, D. E. (1995). Deduction from uncertain premises. *The Quarterly Journal of Experimental Psychology, 48A*, 613–643.

Stewart, T. R. (1988). Judgement analysis: Procedures. In B. Brehmer & C. R. B. Joyce (Eds.), *Human judgement: The SJT view* (pp. 41–74). Amsterdam: Elsevier.

Stone, V. E., Cosmides, L., Tooby, J., Kroll, N., & Knight, R. T. (2002). Selective impairment of reasoning about social exchange in a patient with bilateral limbic system damage. *Proceedings of the National Academy of Sciences*, 11531–11536.

Sun, R. (2001). *Duality of mind: A bottom-up approach towards cognition.* Hillsdale, NJ: Erlbaum.

Sun, R., Slusarz, P., & Terry, C. (2005). The interaction of the explicit and the implicit in skill learning: A dual-process approach. *Psychological Review, 112*, 159–192.

Teigen, K. H. (1998). When the unreal is more likely than the real: Post hoc probability judgements and counterfactual closeness. *Thinking & Reasoning, 4*, 147–177.

Teigen, K. H. (2004). Judgments by representativeness. In R. Pohl (Ed.), *Cognitive illusions* (pp. 165–182). Hove, UK: Psychology Press.

Thompson, V. A. (1994). Interpretational factors in conditional reasoning. *Memory and Cognition, 22*, 742–758.

Thompson, V. A. (1996). Reasoning from false premises: The role of soundness in making logical deductions. *Canadian Journal of Experimental Psychology, 50*, 315–319.

Thompson, V. A. (2000). The task-specific nature of domain-general reasoning. *Cognition, 76*, 209–268.

Thompson, V. A., & Byrne, R. M. J. (2002). Reasoning counterfactually: Making inferences about things that didn't happen. *Journal of Experimental Psychology: Learning, Memory, and Cognition, 28*, 1–14.

Thompson, V. A., Striemer, C. L., Reikoff, R., Gunter, R. W., & Campbell, J. I. D. (2003). Syllogistic reasoning time: Disconfirmation disconfirmed. *Psychonomic Bulletin and Review, 10*, 184–189.

Toates, F. (2006). A model of the hierarchy of behaviour, cognition and consciousness. *Consciousness and Cognition, 15*, 75–118.

Todd, P. M., Fiddick, L., & Krauss, S. (2000). Ecological rationality and its contents. *Thinking & Reasoning, 6*, 375–384.

Tooby, J., & Cosmides, L. (1992). The psychological foundations of culture. In J. H. Barkow, L. Cosmides, & J. Tooby (Eds.), *The adapted mind: Evolutionary psychology and the generation of culture* (pp. 19–136). New York: Oxford University Press.

Tversky, A. (1972). Elimination by aspects: A theory of choice. *Psychological Review, 79*, 281–299.

Tversky, A., & Kahneman, D. (1992). Advances in prospect theory: Cumulative representation of uncertainty. *Journal of Risk and Uncertainty, 5*, 297–323.

Tversky, A., & Kahneman, D. (1973). Availability: A heuristic for judging frequency and probability. *Cognitive Psychology, 5*, 207–232.

Tversky, A., & Kahneman, D. (1974). Judgement under uncertainty: Heuristics and biases. *Science, 185*, 1124–1131.

Tversky, A., & Kahneman, D. (1983). Extensional vs intuitive reasoning: The conjunction fallacy in probability judgment. *Psychological Review, 90*, 293–315.

Tversky, A., & Koehler, D. J. (1994). Support theory: A nonextensional representation of subjective probability. *Psychological Review, 101*, 547–567.

Tversky, A., & Shafir, E. (1992). The disjunction effect in choice under uncertainty. *Psychological Science, 3*, 305–309.

Tweney, R. D., Doherty, M. E., Warner, W. J., Pliske, D. B., Mynatt, C. R., Gross, K. A., et al. (1980). Strategies of rule discovery in an inference task. *Quarterly Journal of Experimental Psychology, 32*, 109–123.

Verschueren, N., Schaeken, W., & d'Ydewalle, G. (2005a). A dual-process specification of causal conditional reasoning. *Thinking & Reasoning, 11*, 239–278.

Verschueren, N., Schaeken, W., & d'Ydewalle, G. (2005b). Everyday conditional reasoning: A working memory-dependent tradeoff between counterexample and likelihood use. *Memory and Cognition, 33*, 107–119.

Wagenaar, W. A. (1972). Generation of random sequences by human subjects: A critical survey of the literature. *Psychological Bulletin, 34*, 348–365.

Wagenaar, W. A. (1988). *Pardoxes of gambling behaviour*. Hove, UK: Erlbaum.

Wason, P. C. (1960). On the failure to eliminate hypotheses in a conceptual task. *Quarterly Journal of Experimental Psychology, 12*, 129–140.

Wason, P. C. (1966). Reasoning. In B. M. Foss (Ed.), *New horizons in psychology I* (pp. 106–137). Harmondsworth, UK: Penguin.

Wason, P. C. (1968). On the failure to eliminate hypotheses: a second look. In P. C. Wason & P. N. Johnson-Laird (Eds.), *Thinking and reasoning* (pp. 165–174). Harmondsworth, UK: Penguin.

Wason, P. C., & Brooks, P. G. (1979). THOG: The anatomy of a problem. *Psychological Research, 41*, 79–90.

Wason, P. C., & Evans, J. St. B. T. (1975). Dual processes in reasoning? *Cognition, 3*, 141–154.

Wason, P. C., & Johnson-Laird, P. N. (1972). *Psychology of reasoning: Structure and content*. London: Batsford.

Wason, P. C., & Shapiro, D. (1971). Natural and contrived experience in a reasoning problem. *Quarterly Journal of Experimental Psychology, 23*, 63–71.

Wetherick, N. E. (1962). Eliminative and enumerative behaviour in a conceptual task. *Quarterly Journal of Experimental Psychology, 14*, 246–249.

Wigton, R. S. (1996). Social judgement theory and medical judgement. *Thinking & Reasoning, 2*, 175–190.

Wilkins, M. C. (1928). The effect of changed material on the ability to do formal syllogistic reasoning. *Archives of Psychology, 16* (102).

Wilson, T. D. (2002). *Strangers to ourselves*. Cambridge, MA: Belknap Press.

Wilson, T. D., & Dunn, E. W. (2004). Self-knowledge: Its limits, value and potential for improvement. *Annual Review of Psychology, 55*, 493–518.

Wilson, T. D., Lindsey, S., & Schooler, T. Y. (2000). A model of dual attitudes. *Psychological Review, 107*, 101–126.

Wilson, T. D., Lisle, D. J., Schooler, J. W., Hodges, S. D., Klaaren, K. J., & Lafleur, S. J. (1993). Introspecting about reasons can reduce post-choice satisfaction. *Personality and Social Psychology Bulletin, 19*, 331–339.

Wilson, T. D., & Schooler, J. W. (1991). Thinking too much: Introspection can reduce the quality of preferences and decisions. *Journal of Personality and Social Psychology, 60*, 181–192.

Woodworth, R. S. (1938). *Experimental psychology*. New York: Holt.

Wu, G., Zhang, J., & Gonzales, R. (2005). Decision under risk. In D. J. Koehler & N. Harvey (Eds.), *Blackwell handbook of judgment and decision making*. Oxford, UK: Blackwell.

Yama, H. (2001). Matching versus optimal data selection in the Wason selection task. *Thinking & Reasoning, 7*, 295–311.

Author index

Subject index